COMING
INFORMATION AGE

ANNENBERG/LONGMAN COMMUNICATION BOOKS
George Gerbner and Marsha Siefert, Editors
The Annenberg School of Communications
University of Pennsylvania

Wilson P. Dizard

THE
COMING
INFORMATION AGE

*An Overview of Technology,
Economics, and Politics*

Second Edition

Longman
New York & London

302.2
D62c2

The Coming Information Age, second edition
An Overview of Technology, Economics, and Politics

Longman Inc., 1560 Broadway, New York, N.Y. 10036
Associated companies, branches, and representatives
throughout the world.

Developmental Editor: Gordon T.R. Anderson
Editorial and Design Supervisor: Thomas Bacher
Production/Manufacturing: Ferne Y. Kawahara
Composition: Graphicraft Typesetters, Ltd.
Printing and Binding: The Alpine Press, Inc.

Library of Congress Cataloging in Publication Data

Dizard, Wilson P.
    The coming information age.
    (Annenberg/Longman communication books)
    Bibliography: p.
    Includes index.
    1. Communication—United States.   I. Title.
II. Series.
P92.U5D5   1984   001.51′0973   84-12625
ISBN 0-582-28522-4

Manufactured in the United States of America
Printing: 9 8 7 6 5 4 3 2 1   Year: 92 91 90 89 88 87 86 85

For Lynn

CONTENTS

FOREWORD

WILSON DIZARD COMMUNICATES. There are many of us, students of communications, who may know a lot about bits, baud, repeaters, cables, optical fibres, WARCs, and CCITT, but what we know is hard to communicate. Many of us wish we could communicate what we think we know as well as this book does.

What follows is, as the title tells us, an overview. It describes for nontechnologists the new technologies of computers, semiconductors, satellites, and light guides. It introduces us to the burgeoning industry of electronic communications, the giants in it, and the challengers. It summarizes the political debates about communications policy in the Congress and the FCC. And at the end we learn about the international controversies on free flow of information, direct satellite broadcasting and international data networks.

But the book is not just an overview. There is a consistent line of argument. The technical and economic review leads up to a political conclusion, one with which I am not sure that I agree. The conclusion seems to be that the United States needs to restructure its government to enable it to reach more coherent communications policies.

Dizard tells us about the erosion of the American lead in computers and electronics, and in particular about the Japanese challenge. He explains the inadequacy of the Communications Act of 1934 and its inappropriateness to the present era of communications abundance. He describes the attempts to reach coherence of policy through the White House Office of Telecommunications Policy and then the National Telecommunications and Information Agency; he also reports their failure. He explains the essential diversity and pluralism of this nation and recognizes that as one of its strengths; he also takes full note of the tradition of the First Amendment.

Given these facets of our national philosophy, there are, I would argue, severe limits to how much coherence of communications policy there can or should be. Nor is it clear what kinds of persons have the competence to create such policies. The technicians in the spectrum allocation game, for example, rarely grasp the political and economic issues with which they deal; the foreign service officers in the State Department rarely understand the technological implications of what they are doing. (Dizard when he was in the foreign service was a rare exception.) Perhaps a certain amount of robust debate among the different parties is not a bad thing. In any case, the issue is raised in the chapters to follow; it will be an active issue of national policy for decades to come.

The question of the United States's lead in information technology is one that needs to be looked at with detachment and sophistication. This country has been the source of the computer and telecommunications revolution. It leads the world in levels of penetration of such devices as computers, telephones, word processors, satellites and CATV: Its cultural products ranging from scientific books to television shows are first in the world market. Is that a good thing, a bad thing, or a morally neutral fact about which there may nonetheless be conflict of interest?

In the United States, the erosion of our lead in information technology has been a subject of alarm. It is in part a reflection of declining productivity. It is also a threat to one of our top sources of foreign exchange earnings. Politically, too, we tend to view the export of our cultural products as a healthy influence towards world understanding and democracy as well as a lever of influence for ourselves.

The same coin turned over is sometimes viewed by others as a threat. Our major totalitarian adversaries, of course, view American world communications with alarm. That need neither surprise nor disturb us. More serious is the fact that from countries we feel to be friends we hear complaints about a threat to their culture or their autonomy.

Dizard, I believe rightly, does not accept that line of argument. Nor is it just a matter of whose ox is gored. It is not a zero sum game. All countries are benefited as any country improves its facilities for communicating or produces interesting cultural products. It is thus appropriate for Americans to be alarmed if we are doing less well than we have in the past in moving mankind's technologies of knowledge forward or in providing books, plays, and music that all enjoy. Nor are we hurt, but rather benefited if other countries advance more rapidly than they have in their information activities. We gain by using their data bases, being able to phone or telex them cheaply and easily, or enjoying their works of art.

There is thus nothing parochial in Dizard's warnings as to problems in America's effectiveness in the world information market. One would hope that the warnings will be pondered, and at the same time one would hope that in every other country there are people giving similar warnings and urgings to their own people to move ahead in creating a freer and better flow of information.

In all that we have said above we have talked of both computing and communications. As this book and many other sources tell us, these technologies are converging to the point where they are hard to distinguish. Dizard quotes Anthony Oettinger's coinage, "compunications." The point about convergence is certainly true; these two technologies interpenetrate to such a degree that it is impossible to formulate policy for one and not for the other — as the F.C.C. has discovered. Yet historically they are two technologies quite distinct.

Starting in the middle of the nineteenth century a revolution in communications began with the telegraph, later expanded by the telephone, then radio and television. By using electronic signals instead of visible marks on a surface, it became possible to transmit messages instantaneously to a distance and to do that not only for written words, but also for representations of voice and graphics, too. That was a revolution in information processing as significant as the two previous great revolutions in that field: the invention of writing, millennia ago, and the invention, 500 years ago, of a way to produce written messages in multiple copies.

The computer, in the middle of the twentieth century, was just as revolutionary to communications, but in a different way. For the first time an artificial intelligence was able to create or modify the messages that were transmitted. Every communications device before that took a message that had been composed by a human being and (with some occasional loss) delivered it unchanged to another human being. The computer for the first time provides a communication device by which a person may receive a message quite different from what any human sent. Indeed, machines may talk to each other.

Thus two revolutionary developments in communications within a century of each other have converged to create a kind of communications system quite unlike that which has ever existed previously. This book introduces us to some of the implications of those technological developments.

Ithiel de Sola Pool
(1917–1984)

PREFACE

ARNOLD TOYNBEE ONCE suggested that the twentieth century is the first time that mankind can seriously consider the welfare of the entire race. If this is true, it is largely because of events described in this book. These events involve the evolution, perhaps within the next half-century, of a universal electronic information network capable of reaching everyone everywhere. It is the beginning of the information age.

This book is an interim report on these developments; Interim because there are still formidable hurdles to realizing the network. Dramatic developments within the past two decades have assured that technology is no longer a serious obstacle. The problems are now almost wholly in the areas of economic and social affairs. We need to triangulate these two factors with technology in ways that will better identify the opportunities and the barriers to a new kind of information-rich civilization. There is an element of insistence in this task, now, as the framework of the new communications and information structure begins to develop at a faster pace.

In providing an overview of these issues, I have tried to tread a thin line — supplying sufficient facts to clarify the issues while avoiding elaborate details that may obscure them. I have tried to keep in mind W. H. Auden's commandment. "Thou shalt not commit social science." Another pitfall to be avoided is the shimmering thin generality, a particular hazard in discussing such broad subjects as information and communications.

The emphasis throughout is on American ideas and actions. This is not chauvinistic conceit. It is rather a recognition of the fact that the fullest concept of the information age is being applied first in this country. I hope to correct any imbalance in a later book that will examine more fully the impact of the information age abroad among our industrial allies, in the developing nations, and in the communist states. The Europeans and Japanese may, in fact, move ahead of us in many applications of the new network during the coming decade. Their governments' centralized direction of communications affairs often permits faster decisions and actions. The American approach is, of course, different, with decision making shared by government and a complex private sector. This involves a considerable amount of confusion and overlapping. But the results are often more innovative, more exciting and, in the long run, probably more effective in providing a wider range of resources to more people.

We do need a stronger national consensus about our goals and actions in the communications and information area. However, in addition to better planning mechanisms, we also need, in Nigel Calder's phrase, "all the fallibility we can get . . . to preserve the absolute unpredictability and total improbability of our connected minds." This is a lovely paradox and a saving one. In the final analysis, our ability to adapt the powerful new communications and information machines to these intensely human qualities will be the best measure of our success in the new age.

I owe a large debt of gratitude to many people who, in different ways, helped me with this work. They include the faculty and staff of the two institutions at which I taught while researching and writing — the National War College and the School of Foreign Service at Georgetown University. In particular, the staff at Georgetown's Lauinger Library, under the direction of Joseph E. Jeffs, was most helpful in meeting my research needs. I was able to complete the book while a Research Affiliate at M.I.T.'s Center for International Studies. Dr. Eugene Skolnikoff, director of the Center, and his staff provided invaluable assistance.

I want to note the special influence the late Dr. Ithiel de Sola Pool had on my thinking. It was my great good fortune to be associated with him, as a friend and as a professional colleague, for more than twenty years. In addition to his superb research and teaching skills, Ithiel Pool was a formidable defender of the principle that the new information and communications technologies will be valuable only to the degree that they expand the range of informed dialogue between individuals. It was a principle he defended with consummate skill throughout his professional life.

I must also acknowledge the helpful comments, both formal and informal, of Carroll Bowen, Philip Dizard, Herbert Dordick, Alex Edelstein, Glenn Fisher, Oswald Ganley, George Gerbner, Jonathan Gunther, Carol Lee Hilewick, Roland Homet, Neil Hurley, Kas Kalba, Donald LeDuc, Brenda Maddox, Leonard Marks, Anthony Oettinger, Edwin Parker, Joseph Pelton, William Read, Jim Richstad, Glen Robinson, Wilbur Schramm, Anthony Smith, and Jon Vondracek, among others. Students in my Georgetown seminars on communications who assisted with specific research include Cynthia Cox, Hugh Dugan, Keelan Hadley, Bridget Kirwin, Susan Klinges, Peter Ling-Vannerus, Ann Llop, Ellen O'Connor, Eileen O'Hara, Jeff Perez, Laura Picchetti, Tamara Schiebel, and Jennifer Shupp. My four sons, John, Stephen, Wilson, and Mark, each provided useful comments. Finally, a special acknowledgement goes to my wife, Lynn, who brought to my efforts the invaluable chemistry of loving interest and informed criticism.

Wilson P. Dizard

CHAPTER ONE

THE INFORMATION AGE

THE WRIGHT BROTHERS' flying machine was an unstable device, designed with just enough new information to permit it to move through a turbulent three-dimensional environment under its own power. The result was a successful 59-second flight on a windswept North Carolina sand dune. Previous experimenters had failed, many of them crashing because they could not match the available facts with the needs of powered flight.

The analogy is apt in describing the turbulence through which American society will be moving in the coming years. Our passage through difficult times involves infinitely more complex factors than the mechanics of wings, struts, and rudders in the Wright airplane. But the critical question will be the same: Do we have sufficient information resources to carry us through the turbulence? As with the Wright brothers, the answer will tell whether we crash or soar, whether we are headed for a life-enriching culture in the twenty-first century or whether we collapse into political lassitude, economic stalemate, and social fragmentation.

These choices come at a time when technology offers a wider range of information and communications resources than people have ever had. The resources are so pervasive and influential that it is now becoming clear that the United States is moving into a new era — *the information age*. Ours is the first nation to complete the three-stage shift from an agricultural society to an industrial one and to a society whose new patterns are only now emerging. One characteristic of the new age stands out among the welter of trends. This is the increasing emphasis on the production, storage, and distribution of information as its major activity. Our strategy for organizing the transition to this new environment will set the pattern and quality of American life well into the new century.

Information age is the kind of trendy label that satisfies our national penchant for slogans. It is, at best, an arbitrary name, useful primarily for identifying a set of ideas. The persistent structural problems of American society will not be dispersed by slogans. A cliché label is less important than a real perspective on where we are and where we want to be, as individuals and as a society, during the coming years.

1

The purpose of this book is to examine the transition to the new age, to test its implications, and to suggest strategies for managing it. The survey of developments presented here will show that what is happening is not simply a linear extension of what has gone on before. We are experiencing instead a qualitative shift in the thrust and purpose of American society in ways that call for a dynamic response.

The United States is the primary incubator of the changes pushing the world towards an information age. The energies of most societies are still largely absorbed in farming or early industrialization. Japan and the advanced nations of Europe are beginning the transition to a new communications and information environment, although they are not yet as deeply involved as we are. Like the rest of the world, they are watching the United States, in Michel Crozier's phrase, as "the society which is inventing the future."

This is not a flag-waving conceit. The technologies of the information age were largely developed here, and they are being applied here first. This advantage is temporary, however. In the fast-moving new technocentric order, the lead time for innovation that can monopolize the market has been narrowed down to a few years at best. Technology transfer, legal or larcenous, is the order of the day. The research breakthrough made in a California laboratory shows up very quickly on production lines in Cologne or Osaka, often in an improved version. Technological isolationism — the kind that led Chinese emperors to decapitate subjects who sold secrets — is no longer possible. America's lead in high technology gives us an edge in the transition to the new information environment. Our lasting influence, however, will depend on our ability to design political and social strategies to match our technological potential in the coming years.

The rush to identify the new information age has resulted in a wide array of adjectival clichés. There are George Lichtheim's *post*-bourgeois, Rolf Dahrendorf's *post*-capitalist, Amitai Etzioni's *post*-modern, Kenneth Boulding's *post*-civilized, Herman Kahn's *post*-economic, Sidney Ahlstrom's *post*-Protestant, Lewis Feuer's *post*-ideological, and Roderick Seidenberg's *post*-historic societies. Richard Barnet adds a pragmatic note with his contribution: the *post*-petroleum society. Most of these epithets have been left at the *post* by a phrase popularized a decade ago by Harvard sociologist Daniel Bell: the *post*-industrial society. The common prefix of these labels suggests an autumnal quality to our age, a sense of ending. Neither Bell nor the other future watchers have projected a grand design for what is to come, either out of intellectual prudence or simply out of awe at the many contentious prospects available.[1]

Nevertheless, each of them assigns great significance to the prospects examined here — the evolution of a more complex information and communications environment. They may approach the phenomenon from varying perspectives and draw different conclusions, but they share a sense of its importance. Professor Bell, in particular, puts the information factor at the center of his concept of the post-industrial society. He sees a seismic shift of the economy from goods production to information-based services, with professionals and technicians replacing business entrepreneurs as the preeminent social class. Knowledge becomes the pivot of innovation and policy making and technology the key to controlling the future. In Bell's view, a new intellectual technology will be created based on computers; problem-solving devices will replace intuitive judgments.

The future, Dr. Bell suggests, belongs to the eggheads. It is an intriguing notion, inevitably challenged by the eggheads he exalts. These challenges are in the tradition of Lewis Mumford, the most perceptive critic of twentieth-century industrial society. Early in his career, Mumford projected the growth of a humane, technology-based civilization. In his later years, he drew back, predicting instead a massive information-based military-industrial establishment run by an expanding, oppressive bureaucracy.[2] More recent critics, like Peter Stearns and Michael Harrington, continue to challenge euphoric projections for our collective future, sounding a warning against the assumption that powerful, resistant social structures can be readily modified to meet new demands.[3] All theory is gray, as Goethe reminds us, and most of what Dr. Bell and his academic defenders and detractors tell us is theory. However, out beyond the academic forums and lecture halls, massive changes in the information environment are changing the shape and thrust of American society in very concrete ways.

Until recently, there was little solid evidence of the dimensions of this change. Researchers relied primarily on the useful but incomplete studies of the Princeton economist, Fritz Machlup, two decades ago. Machlup looked at what he called "the knowledge industries" — an umbrella phrase covering the educational system, the media, libraries, research institutes, and the like. He suggested that these industries and services were becoming a major force in the United States economy and were expanding at a much faster rate than the industrial and agricultural sectors. In the early sixties, he estimated that the knowledge industries accounted for over 40% of the work force and about one-third of the annual gross national product.[4]

Machlup's study was an important first step in identifying the dimensions of information-based activities in the United States. Like most ground-breaking research, it raised more questions than it answered. A detailed survey of the changes identified by Machlup did not become available until 1977, when the United States Department of Commerce published a nine-volume report entitled *The Information Economy*.[5] Written mainly by Stanford sociologist, Marc Uri Porat, the study confirmed and strengthened Machlup's thesis that the dominant trends in the United States economy involved information-related activities. The Commerce Department's study used different criteria than Machlup's in projecting a new view of the economy in which over 45% of the gross national product is tied to information production and distribution, while nearly half the labor force is engaged in these activities. The study refined Machlup's analysis by dividing the information economy into two parts: a primary sector made up of the direct producers and distributors of information in the marketplace and a secondary sector consisting of the private and public bureaucracies that manage or regulate the economy. The distinction is significant, particularly because it identifies the heavy impact of bureaucratic activities, as distinct from marketplace factors, in the new information environment.

The Commerce Department study will be examined more closely in a later chapter. It is useful in providing a data base with which to identify the salient characteristics of a new kind of economy, increasingly concerned with the production, storage, and distribution of information. This development has all the characteristics of a permanent shift, and it is one whose implications are difficult to grasp. Some of the implications were defined in broad terms some years ago by the theologian–paleontologist Teilhard de Chardin when he described

> the increasing degree in which present-day thought and activity are influenced by the passion for discovery: the progressive replacement of the workshop by the laboratory; of production by research; of the desire for well-being by the desire for more being. . . . Research, which only yesterday was a luxury pursuit, is in the process of becoming a major, indeed the principal, function of humanity. As in the case of all organisms preceding it, but on an immense scale, humanity is in the process of "cerebralizing" itself.[6]

De Chardin's vision still seems utopian. Nevertheless, it is an early warning of the cultural changes implicit in the dry columns of statistics in the Department of Commerce report and other studies of the new information environment. Given the momentum with which we are moving into this environment, we need to get our bearings now and to develop a strategy for managing it.

What scenario can we project for an information-oriented society in the coming years? None of the theory or the research of the academics gives us clear indications. The closest historical precedent is the introduction of printing, an event to which the reaction was delayed and spread out over centuries.

Unlike printing, today's technologies have an almost instantaneous impact. The computer pioneer, John von Neumann, pointed out that modern technology increases the rate of change not so much by shortening the time involved as by expanding the areas — political, economic, and cultural — that are affected. In the communications and information fields, new technologies no longer develop in a linear fashion, separated by decades, with enough time in between for their implications to be sorted out and for them to be brought into active use. Now we are dealing with a wide range of converging technologies, forcing us to make immediate choices and allowing considerably less margin for error.

Forecasting change under these conditions is a risky business, particularly when it involves, as in this country, an already complex information and communications structure. Nevertheless, a general pattern is emerging. It can be seen roughly as a three-stage progression, beginning with changes in the basic information production and distribution industries, leading to a greater range of services available for other industries and for government, and resulting in a vastly expanded range of information facilities at the consumer level. It will be useful to take a summary look at this progression.

The first stage of transformation is already well underway. It is concentrated in what the Department of Commerce's 1977 study called the "primary information sector." This sector is dominated by a relatively small group of large corporations that are the builders and operators of the basic information and communications infrastructure. Their size and influence are awesome. The largest of them, the American Telephone and Telegraph Company, had a gross income greater than the individual gross national products of 118 foreign countries before the 1982 decision to split up the company. The industry is dominated by acronymic giants — IBM, ITT, RCA, GE, CBS, and so on. Clustered around them are groups of smaller firms with little-known names such as Digitech, Valtec, Transnet, and Micom. These minor players are no match for the giants in terms of economic power, but they represent an important trend. Many of them compete successfully against the established leaders by introducing innovative ideas and techniques with a flexibility and flair often lacking in the old-line companies. The result is a newly competitive tone in what has heretofore been a cautious, conservative sector of the economy. But whether with established firms or feisty new challengers, the industry is building the high-technology infrastructure that will form the basic pattern for the information economy. A large part of the structure is already in place. Much of the rest of it is on the drawing boards, ready to be built and completed well before the end of the century.

Meanwhile, the next stage of the new information economy is emerging. It involves the industries and organizations, both private and public, that will be the primary users of the new high-technology network. Their dependence on the services of the new technology is already extensive, and it is increasing exponentially. The banking industry, for instance, is moving towards a universal electronic funds-transfer system that will gradually replace most of its paper transactions, including the more than 40 billion checks written every year in the United States. The national health-delivery system will be supported increasingly by automated, computer-based data systems whose functions range from storage of medical records to long-distance monitoring of patients. The education industry, with its $230 billion annual budget, will move more rapidly into electronic learning systems. Hopefully, this industry will benefit from lessons learned in the sixties, when it attempted to automate instruction for the wrong reason, that is, to save money rather than to improve the learning process.

Computer-assisted instruction, already used by millions of students, is becoming commonplace. Computer literacy will be taught as a basic skill. The driving force for this will be the increasingly ubiquitous personal computer. At mid-decade, there were over 20 million of them installed in American offices and homes. By 1990, this number will have tripled.

Some of the most extensive changes will take place in business offices. The trend toward automated office operations is already running strong in large organizations. Within this decade, it will encompass even the smallest firms, making them essentially computer-based communications centers. It took the telephone 75 years to reach the level of penetration in offices that the small computer will attain in 10. The automation of office procedures will probably account for the largest dollar-volume share of the expanded information sector in the next few years.

Meanwhile, the vast public sector bureaucracy is adapting to the new technologies. The United States Government is now the world's largest repository and dispenser of information, from cookbooks printed by the Government Printing Office to maps of Mars produced by the Space Administration. One small federal agency, the National Technical Information Service, is the largest publisher of books and reports in the world, using a computer-based system that has almost nothing to do with conventional printing presses.

The third and most far-reaching stage of the information age will accelerate during the coming decade. This is the mass consumerization of high-technology information services. Communications and information resources in the United States are more complex than in any other society. They are relatively primitive, however, considering the prospects created by the application of available technology to a new kind of mass information network. As inventor Peter Goldmark put it, our communications are still in the "tom-tom stage." The changes are coming fast, however. Advanced information and communications resources, now limited largely to use by big business and big government, can be extended to homes and small organizations, providing a wide range of computer-based information resources that is well beyond anything now available. Nearly half of all American homes are already linked to cable or direct-broadcast satellite systems.

This possibility conjures up visions of whirring, blinking computers in the living room and other Sunday-supplement dreams. The reality is somewhat different — and more reassuring. Most of the new services will be made available through two devices already present in most American homes — the telephone and the television set. These familiar instruments can be the links to a new kind of information richness.

In Britain, an information network with the unassuming name of Prestel already supplies thousands of homes and offices with a full range of computerized information services. The system is based on the telephone, the television set, and a "black box" attachment that costs less than $200.

The service is linked to hundreds of data bases, providing hundreds of thousands of "pages" of information which can be ordered up on the television screen by dialing the appropriate computer through the telephone system. The data ranges from the frivolous to the practical to the profound: *What is my horoscope for today? Who won the fifth race at Ascot this afternoon? Which library provides the best bibliographic information on the combinatorial mathematics of scheduling?* Prestel tells all, for a fee that is added to one's telephone bill at the end of the month. It is a working system that is being replicated in a half-dozen other European countries. After considerable experimentation and a few expensive false starts, several networks for merchandizing similar services have been developed in this country.

Prestel and other projects that plug millions of people into a vastly expanded system of information services are Model T versions of what may be a taken-for-granted part of daily life by the end of the century. The present systems can only connect their subscribers to relatively large central computer banks. The next step, well within the capacity of present technology, will be to allow subscribers to develop their own data banks. This information can be sent to central data banks, passed on to other subscribers directly as a public service or for a fee, or stored for future reference. Here we will have a new kind of First Amendment democracy — every person his own data collector and publisher, unmediated by any authority, public or private, as long as he pays the telephone–computer service bill at the end of the month.

The full possibilities of this technology will be felt only in those democracies — a discouraging minority of the world's nations — that are committed to open inquiry and the ambiguity of conflicting challenges to authorized, conventional wisdom. The United States and like-minded societies have had only limited experience with such an environment until now because of technical and economic constraints on universal information access. But, we are beginning to grapple with the implications of the changeover. It will, for instance, affect the way in which we learn, not only in school but in the long years afterwards. For all our commitment to mass education, we are still living in a time of educational incapacity. Formal learning for adults is generally cut off in the late teens or the early twenties, leaving most of us diminished in an environment that requires lifelong retraining. With the new technology, continued learning will be more than a question of refresher courses and other "adult education." It will involve, rather, an environment that adds a stunning dimension to information seeking and creative thinking. Norman Macrae, an editor of the *Economist*, asks what will happen if the new technologies are applied in ways that remove the present limitations on life-time access to information.

> The prospect is, after all, that we are going to enter an age when any duffer sitting at a computer terminal in his laboratory or office or public

library or home can delve through unimaginable increased mountains of information in mass-assembly data banks with mechanical powers of concentration and calculation that will be greater by a factor of tens of thousands than was ever available to the human brain of even an Einstein. From the 99 percent perspiration and one percent inspiration that was Edison's definition of inventive genius before he died in 1931, we have in the four decades since his death already provided the machines that can reduce the main part of that perspiration much more than 99 times over. Because this will eventually make research a task that can be undertaken more effectively (even part-time) by many more people, this must surely increase the prospect by unearthing more people with Edison's or Einstein's divine afflatus. I do not believe that heretofore more than a small fraction of mankind's potential geniuses have ever had a chance to indulge in research work if they wanted to.[7]

The prospect of crowds of Einsteins and Edisons is enough to give us pause. More immediately, a full-scale information network will break the old constraining bonds of limited access to information resources. Computer scientists have a phrase that fits the new situation, "distributed intelligence." Until a few years ago, Norman Macrae's future geniuses were limited to large, centralized data bases. The new technologies — minicomputers and high-speed data networks — are changing this, making possible a new kind of flexibility and creative individualism. Geographically dispersed data terminals, each with its own information storage and computing capability, can operate independently, be linked to each other, or be linked to large central data sources. The focus in computer development has moved from the relatively simple management of central data bases to new patterns of "distributed intelligence" — a phrase that defines much of the creative promise of the coming information age.

The image of the genius working at a computer terminal in a small room appeals to our pride of technological prowess as well as to our democratic faith in individualism. What is difficult to imagine is its replication tens of thousands or even millions of times. This calls for a quantum leap of both imagination and of faith in the promise of a new information environment. Our understanding of freedom, creativity, and democracy will take on different dimensions in the new era.

British communications scholar, Anthony Smith, predicts a seismic effect of these changes on the notion of authorship as an individual process and the protection of information property rights as a result of the new technologies. He points out that, whereas in the age of Gutenberg print, the author became supreme and the machinery of information was under the control of the author, the computer age is beginning in many ways to unwind this concept of information. More and more, he notes, research and authorship are being recognized as collective acts, not individual ones. Moreover, he adds, the information age is a transnational age. Information systems that were national, *uni*lingual and *uni*confessional are giving way to systems that are *multi*national. Inevitably, governments and societies will act to preserve national voices and channels, particularly in reaction to societies like the United States that export vast amounts of information in many forms.

The promise of the information society is intangible and elusive. We are not going to vote on it one day any more than our eighteenth-century ancestors voted on the industrial age. There is no specific critical moment when we can decide how we want to handle the new environment. The issues are spread out in time and place, across a fragmented array of institutional decisions. As we shall see, this makes development of a broad strategy for the new age problematic. We have, in any event, moved beyond easy notions that we can fill our information needs simply by plugging in bigger and better machines. To be sure, the technology for such machines is available. The challenge is in applying them with a clear perception of social needs and in giving emotional texture to the new environment they will create. As Jacques Maritain once noted wryly, "The telephone and the radio do not prevent man from having two arms, two legs, two lungs, falling in love and searching for happiness."[8]

The technocratic visions of the thirties and forties, in which communications were a mechanistic linear process, collapsed under their shaky assumptions about human behavior. Many of the subtleties of the communications process still elude us and probably always will. However, its human dimensions are better understood now as a result of the increased attention given them by researchers in all disciplines from animal biology to mathematics. One of the most fruitful research areas has been the study of how animals, from dolphins to chimpanzees, communicate in elaborate patterns. Another has been the study of nonverbal human communications, the use of body gestures and other signals which, according to anthropologist Edward Hall, make up 70% of our communication patterns. The result, as Harold Lasswell noted, has been to reduce the parochialism of the larynx in our understanding of communications.

If it has not come up with final answers, the new research has emphasized the complexity of the communications process. Human beings are not information processors, but code crafters. They don't think straight, if "straight" is taken to mean adhering to standards of right-thinking predetermined by some higher authority. This ambiguity is the most subtle and useful quality we bring to the task of fashioning a truly creative information environment. In this work, we are heirs to the great tradition of men and women who, through the ages, have sought to organize knowledge for civilizing purposes.

Success in our generation will depend on the degree to which we shape the new information technologies in accordance with human values. For most of this century, futurists and planners have imagined human progress in terms of a technological society, a chromium wilderness in which emotional richness has been overtaken by programmed happiness. H. G.

Wells, among others, described this solemnly in his works. Aldous Huxley added the saving grace of satire in *Brave New World*. We have moved away from these monstrous models towards more humanistic ones, in which machines are a subordinate rather than a controlling factor. The cold metaphor of the impersonal, technocratic machine is being replaced. The new metaphor is a blooming, buzzing garden in which each of us — including those new Einsteins and their computers — can cultivate a personal plot. This involves combinations of order and disorder, as well as the surprises that spring from the widened boundaries of creative imagination.

Programmed utopia or blooming, buzzing garden — these are, in simplified form, the alternative ways in which we can begin to understand our choices in the emerging information environment. It is a familiar problem for Americans. The tensions between democratic, humanistic ideals and technocratic imperatives thread through our history. However, the new information machines add an insistent, even urgent, dimension to this conflict. They do this by amplifying intelligence dramatically in much the same way that the machines of the Industrial Revolution amplified physical strength. Computers and other information machines are the new motor power, pulling us toward a transformed society faster than we can understand where we are going. The machines can help to orient us in these ambiguous passages, but they are not panaceas. Their mechanical innards do not contain certain formulas for surviving and thriving.

Neither will we find the answers at the Delphic shrines of the technocrats and their systems analysis dogmas. As Herbert Stein has pointed out:

> The dream of thinking everything out before we act, of making certain we have all the facts and know all the consequences, is a sick Hamlet's dream. It is the dream of someone with no appreciation of the seamless web of causation, the limits of human thinking, or the scarcity of human attention. The world outside is itself the greatest storehouse of knowledge. Human reason, drawing upon the pattern and redundancy of nature, can predict some of the consequences of human action. But the world will always remain the largest laboratory, the largest information store, from which we will learn the outcomes, good and bad, of what we have done. Of course, it is costly to learn from experience, but it is also costly, and frequently much less reliable, to try through research and analysis to anticipate experience.[9]

Who sets the social directions and policies in this complex new environment? Government is only one of the major actors in the process. Industry, labor, the financial community, and universities all play critical-roles. Given the sensitivity of the subject, the process demands a new kind of awareness of the relationship between technology, economics, and social needs. Decisions on the future pattern of communications and information resources differ from those dealing with, for example, medical care or housing. Communications and information policies involve basic questions of personal identity and values. The overriding concern should not be specific programs or techniques but rather the pattern by which influence is exerted and information becomes effective in a pluralistic society. Strategic decisions will depend on how we see ourselves and project our own interests as we face an uncertain future. A large democracy thrives only when its citizens share enough information, beliefs, and assumptions to function together in a rough consensus. This consensus becomes more important as the pace of change accelerates, upsetting present assumptions and clouding future expectations. We need to collectivize our intelligence, not in centralized, authoritarian fashion, but by encouraging dialogue based on shared information and leading toward agreement on strategies for surviving and thriving as individuals and as a society.

This imperative for both personal and communal awareness is underscored by political scientist, Karl Deutsch.[10] He suggests that we are coming closer to the boundaries within which our intellectual equipment is able to cope with present complexities. He calls for greater emphasis on "intelligence amplification," using information technologies to increase human understanding. Part of the problem with this is our ignorance about the capabilities of the new machines. We tend to see them primarily as improved means for storing and distributing information. Their greatest value, however, may be as satellites of consciousness, monitoring and identifying social needs in much the same way as the NASA Landsat satellite monitors earth's environmental conditions. This calls for a new kind of information and communications pattern well beyond our present limited system, one that is universal, interactive, and accessible to everyone.

One advantage we have is in not being bound by the easy assumptions of earlier generations about the value of technical progress; we see more clearly the contradictions involved in this process. The French sociologist, Jacques Ellul, has developed a sobering catalogue of these paradoxes. He points out that

- All technical progress exacts a price; that is, while it adds something on the one hand, it subtracts something on the other.
- All technical progress raises more problems than it solves, tempts us to see the consequent problems as technical in nature, and prods us to seek technical solutions to them.
- The negative effects of technological innovation are inseparable from the positive. It is naive to say that technology is neutral, that it may be used for good or bad ends; the good and bad effects are, in fact, simultaneous and inseparable.
- All technological innovations have unforeseeable effects.[11]

These strictures apply with particular sensitivity to the spread of communications and information technologies. For all our willingness to assume that the new networks are a good thing, there are warning signals to the contrary. Consider, for example, Citizen's Band (CB) radio, that new form of electronic populism which has given over 30 million Americans their own two-way broadcasting capabilities. Advertisers of CB sets stress safety and convenience as benefits of their products. There may be such advantages, but they mask the deeper reasons for the CB craze. The less advertised factor is CB's appeal to more personal needs. Communications researcher, Bert Cowlan, sees the CB phenomenon as

> a desire to overcome alienation and to have the opportunity to manage one's own communication system, coordinate one's own resources to survive in what many perceive as an increasingly hostile, bureaucratic, and depersonalized, costly, inefficient and high-risk environment.[12]

The CB user may broadcast in an urgent megavoice, but he or she often displays a penchant for anonymity with a glamorized pseudonym. Tom, Dick, Harry, and Mary Jones turn into Crusader Rabbit, Super Stud, the Ace of Spades, and Crazy Mama. As one of the characters in the perceptive 1977 film, *Citizen's Band*, says about CB's influence in a small town: "Everyone in this town is somebody they're not supposed to be."

The tendency to hide one's identity behind an electronic shield can be found in another well-known phenomenon — the unlisted phone number. Once the preserve of a self-conscious minority, the unlisted number is now common. Almost a million phone numbers in New York City are not listed.[13] The private number is a symbol, albeit an absent one, of the dark side of our assumptions about the importance of being in touch, of being part of the network. It is a reminder that, for many people, the openness promised by new communications technologies is a threat, not a promise.

These examples are not aberrations, but merely some of the doubts, fears, and other human frailties we bring with us to the expanded information environment. The promising aspect of the new technologies is that they may expand democratic humanistic options, allowing more sharing of responsibilities and rewards. They can, obversely, have less rewarding effects, propping up outmoded institutions and narrow interests. Such rigid use of technology leads to political alienation and social unrest, resulting in the kind of bloody-minded Ludditism that characterizes so much of the popular attitude toward impersonal technologies and the managers who control them. In the short run — the next decade or two — the first attempts to apply the information machines effectively will compound this problem. This process will call not only for technical efficiency but also for a new kind of democratic equity, a person-centered perspective that assumes neither men nor machines need to be changed radically before human progress can take place.

We are moving into a new ecology of information, defined in large part by the computer's ability to amplify intelligence. This liberating potential of the information machines is still only partially understood. In these first decades of computer technology, the machines have been regarded primarily as useful, somewhat exotic storage bins and calculating devices.

Their misuse and underuse is characteristic of our technological and social illiteracy. The problem is computer literacy, a subject commanding more and more attention from researchers and educators.

British critic, George Steiner, has observed that computer language may be a more logical common tongue than English or any other so-called world language. Probably, a new polyglot will develop from computer-oriented English and ideograms. A sort of universal Pidgin may emerge, similar to the special patois that airline pilots use as they take off and land in a multilingual range of cultures.

Developing a comprehensible, comprehensive language is only part of the problem of computer literacy. Equally important is developing a level of literacy that will stimulate creative use of the machines as intelligence amplifiers by nontechnical users. As computer scientist, Alan Kay, puts it: "Simple tasks must be simple and complex ones must be possible."[14] Kay and his colleagues at the Xerox research center in Palo Alto are among the groups studying ways in which to expand creative application of personal computing systems. Significantly, they have turned to the inventiveness of young children for their insights. The project, known as SMALLTALK, involves hundreds of children, ranging in age from 6 to 15, who are given wide latitude to program computers. Along the way, the Xerox researchers have learned a lot about learning, particularly about the fragile balance between free exploration and structured curricula. Similar research at M.I.T.'s Artificial Intelligence Laboratory confirms the computer's simulating value in expanding the prospects for imaginative learning.[15]

Children have taught the SMALLTALK researchers to program more imaginative uses of the simulating property of computers. Most adults use computer simulation as a crutch to confirm their versions of reality. Children have far fewer inhibitions. They use the computer to create what Kay and his colleagues call "splendid nonsense," simulations that stretch the limits of human imagination beyond conventional ideas. This may be the greatest force unleashed by the new high-capacity information machines, with games played by children pointing to a new kind of expanded human creativity. The computer programs created by children in the Xerox lab are the modern equivalent of the "splendid nonsense" with which the movers and shakers of civilization have always challenged conventional thinking.

The stumbling blocks to realizing this potential lie not in those who exaggerate the computer's capability, but in those who fear it. There is a disturbing tendency to retreat from the implications of the new machines, to deny the possibility of a viable technology-powered democratic society. These antitechnology forces, the new Luddites, seek solace in astrology, artificial Waldens, and bad poetry. Most of us still accept, if with some reservations, the traditionally American secular faith in technology and its benefits. We recognize that technology is not an all-purpose solution. In a divided world, it exerts a powerful influence in keeping us divided.

Nevertheless, as Harold Lasswell has noted, an effective information and communications system, at home and abroad, is needed to sustain the powerful trends pushing us toward a new form of world order — the shaping and sharing of basic values and the introduction of specific procedures for more stable social and economic development.[16]

Whether such a pattern can be realized will depend not only on our own efforts but ultimately on decisions made in 150 highly diverse societies beyond our borders. Each of them must deal, in its own cultural context, with the new information machines and with the need for difficult institutional changes at the political, economic, and social levels. American experience has a powerful attraction for other societies searching for their own versions of a new Eden. The difference now is the renewed strength and universality of the search. There is, as Janet Flanner said, a strong wind blowing for all men of different colors on different parts of the globe with a steady, unending velocity, unlike the limited cyclonic gusts of the past. Americans have had practical experience with this liberating spirit for more than two centuries; for others, it is a traumatic new experiment.

In its "export" overseas, the American example has taken on a wider identity. It is the gospel of modernization. Since modernization describes much of the psychic environment in which the global information age is developing, it is an important part of our story. Modernization is the doctrine of organized universal betterment. As a worldwide civil religion, it is more influential than nationalism or such limited movements as democracy, fascism, or communism. It shows itself as a psychic mass migration toward a better life. Once this idea makes contact with a society, it diffuses in ways that irrevocably affect traditional institutions and values. It becomes the universal social catalyst, changing everyone it touches.

The gospel of modernization has had to undergo adjustment to some persistent realities since it was first proclaimed in the 1950s. The tone then was one of unalloyed missionary zeal, involving the transformation of the world's underdeveloped areas into local versions of middle-class American suburbs. Reluctantly, its proponents have had to scale down this vision considerably in recent years. Modernization now tends to be described in such uninspiring terms as the New International Economic Order. The emphasis is on sober subjects such as technology transfer, export subsidies, protection prices for raw materials, and the like. Nevertheless, behind the facade of this new sobriety, faith in modernization remains strong. It is a gospel that speaks to the common desires of human beings, as the British critic, Malcolm Muggeridge, once stated:

> What they all want...is what the Americans have got — six lanes of large motor cars streaming powerfully into and out of gleaming cities; neon lights flashing, and juke boxes sounding and skyscrapers rising, story upon story into the sky. Driving at night into the town of Athens, Ohio (pop. 3,450), four bright colored signs stood out in the darkness

— "Gas," "Drugs," "Beauty," "Food." Here, I thought, is the ultimate, the *logos* of our time, presented in sublime simplicity. It was like a vision in which suddenly all the complexity of life is reduced to one single inescapable proposition. These could have shone forth as clearly in Athens, Greece as in Athens, Ohio. They belonged as aptly to Turkestan or Sind or Kamchatka.... There are, properly speaking, no Communists, no capitalists, no Catholics, no Protestants, no black men, no Asians, no Europeans, no Right, no Left and no Center.... There is only a vast and omnipresent longing for Gas, for Beauty, for Drugs and for Food.[17]

Western democratic capitalism has undoubtedly fostered and diffused the modernization idea faster than any other system. However, it would be wrong to equate modernization exclusively with America's own political and economic experience. Many of our mistakes in dealing with the Third World are based on this kind of misperception. Nevertheless, the American example stands as a major force, despite the apparent erosion of our political and economic influence abroad in recent years. "America is a gigantic theater," wrote Ceasare Pavese, "where, with greater candor than elsewhere, is being played out the drama of us all." The drama others are observing now is an America moving beyond the conventional modernization process into an advanced evolutionary phase in which information rather than material production is the focus.

This is usually demonstrated in economic terms, but the American contribution goes further in defining its social dynamics. We add the hitherto startling notion that we expect to live through two or more sets of futures in one lifetime. This is reflected in an educational system that, at its best, prepares for a future that is unpredictable, different, and — still the American hope — qualitatively better. This is a long psychic jump, not without peril, from the assumptions of most other societies with their still-powerful legacies of hierarchal immobility. Such traditions are being eroded everywhere as the gospel of modernization spreads.

Americans proselytize most effectively when they do so least consciously. In his masterful work on propaganda systems, Jacques Ellul emphasizes that unstructured "social propaganda" as expressed in Hollywood films or the *Reader's Digest* has far more impact than the highly organized propaganda attempts of the Nazis, communists, or even our own government's programs of official political persuasion aimed at overseas audiences through the Voice of America. The impact of unintended American social influence — from Levis jeans to IBM computers — is a potent part of the dynamics of modernization.

The coming of the information age complicates the modernization process. Even the limited communications channels available over the past three decades served as powerful diffusers of the new gospel. The new communications and information machines will speed this diffusion dramatically. The developing high-technology networks around the world are

predominantly American in style, as is the tone of most of the modernization messages flowing through them.

A new map of the globe is being drawn. It is an information map,
comparable to a weather map in that it indicates environmental conditions
rather than linear directions. The map shows a dense mass of organized
information over North America, with smaller masses over Europe, Japan,
and the Soviet Union. Elsewhere the density of information shades off into
thinness. The new technologies can change this map radically by helping
create a global knowledge grid. How much of the grid can be in place by the
end of the century? By the year 2010? To what extent will political,
economic, and ideological factors cause delays?

The answers will depend on the strategies and actions we choose during
the coming decade, both within our domestic framework and in our
relations with other societies. Americans have tended to see the modernization process in terms of the political and economic power it may confer on
us. This view is shortsighted. The end benefit, to us and to every other
society, will be a stunning global dimension to learning and knowledge.
This new dimension can convert our fixation on modernization into a
powerful civilizing force.

We are heirs to a great tradition of men and women who saw the
organization of available information as a basic condition of human
progress. It is the tradition of Ptolemy I Soter (305–283 B.C.) who founded
the great library of Alexandria, the first attempt to gather all the world's
books in one place and catalogue them scientifically. Its collection of
perhaps 700,000 volumes was not matched again until the past century. The
destruction of the library in 391 A.D. was a major disaster for Western
civilization, reducing the stock of organized knowledge to a few hundred
manuscripts. Fortunately, the tradition was kept alive by small groups of
Benedictines and other monks, who copied and preserved the few works
that survived. The next great step, following the invention of printing and
cheap paper, was the work of the French Encyclopedists and their equally
enlightened Scottish counterparts, the creators of the *Encyclopaedia Britannica*. Both attempted to summarize the world's knowledge in one set of
books. Theirs was an astonishing effort, with (in the case of the French)
direct revolutionary implications. The concept spread to the development of
the modern Alexandrine counterparts — the Library of Congress, the
British Museum library, and other great library centers.

In the early part of this century, H. G. Wells proposed the development
of a World Brain, a project for gathering and storing all information in one
place, using the latest technologies. His World Brain was dismissed as
fantasy at the time, but the concept is realizable today in the computer,
whose capabilities go well beyond those he proposed. The contents of the
Library of Congress, over 30 million volumes, could now be stored
microelectronically in a relatively small room. Reduced to digital comput-

erized form, the Library's total holdings could eventually be transmitted in a few minutes over high-capacity networks. These may not be practical possibilities, but the growth of massive data banks, linked to users throughout the world by high-speed circuits, already constitute a new civilizing force in the great tradition of Alexandria, Monte Cassino, the Encyclopedists, and the great modern library centers.

Here is a challenge to match the promise of our democratic society as we move towards a new century. In little more than a generation, the technology to match this challenge has moved from the laboratories into everyday use. Our applications have been primitive compared to the potential of the new machines. The United States has expanded its information production to the point that it is now the repository of the largest share of the world's organized knowledge. Greater benefits may come, however, not from the knowledge we give or sell to other societies, but from what we receive over the new electronic circuits from them. We need these outside resources not simply as accretions to our own knowledge inventory but for the health of our society. They are needed, as the veteran diplomat George Kennan once said:

> just as rain is by the desert and needed... for our sakes alone, for our development as individuals and as a nation, lest we fall into complacency, sterility and emotional decay; lest we lose our sense of the capabilities of the human spirit, and with it much of our sensitivity to the possible meaning and wonder of life itself.[18]

The American influence on a global knowledge network will depend primarily on what we do as a nation. The issue is the development and application of technologies vital to the future of our democratic society and its place in the world. A strategy will emerge either by design or default; for the present, we have not decided which it will be. Given our reluctance to turn over the decision and control functions in this area to government, we have relied largely on haphazard, unstructured decision making, driven primarily by economic forces that have given us the most advanced communications and information structures in the world. The question is whether we can continue on the same course in the same manner or whether we have arrived at a moment when a different national strategy is needed.

How does a society shape strategies for its survival? There is no formula to guide us into an uncertain future with its combination of enhanced intelligence capabilities and greater social ambiguities. Our greatest resource in meeting the challenge is a 3-pound electrochemical device, slightly alkaline, which runs on the power of glucose at 25 watts. It is the human brain. It has one striking advantage which even the most sophisticated computer will eternally lack — the power of divine afflatus, imagination, or even just common sense.

NOTES

1. Daniel Bell first outlined his post-industrial thesis in *The Coming of Post-Industrial Society* (New York: Basic Books, 1973), p. 212 *et passim*. For a more recent version of Bell's ideas, see his "The Social Framework of the Information Society," in The *Microelectronics Revolution*, Tom Forester ed., (Cambridge, Mass.: M.I.T. Press, 1981), pp. 500–549.

2. Lewis Mumford, *The Pentagon of Power* (New York: Harcourt Brace, 1970), pp. 293–299.

3. Peter Stearns, "Is There a Post-Industrial Society?" and Michael Harrington, "Post-Industrial Society and the Welfare State," in *Libraries in Post-Industrial Society*, Leigh Estabrook ed. (Phoenix: Oryx Press, 1977), pp. 8–18; 19–29.

4. Fritz Machlup, *The Production and Distribution of Knowledge in the United States* (Princeton, N.J.: Princeton University Press, 1962).

5. U.S. Department of Commerce, *The Information Economy* (9 vols.), (Washington, D.C.: Government Printing Office, 1977).

6. Teilhard de Chardin, *The Future of Man* (New York: Harper & Row, 1969), pp. 166 and 173.

7. Norman Macrae, "Multinational Business," *The Economist* (London) (January 22, 1972), p. 10.

8. Julie Kernan, *Our Friend, Jacques Maritain* (New York: Doubleday, 1975), p. 177.

9. Herbert Stein, "Designing Organizations for an Information-Rich World, in *Computers, Communications and the Public Interest*, ed. Martin Greenberger (Baltimore: Johns Hopkins University Press, 1971), p. 47.

10. Karl W. Deutsch, *The Nerves of Government* (New York: The Free Press of Glencoe, 1963).

11. Jacques Ellul, "The Technological Order," *Technology and Culture*, 3 (Fall 1962): 394.

12. Bert Cowlan, "Communications for the Individual and Extension of Choice" (Paper presented before the annual conference of the International Institute of Communications, Washington, D.C., September 1977), p. 4. See also Jon T. Powell and Donald Ary, "Communications Without Commitment," *Journal of Communication*, 27, no. 3 (Summer 1977): 118–21.

13. "The Unlisted Numbers List Is Growing." *New York Times*, 17 December 1977, p. 35.

14. Alan C. Kay, "Microelectronics and the Personal Computer," *Scientific American* (September 1977): 231.

15. See Seymour Papert, *Mindstorms: Children, Computers and Powerful Ideas* (New York: Basic Books, 1980) for a description of pioneering research on computers as learning tools conducted at the MIT Artificial Intelligence Laboratory.

16. Harold G. Lasswell, "Communications in a Divided World" (1977 Louis G. Cowen Lecture, sponsored by the International Broadcast Institute, London, 1977).

17. Malcolm Muggeridge, *Things Past* (London: Collins, 1978), p. 125.

18. Quoted in Wilson Dizard, *The Strategy of Trust* (Washington, D.C.: Public Affairs Press, 1961), p. 172.

CHAPTER TWO

THE AMERICAN STAKE

IN CONSIDERING STRATEGIES for the information age, we must be aware of the psychic forces that have created the new environment. The most important of these is the American technological myth, the search for a new Eden through the melding of nature and the machine. This machine-in-the-garden is a persistent vision from the beginnings of American thought. At once utopian and pragmatic, millenial and immediate, it is a view of society as a progression towards an earthly ideal, not, as in older civilizations, an acceptance of unchangeable conditions.

Benjamin Franklin, kite in hand, may be the best-known symbol of the search for an electrically powered paradise. Thomas Jefferson, the farmer–philosopher who distrusted the new industrialism, saw America as sufficiently removed from the evils of European society to be the model for fusing spiritual values with technology-based wealth. A half-century later, the quintessential national philosopher, Ralph Waldo Emerson, wrote, "Machinery and transcendentalism agree well....Our civilization and these ideas are reducing earth to a brain. See how by the telegram and steam the earth is anthropologized." This is the rhetoric of the "technological sublime," in Leo Marx's phrase, and it runs like a golden thread through the national uplift literature.[1]

This American faith has been a powerful force propelling us toward new forms of post-industrialism. Its focus has changed somewhat as American society has become more complex, and particularly as it has expanded its global interests. However, even the recent lowering of expectations about the United States' role in world affairs has not seriously affected the myth. The lure of the Western frontier has been largely replaced by the lure of the equally elusive global village. This folksy creation of the late Marshall McLuhan appeals to our desire to reduce the wide world to familiar proportions. McLuhan is, significantly, one of the best-known of the present generation of believers in the transforming power of electricity. (Others of the faith have included biologist, Julian Huxley, theologian, Teilhard de Chardin, and engineer, Buckminster Fuller.) In a metaphysical flight, McLuhan once declared that the computer "promises by technology a Pentecostal condition of universal understanding and unity."[2]

Social salvation through better communications and information has been a steady promise within the American technological myth. The promise has, moreover, been translated into practice here on a scale never attempted by other societies. The statistical measures of growth toward a new kind of information society are awesome — in numbers of telephones, computers, and other devices. The newly proclaimed information age is, however, less an accretion of machines and techniques than a declaration of faith that electronic salvation may well be within our grasp. The proofs of the faith are found these days in the pea-size products of the microelectronics industry — the stunning range of technologies that began with the transistor in the 1950s and came of age with the integrated circuit, tiny semiconductor devices which are the building blocks of the post-industrial era.

With all its sophisticated capabilities, the new technological environment includes some stubborn problems. Its initial impact has been to raise the level of social complexity. We try to temper this, often by anthropomorphizing the new machines. Where but in America, to use the old lead-in, would a bank try to sell the services of its computerized teller machines by advertising a mechanical pal named "Tillie the Teller" — and succeed? "We promoted her personality," says an official of the First National Bank of Atlanta. "She's a bubbly, giggly kind of character."[3]

Tillie the Teller aside, we will have to come to terms with some changing realities in our search for the electronic Eden, the machine-in-the-garden. And here the dark side of the technological myth has to be faced. Henry Adams was one of the early doubters. In *The Education of Henry Adams*, he saw the dynamo, the symbol of technology, as a threat and sought refuge in the virgin cult of the Middle Ages. Mark Twain expressed his skepticism by having Hank Morgan, the hero of *A Connecticut Yankee in King Arthur's Court*, become trapped by an electrical fence which he had intended to use as protection against the primitive Britons.

In more recent times, an incisive critic of the technological myth has been Lewis Mumford. In his early career, Mumford accepted the optimistic view of technological benefits espoused by his teacher, Patrick Geddes, the Scottish biologist and urban planner. In *Technics and Civilization* (1934), Mumford declared that electricity would be the great instrument of social balance in American civilization. But in his last great book, *The Pentagon of Power* (1970), he attacked easy optimism about the benefits of technology, including those associated with communications and information. Whatever its early promise, he declared, the new technologies were being used to magnify and vulgarize the dominant components of the power structure, making it easier for a small elite to dominate large populations.[4] His conclusions were anticipated some years before by a Canadian scholar, Harold Innis, who challenged the idea that communications would lead to a democratic diffusion of power. Innis saw what he termed the tragedy of modern culture here and in Europe as the influence of print and electronic media undermining space and time in the interests of commercial and political power.[5]

The warnings of Mumford, Innis, and other critics have continued in recent years. Victor Ferkiss of Georgetown University believes American society is at a critical juncture in its inability to understand adequately the political consequences of technological change.[6] At the popular level, Alvin Toffler sees the prospect of social breakdown as the result of uncontrolled information overload.[7] University of California researcher, Herbert Schiller, maintains that the manipulation of communications and information resources by a military-industrial establishment is undermining the prospects for democratic society in this country.[8] One of the most striking criticisms of the perils of microelectronic technology is found in a study sponsored by an organization with certified establishment credits — the New York-based Conference Board, a business research group. Its report, *Information Technology: Some Critical Implications for Decision Makers*, takes a somber view of our ability to cope with the choices opened up by computers and other information technologies.

> We may create and strengthen the power of management elites, circumscribe the freedom of man, and create a new kind of rich–poor gap between those, regardless of economic status, who know how to command information and those who do not.[9]

Although their approaches to the subject vary, these post-Mumfordian critics concur in their assessment of technology as a double-edged weapon which is being misused. Their pessimism is grounded in the dark perceptions of technological consequences outlined by French sociologist, Jacques Ellul, in the five sobering precepts listed in Chapter 1. None of these critics has stated the case of unintended consequences more sharply than the distinguished American philosopher, Morris Raphael Cohen. He would propose a dilemma for his students: If there was an invention that would enormously increase individual freedom and mobility but demanded the sacrifice of 30 thousand human lives annually, would you take it? The invention was, of course, the automobile. No one in the early years of this century could have assessed its benefits and costs. The new information technologies will, if anything, have a greater impact — although perhaps not involving the direct loss of lives in quite the same way.

This unease spreads well beyond the problems posed by those few individuals who ponder the philosophical implications of change. It is reflected in the ambivalence ordinary men and women feel about the new environment. The extreme form of this ambivalence is the Ludditism and other types of defiance exhibited by countercultural critics of the system. But it is also present, less dramatically, in the general attitude or feeling that something is wrong, that a ubiquitous "they" is ganging up on the rest of us.

This attitude breaks through in daily irritations about computerized credit card mix-ups, erroneous bank statements, wrong numbers on the telephone, transportation delays, and shoddy "quality-controlled" products in the stores. These incidents feed into a vague sense that technologies have now crossed the threshold into uncontrolled power and consequences from which there may be no turning back. It is reinforced by the piling up of larger problems, such as diminishing energy resources and environmental pollution, where technology emerges as cause rather than cure. Taken together, these problems are seen not as minor obstacles but rather as the end result of a serious, persistent disequilibrium. As Victor Ferkiss has noted, this attitude highlights the difficulties of fashioning viable social institutions and processes to deal with a more complex, technology-driven structure.[10]

If Americans are being currently denied the sunny certainties of onward-and-upward technological progress, we have some sober compensations. These take the form of a greater, if still reluctant, readiness to face up to the situation. Under the pressure of events, there is somewhat less wandering in the meadows of easy assumption about the changed environment of post-industrial society. We have succeeded in shucking off some of the more romantic notions of the technological myth. Hopefully, we have begun to see more clearly the prospects of a free society in which technology can be applied more effectively on a mass scale to serve both material needs and those intangibles that enrich the quality of life. To deny this hope, or not to act on it, would be to erode — perhaps beyond repair — the social mystique holding us together as a civilization that has moved beyond the traditional cultural ties of race or place. The electronic Eden, the machine-in-the-garden, still has a powerful role to play, newly revised to suit conditions that our forebears could not imagine. The question is whether this new reality can be matched with old values in a way that strengthens our prospects for a humanistic democracy.

Here is where the new capabilities of communications and information become critical. They are not simply microelectronic add-ons to the economic structure. They are a controlling resource, the social brain and nervous system holding society together and keeping it in some sort of working equilibrium during a difficult transition. Again, the Wright brothers' unstable flying machine is a useful analogy. It was designed with enough new information input to allow it to move through a turbulent three-dimensional environment under its own power. We have the same problem in our own turbulent times. Do we have sufficient information and adequate communication to navigate this perilous passage? To a considerable degree, the deciding factor will be the effectiveness of our communications and information tools.

Since the focus here is on the American stake in communications and information, we must take the somewhat risky step of separating developments in these fields from those in other technologies. The risk is in trying to factor out the implications of one set of technologies as if they were independent variables. They are not, of course. The cautions are particularly apt in the study of communications and information patterns. These patterns involve fundamental chemistries of change, infusing all other elements of our lives and altering them. Moreover, these patterns are themselves changed as they affect human attitudes, values, and actions, which then feed back into the entire process.

Such analytical pitfalls must be kept in mind in assessing the American stake in a new strategy for communications and information. The task requires triangulating economics, technology, and politics to arrive at an integrated view of the problem. This kind of overall assessment has, until recently, been curiously neglected. The volume of research in communications and information has risen steadily in recent years. It is still largely conducted, however, in tight clusters of academic disciplines — among the graph-riddled economists, the mouse-maze psychologists, the group-dynamic sociologists, and so forth.

One of the pioneers in modern communications research, Wilbur Schramm, reminded his colleagues many years ago that communications is the crossroads where all the disciplines meet. He was trying to tell them that, essentially, they were all talking about the same thing. They duly noted his maxim and turned back to their narrow projects. Fortunately, in the past decade a hardy group of interdisciplinary souls heeded Schramm's advice and moved toward more integrative studies. They included Ithiel de Sola Pool at M.I.T., Anthony Oettinger at Harvard, George Gerbner at Pennsylvania, and Edwin Parker at Stanford. Their respective angles of vision on the subject were different, but they all accepted the complexities of a new environment where human communications — and therefore understanding — were increasingly mediated through high-technology machines. They shared a fascination for, and an increasing body of research and insights about, the implications of this change.

Meanwhile, real world events did not wait on the promise of better understanding. The new microelectronics-based grid is being assembled without the benefit of clear-cut projections of its many impacts. Even with the most careful studies, the breadth and depth of these impacts make any precision difficult. This should not excuse us from trying to identify where we are now and where we are going in this area. The stakes are too high to justify any Micawberish hopes that something will turn up. A century ago, the historian Jacob Burkhardt warned that the denial of complexity is the beginning of tyranny. The best approach, as proposed above, is to attempt an integrative look at this complexity in communications and information affairs by triangulating their economic, political, and technological aspects.

Microelectronic technology is, for the present, the driving force among these factors, with its active promise of a new era of abundant resources. Economics is next, as industry demonstrates its ability to transform technological capabilities into marketplace realities. The most critical side of the triangle is the political one. Here is where understanding and actions are weakest, threatening the chances that viable strategies for dealing with the new environment will emerge. The choice, in simplest terms, is whether resources adequate to meet our needs can be assured through a linear extension of past political and social practices or whether a new set of strategies is needed. The argument is a common one in discussions of post-industrial problems, but it has particularly sensitive relevance in the communications area.

The dispute runs across the political and social spectrum. At one end are those who would leave present policies and practices essentially alone, adjusting them in small ways as specific conditions change. There is some nostalgia for laissez-faire, muscular capitalism by proponents of this approach. The more compelling arguments, however, involve the recurrent suspicion that, whatever the beneficent intentions of political and/or social actions in this area, such intervention is inevitably counterproductive and even dangerous. The unique American experiment in restraining public intervention in communications and information affairs has worked so far, proponents of this view say. The duplications, confusion, and other inefficiencies of the system, they argue, are a small price to pay, now or in the future, compared to the costs of public actions based on doubtful premises of social efficiency and economic rationality.

At the other end of the spectrum are a small, persistent band of interventionists. Some of them draw their inspiration from various forms of socialism, native to America and otherwise. Another faction is the heirs of a 1930s type of technocratic thinking in which it is believed that the only way through the current rough passage is by applying more rigorous social engineering, based on centrally directed technology.

The answer lies between these ideological extremes. In this society of compromise and deal-making, our real strategic options can be found toward the center of the spectrum. What is clear is that, for all their power, technological and economic forces themselves cannot make the overriding social decisions needed to assure a viable environment in which communications and information resources match our needs. The decisions involve factors well beyond technological advances or marketplace economics. In the last analysis, the issues are strategic and political.

What are the policy choices for the new information environment? Finding out requires the kind of basic assessment that Americans are generally reluctant to make. For all our attachment to efficiency and planning, we are not moving in an orderly fashion into the new environment. We are backing in, with, at best, an over-the-shoulder view of things to come. And there are few junctures along the way that will permit us to get our critical bearings.

In assessing planning efforts in this area, a Harvard study group has declared:

> Decisions of vital importance — national, international, corporate and personal — are being fought out in dimly lit arenas under rules that are not clear even to the lawyers, engineers, economists and bureaucrats who devised them. Rosters and score cards are rare. Some of the players are unnumbered; others wear the wrong numbers.... There are many kinds of information technologies, but it is becoming clear that there is really only one information system, no matter how disconnected the parts may seem. Information is a basic resource, fully as important as materials or energy. While materials and energy have not lacked for public scrutiny and policy attention, information resources have developed willy-nilly, their potency overshadowed by their technical details, their pervasiveness so complete they are taken for granted, like the clean air we breathe.[11]

Communications and information policies are a thicket of laws, regulations, administrative decisions, and encrusted practices carried out by hundreds of public entities at the federal, state, and local levels. The pattern is confused and often overlapping and contradictory in both purpose and application. Despite the faults of the system, it reflects — not always clearly — a rough consensus. This includes the agreement that there is a need to limit the growth of a central authority that could undermine First Amendment rights and the wide-ranging interpretation of these rights, both in law and tradition, which has been developed over two centuries.

As a result, no one is in charge, by design. Moreover there is no firm consensus on how to proceed in adjusting the system to new realities, or whether to do so at all. One striking example of this confusion can be seen in the recent attempt to revise the only basic communications legislation ever approved by Congress, the Communications Act of 1934. Simple logic argued that a law, which was written over a half century ago, to define telephone, telegraph, and radio broadcasting regulations should be brought up to date in the age of computers, satellites, and other exotic technologies. Congressional hearings on such a revision began in 1976. They have involved millions of words of testimony by hundreds of experts. Long years and many rewrites later, the process continues with no prospect of a comprehensive solution yet in sight. Significantly, the debates have not involved disputes over the issue of First Amendment rights. No one has seriously proposed any widening of government controls over communications and information. The vast bulk of the proposals have proposed weakening the public role.[12]

There are many reasons for this policy immobility. In part, it involves a general lack of public discussion of the issues. In a hyped-up media environment which thrives on sensationalism, sober discussions of communications policy attract little attention. The more immediate reason for the legislative impasse, however, has been the inability of the major vested interests to agree on a formula for compromise. If a solution is found, it will be primarily through the interplay of these economic forces.

And there probably will be something missing. The debate over this so-called rewrite legislation (that is, the rewriting of the 1934 Communications Act) has been long on economic arguments, but it has been short on substantive discussion of overall national needs, beyond ritualistic incantations in support of a bigger, better communications system. To a considerable extent, this reflects a lack of firm social indicators that could give direction to a full public discussion of the issue. Such indicators would not be definitive or determining, but they could provide raw material for a more meaningful debate on policy options than has been the case up to now.

The idea of social indicators for communications and information is not new. The Japanese and Swedes, in particular, have been experimenting with such projects for some time. The results have enabled them to identify conditions on a national scale with some precision. The Japanese knew before they started that they had an annual 10% increase in the rate of information production. What they found out through their indicators project was that there was only a 3% annual increase in the use of this information. Thus, questions were raised: Did this mean that more than half of the information produced went to waste because people lacked the time to handle it? What was useful information and what wasn't? The Japanese had no easy answers to these and other issues raised in their indicators surveys, but they did have a new set of questions. In Sweden, there is a similar interest in the day-to-day pattern of information use, especially in the present and potential impact of computer communications on ordinary citizens.[13]

No country turns out more social research on communications and information than the United States. It piles up in mountains of monographs, books, computer tapes, and microfilms — some of it very good, some of it very ordinary, and most of it written in the special corkscrew prose through which social scientists attempt to communicate with one another. The problem lies not merely in its bulk or its uneven quality but in the fact that it is so fractionalized. There is every reason to encourage independent and even adversary research. The question is whether, or how, it can be made more useful and comprehensible in the public policy debates in this field.

Plans for some sort of comprehensive social-indicators system crop up perennially. Numerous proposals for funding such a project have been launched, most of them aimed at the Treasury Department in Washington. In the euphoric days of his "Great Society" program, Lyndon Johnson proposed a federally sponsored annual social-indicators index. The idea was promptly rejected by Congress, which did, however, permit the Census Bureau to issue occasional reports. Over and above charges of academic boondoggling, the idea of an annual assessment ran into entrenched suspicions about so-called social engineering.[14] In this area, most Americans have a vested interest in ambiguity. For all our professed devotion to facts and figures, we back away from official attempts to track and measure the conditions of social consensus. In the American version of participatory democracy, with its emphasis on special-interest negotiations, we do not want to be tied down to any plan which purports to codify, under the rubric of objectivity, the social alternatives open to us. As a result, communications and information policies and actions evolve generally without firm indicators of the social conditions involved or the full range of options available.

The lack of a firm consensus on communications and information needs does not excuse us from more precision in defining them. There is a tendency to identify with simple options, from a Pollyannaish everything-will-turn-out-fine attitude to the somber scenarios of Lewis Mumford and other pessimists. As noted earlier, Mumford saw American society moving towards a fascistic magamachine future because of the lack of adequate social controls over technology. (His analogy was that of a locomotive, with neither brakes nor engineer, inexorably gathering speed and heading toward a crash.) But he underestimated the role of the web of checks and balances in American society in preventing such an extreme course. This system has worked tolerably well up to now. However, there is serious doubt as to whether it can maintain its resiliency in coping with the information needs of a more complex technological society.

The political implications of this problem were identified almost two decades ago by Karl Deutsch in *The Nerves of Government*.[15] Information is power, Deutsch noted, and — equally important — it is a multiplier of power. In a high technology society, he argued, control of access to information is more important than control of physical forces such as the police or the military. One of our democratic assumptions is that everyone has equal access to information. In reality, of course, access to information is highly uneven for many reasons. The problem is complicated, Deutsch noted, by an increasing flood of information, which pushes us toward the limit of human capacity to cope. The solution, Deutsch suggests, is a new approach to what he calls "intelligence amplification" through computers and other information technologies that can provide a greater sharing of access to the data that allows us to survive and thrive.

Intelligence amplification in the service of a democratic society is the goal of a strategy for the information age. It is a goal squarely within our national mythos. It identifies and illuminates the psychic bounds of a new kind of post-industrial society whose energies are moving away from the production of things toward the production and distribution of ideas. The objective, after all, is the construction of a national (and eventually global) interactive information grid, capable of connecting everyone on earth with everyone else and with a wide array of information resources. The microelectronic base for the network is essentially proven and available. If a strategy combining technology, economics, and politics can be worked out, this high capacity grid can be in place in North America well before the end of the century, and in most of the rest of the world early in the new century.

And such strategy can benefit from lessons already learned in the building of a smaller mass communications grid during the past century — namely, the telephone system. The phone network services 95% of the populace directly and most of the remaining 5% one step removed — that is, with pay phones. Over 750 million voice calls are made through the system every working day. Only Canada, among major countries, matches the United States system in its coverage and use. The phone network offers, moreover, a wide array of communications services over and above what the engineers call POTS — Plain Old Telephone Service. POTS will probably be displaced by data communications as the chief source of the network's revenues before the end of the eighties, and what we now call the telephone system will be called something else because of its extended capacities (Infonet? Comnet? Or simply, the Network?). The point is that the telephone network exists as an almost universal grid, and it works very well. More significantly, it is pragmatic proof of the American commitment to the idea of a universal communications system. This commitment will be further tested in the coming years with the 1984 breaking up of AT&T's near monopoly of telephone service. This development (discussed in Chapter 6) will test whether an integrated telecommunications system can be operated on a fully competitive basis in ways that benefit us socially as well as economically. However, as the expanded network develops, it will have the many forms of the present telephone system to use as a reference — technologically, economically, politically, and socially. The new expansion involves upgrading and supplementing an already extensive grid, centered around the AT&T, its former local Bell companies, and 1500 independent phone systems. There are also an increasing number of competing networks, some of them successors to the old telegraph systems and others newcomers either starting from scratch or as spin-offs from other industries. In Chapter 5, I will examine the complex relationship between these many elements, old and new, in the communications and information industries. For now, however, it is useful simply to get an overview of how the expanded network will fit into the new information economy. Although the present network provides some guidelines, these guidelines are inexact when set against the size and complexity of the new grid. The cost of the expanded network will be staggering, measured in hundreds of billions of dollars before it is completed. It will involve technological options on a scale never before tried. Moreover, no one is sure how the system should be configured in terms of its potential use.

Inaccurate estimating of communications and information usage is nothing new. Alexander Graham Bell thought the telephone network would be primarily an entertainment instrument, transmitting concerts and operas to homes.[16] To his credit, he eventually saw the phone's advantages as a device for personal use rather than for mass broadcasting. The developers of the first modern computer in 1945 predicted that six of the machines would serve all foreseeable world needs. In 1980, 30 years after the fact, the IBM

Corporation humbly admitted that in the early fifties it had estimated its market for computers would be limited to about 50 machines.[17] Underestimations of the demand for goods and services has been one of the consistent elements in the communications and information industries since World War II. In fact, these industries are the only areas of the economy which have expanded steadily in recent years, not following the zig-zag course of economic trends.

One result of this has been to confuse economists. In Chapter 1 we looked briefly at a 1977 Department of Commerce report that documented how information related activities now dominate the economy in terms of gross national product and work force. The study identifies a fundamental, and still little understood, shift in the focus of American society away from the production of goods to the production and distribution of information. For all its thoroughness — nine eye-straining volumes of it — the report leaves many details of this new economic environment unexplored. However, curiously little in-depth research has been undertaken to follow up on the Commerce Department study.

The apparent reason for this is that economists are generally not comfortable with the intangibles of communications and information. They acknowledge the growing importance of information-related activities, but the subject does not fit neatly into their formulas the way more measurable resources, such as industrial products or energy do. How do you put a price tag on a fact or an idea? How is information productivity measured when it involves a scholar ruminating in a library or a scientific researcher manipulating computer data? It is probably true that half of the information produced in this country is underutilized, used only a few times or not at all. Does this mean that too much information is being produced, or only too little of the right kind in the right place at the right time? Who decides what is "the right kind" of information? One question leads to another. How will the information economy change living patterns? What kinds of jobs will be available? If so, where will they be?

These are practical questions that go well beyond the difficulties economists may have in providing answers. They involve everyday problems of jobs, family, and community. Deeper down are psychic questions, the doubts of ordinary men and women about the so-called benefits of technology. Here Pollyannaish optimism gives way to concerns about the impact of computers and other information–communications machines on prospects for jobs and professional advancement and on personal status in a society where one is identified by what one does from 9 to 5. These elements have always been present in technological shifts. But they are taking on new force as the United States moves into a period of exponential technological acceleration, particularly in the information and communications fields.

This cycle is just beginning. The fears that computers and other information machines will create hardcore unemployment or down grade job opportunities are still muted. Information machines have generally created new jobs in roughly the same proportion as they have eliminated older ones. But workers are not economic statistics whose lives can be measured in balanced-out equations. Machines eliminate and create jobs, but the shift is never smooth for the men and women involved.

Nevertheless, even in this early stage of microelectronics the shift is being felt. It is particularly striking in those industries and services that have the financial resources and planning skills to take advantage of the new technologies. A good, close-at-hand example is the telephone system. After the federal government, the telephone companies constitute the largest private user of computers and other information machines in the country. Between 1972 and 1977, there was an 18% increase in AT&T telephone calls, but the system's labor force dropped from just over 1,000,000 employees to 940,000. Equally significant was the change in the system's mix of employees in the same period. The number of managers, clerical employees, and semi-skilled workers dropped, while the number of professional specialists increased by 17% and the number of technicians by 50%.

The telephone system is an outsized example of what happens when high technology becomes an integral part of an industry. Its experience is being replicated, in varying degrees, across the range of United States industrial and service enterprises. The banking business is a typical case. Why have a labor-intensive bank branch, usually in an expensive location, when a customer can go to a machine and use the magnetic tape on the back of his bank card to make withdrawals and deposits directly? This system requires fewer tellers, less paper work, and gives better service. Another increasingly familiar example is the computerized check-out counters in supermarkets that add up purchases, monitor inventories, and order new stock in one operation — again, requiring less personnel and giving more efficiency and better service. These are not futuristic fantasies. They are rapidly becoming commonplace. Their advantages are those that have always accrued over the long run when goods and services can be made available to more people with less physical labor. The new information machines will accelerate this process, and the impact on peoples' lives will be more direct than ever before.

Such changes are usually seen as American success stories, modern legacies of the technological myth. The shift to microelectronics can mean more efficient production, lower costs, better products, and a work force with greater professional responsibilities. But there is another side to the story, one which is beginning to be seen more clearly in the light of the economic difficulties plaguing the United States economy. Of the nostrums offered to counter economic sluggishness, none has more crowd pleasing appeal than the idea of "reindustrialization," generally interpreted as the shifting of industrial activity toward more efficient high technology activities. The fact that this has been happening steadily over many years has not restrained its enthusiasts from proclaiming the doctrine as new and revolutionary. Communications and information rank high on the reindustrialization agenda, since these sectors of the electronics industry have been the leading growth area in an otherwise troubled economy in the early eighties. Reindustrialization is, in fact, a short-term cliché for the longer range push to adjust the economy to the needs of an information-based, post-industrial society.

Whatever the trend is called, there is growing agreement within the Western industrial nations that microelectronics is a critical area in their economic projections. "The next century's underdeveloped nations," the authoritative London *Economist* says, "will be those industrial societies which fail to harness the explosion of microelectronics technology to all that they make and to the factories that make it."[18] This borders on editorial hyperbole, justified perhaps by the newspaper's discovery of a report which indicated that only 5% of British firms were using high technology electronics. The report was useful in pushing the British government into more effective support for microelectronic research and development — a step taken earlier by the United States, Japan, France, and other industrial powers. Their motivation was basically the same: the hope that microelectronics could overcome some of the constraints on productivity growth that have hurt their economies. A secondary motivation has been the assurance of their shares of the multibillion-dollar world market for these technologies. Microelectronics research and development have boomed at a rate unmatched by any other technology. A new generation of microelectronic circuits has been developed every 12 to 18 months in this country during the past decade.

The United States holds a commanding position for the present, which would seem to add another chapter to our national success story. However, there are other considerations, involving some negative side effects. As Colin Norman has noted,

> The nostalgic hope seems to be that microelectronics, along with other high technology industries, will lead the way back to the golden days of the postwar era, when the world economy expanded at a rate that provided high demand that in turn created millions of new jobs. Such a development is at best unlikely. . . . The development and application of microelectronics and other technologies will help to stimulate growth, but it will do little to remove the underlying causes of sluggish economic growth.[19]

Norman and other researchers see the need for more effective public strategies to deal with these dislocations. They cite, in particular, the problem of "jobless growth" in industries where production is being automated and workers face layoffs. But the issues are not confined to economics; they will be increasingly political and social as the United States moves more deeply into the new high technology environment.

There are, in short, some disturbing flaws in the vision of information-based high technology sectors strengthening the prospects of social and economic progress. Richard McGahey of New York University's Urban Research Center points out that services and high-tech jobs generally pay less and offer less mobility than older manufacturing jobs: "Dazzling high-tech factories are designed by highly-paid professionals but staffed by low-skilled, low-paid workers." He notes that, in California's Silicon Valley, computer assemblers earn about 70% of the hourly wage of auto workers. Moreover, jobs in high technology industries are not likely to grow as rapidly as they did in the 1970s. The low-skilled nature of many new jobs makes them vulnerable to technological displacement and foreign competition. A highly publicized example of the latter took place in 1983 when Atari Inc. decided to transfer its manufacturing operations from California to Taiwan.[20]

How will the high capacity information network evolve? As noted above, it will be, to a considerable degree, an extension of the present grid — the basic telephone network and the smaller specialized networks that have emerged in recent years. These facilities will be upgraded, widened, and in many cases interconnected over the next decade, primarily in response to specific economic needs. The speed with which this is happening has led economists and others to identify the phenomenon as a distinct new structure defining a network pattern in post-industrial America. They see the evolving grid as radically transforming older, slower economic activities by channelling them through high speed circuits linking buyers and sellers in a vastly expanded electronic market. The concept has been given several name tags, but the one which may stick was developed in the late seventies by a team of University of Southern California researchers led by Herbert Dordick: the "network marketplace." Dordick and his colleagues took a look at the aggregate effect of the many electronics-based information networks being developed or planned and concluded that

> an important industry is rapidly emerging from the marriage of computers and telecommunications. This industry permits users to interact directly with one or more computers, associated data files and problem solving algorithms from remote terminals. It may include access to distributed information systems within and between organizations, remote transaction recording, data base inquiry and computer conferencing.... All the usual services of a marketplace can be offered within a large information network. Products and services can be advertised and sellers can be located; ordering, billing and deliveries can be facilitated; and all manner of transactions can be consummated, including wholesale, retail, brokering, and mass distribution. Indeed the entire range of such products and services for business, industry, the consumer and government can be perceived as a marketplace — a marketplace on a communications network or the network marketplace.[21]

This concept of marketplace will be a critical element in the forming of the expanded information infrastructure of United States post-industrial society. It will not be the product of a master design, however theoretically efficient such an approach might be. It will develop from a pattern of many decisions, large and small, tied to different (and often conflicting) projections of marketplace needs. This is the reality behind the high flying predictions of a universal information grid which have become part of the standard scenario of futurists in recent years. Their vision of a plug-in future, of computers in the living room, of global teleconferences, of robotics factories controlled by telepresence techniques, and of a new quality of life based on access to vast information resources is, nevertheless, too close to possible realization to be dismissed any longer as sci-fi fantasy.

The new network may, however, fail to match these prospects. Its capabilities may be limited to simply providing more efficient communications services to the higher reaches of United States business. On the other hand, it can also become a truly universal service grid with a strong economic base, servicing a full range of economic and social needs of both consumers and businesses. This choice will be critical in the definition of American strategies in the new information age. It is useful, therefore, to look at the factors that will determine how and for what purpose the new grid will be assembled.

The choice of a mass or elite network can go either way. The grid is now only in the very early stages of development. Its present development is comparable to that of the telephone system after World War I. Like the phone system of that era, it is a collection of separate networks, large and small. In fact, it was not until the thirties that all the separate — and often competing — telephone systems in this country were interconnected to permit universal subscriber service. Will this serve as a precedent for a new integrated grid of high capacity communications and information services? There are similarities between the two systems, but many of the details are different. It took a half-century to sort out the economic, legal, and social aspects of a relatively simple integrated phone system. These factors are immensely more complex in the new network, with its expanded capability for voice, visual, and data services. Moreover, in these early years of the grid's development, public policy and pressure from industry strongly favor a competitive system of network diversity.

The United States grid, in short, will not be built following any centralized master strategy. It will be the outcome of many competing plans. Consequently, the first integrated national grids will probably be built in Europe and Japan. Although these countries are currently trailing the United States in high capacity networking, their practice of government control over telecommunications development gives authorities greater leeway in laying out a national strategy for an integrated system. They are generally not tied down by the cat's cradle of legal, economic, and social restraints we have imposed on ourselves, beginning with First Amendment inhibitions about government involvement.

The rapid growth of wide service networking in the past decade has demonstrated United States industry's ability to meet the difficult, usually economically based needs of large government and business bureaucracies. Industry's ability to meet the needs of smaller organizations and individual consumers of information is less clear. Herbert Dordick and his colleagues have noted that this can pose a serious problem for a democratic society. As mentioned earlier, we may be moving toward a new and hazardous form of information inequality, well beyond the traditional gap separating those who have the economic and social means to gain access to information resources and those who do not.[22]

Most of the options favoring a full-access grid are still open. For the present, the network is being designed to meet a variety of limited purposes. Will all these purposes add up to a full range of communications and information services needed by a healthy post-industrial environment? Or should we begin to develop some new kind of national strategy that will assure such a range of services by applying social resources to marketplace economics? For the present, Dordick and his associates point out, "There is not now or in the wings a network policy for the United States."[23]

Right now, there may be no prospect for an all-inclusive national policy in this area, but a network construction boom is in progress, beginning with a series of limited federal government decisions to open the industry to greater competition. Over the past decade, these decisions have exposed a cautious, hidebound industry to new forces — forces that triggered a dramatic expansion of networks and related services in the seventies, which will grow even more rapidly throughout the eighties. Experience to date has confirmed that doing business in the network marketplace can be cost effective, particularly with the rising cost of labor. There are other factors — better overall management control, reductions in energy costs, more effective quality controls over goods and services, plus the intangibles of convenience. However, the ultimate economic prize is the expanded marketplace access gained by buyers and sellers on the network. This will not come automatically; there are still many questions to be resolved as the networks expand. These include pricing of services, public regulatory controls, technical compatability between networks, and capital formation. A number of promising network ventures have already foundered in the midst of such hard realities. A classic case in the mid-seventies was that of the Datran Corporation, a self-styled David that took on the Goliath-like telephone company and, contrary to Biblical form, lost. The additional competitive forces released by the break-up of AT&T in January 1984 will add to the list. The result, a series of shakeouts, will inevitably take place before the network marketplace settles into a long-term pattern.

By that time, the networks will be adequately serving the needs of the United States business and government structure — a major step toward a post-industrial economy. The process, however, will be incomplete if the networks fail to serve efficiently the wider field of mass consumer services as the telephone network succeeded in doing two generations ago.

Universal telephone service resulted from a national strategy decision embedded in the Communications Act of 1934. It came about after a hard-fought struggle between industry and government, in which the two sides traded economic concessions for social gains — a process which has been maintained, with some adjustments, ever since. But the conditions required for replicating such a scenario in the future will not be the same. Nevertheless, there are sufficient similarities to suggest that definitive policy decisions extending high technology, full-service networking to mass consumer levels are needed.

This will involve the integration of economics, technological, and policy factors in new and innovative patterns. Two familiar technologies — those of the telephone and television — are already available in most American homes, schools, and other institutions, providing the physical means for consumer access to the network. The high capacity circuitry to deliver full service is already installed in over one-third of these sites via cable television. This ratio will move to over one-half in a few years, with increased use of thin fiber optic wires in place of expensive copper cables. Other technologies, such as direct broadcasting from satellites and terrestrial multipoint distribution services, are competing with cable systems for the consumer market. This expansion is currently being fueled by the demand for pay-television films. Increasingly, cable home-delivery systems will provide other specialized entertainment and information services, most of them retrieved from computer data banks.

These "wired nation" strategies have been puffed up for years, only to be deflated by the difficulties of fitting the technological, economic, and political pieces together. The difficulties are still there, but the outlook for overcoming them is more favorable now than ever before. Driven by economic forces, the new networks are expanding beyond business and government services into the consumer sector. But the long-term pattern of expansion remains to be seen. Will it be an elite service, aimed at those in the upper income levels, whose information needs are more readily identifiable and marketable? Will it merely reap easy profits from lightweight entertainment services, replicating patterns of commercial television? Will it provide full services to the full range of the population, including people who live in such neighborhoods as Watts in Los Angeles, Liberty in Miami, or East Harlem and Bedford-Stuyvesant in New York City?

In their study of the network marketplace, Herbert Dordick and his colleagues suggest that this problem of neighborhood "local loop" services will be the critical one in determining whether mass consumer-oriented services will be available. The economics of high density business networking is already clearly favorable. The problem will be in so-called "thin route" networking down to homes and smaller institutions, not only in middle-class communities but in inner cities and rural villages. Dordick suggests a 1990s scenario in which Congress is asked to declare a Universal Network Access principle in much the same way as an earlier Congress laid down a similar principle for the telephone system in the 1934 legislation.

The distance between that possibility, a decade from now, and where we are now is considerable. There are too many intangibles, ambiguities, and other surprises involved to predict any firm kind of pattern. Nevertheless, America has too important a stake in the outcome to leave the subject stranded in the belief that everything will turn out all right. It is all too easy to project a flawed strategy in which we may move, in Lewis Mumford's phrase, toward a "mega-machine society" in which a self-serving elite uses information and communications resources to control the levers of power. The old confidence, tied to our technological mythos, that it cannot happen here is no longer as steady as it once seemed. Social erosion, what Alvin Toffler calls "demassification," is taking place; traditional groups are breaking up, leaving their former members drifting and alienated. Communications and information resources as such cannot stem this erosion. They can, in fact, hasten it. However, they can also supply new linkages between the pluralities of United States society in ways that can reinforce communal trust and creativity.

The question is: How can we keep our essential freedoms while developing new information patterns to meet the problems of a more complex post-industrial society? The answer lies somewhere between authoritarian control and laissez-faire drift. It is here that the conflicting pressures of technology and economics must serve the needs of social equity.

Whether successful strategies are designed and followed will depend only in part on technical or economic decisions. The primary decisions are political. They depend on our willingness to adapt basic social institutions to the opportunities of the new information age. How much readjustment must be made and whether we have the collective ability to make it in time, are open questions for the present. Before examining these policy questions, we will look at the technologies that will shape a large part of the decision process.

NOTES

1. Leo Marx, *The Machine in the Garden* (New York: Oxford University Press, 1964), pp. 232–234.

2. The quotation is cited in James W. Carey and John J. Quirk, "The Mythos of the Electronic Revolution," *The American Scholar* (Summer 1970): p. 402.

3. "Banks Promoting a Mechanical Pal," *New York Times*, 8 August 1977, p. 37.

4. Lewis Mumford, *The Pentagon of Power* (New York: Harcourt Brace, 1970), p. 293.

5. Harold A. Innis, *Empire and Communications* (Toronto: University of Toronto Press, 1950), pp. 166–170.

6. Victor Ferkiss, "Technology: The Hidden Variable," *The Review of Politics*, 42, no. 3 (July 1980): pp. 349–355.

7. Alvin Toffler, *Future Shock* (New York: Bantam Books, 1971), pp. 350–354.

8. Schiller has elaborated his theories in a series of works including *Mass Communications and American Empire* (Boston: Beacon Press, 1971), *The Mind Managers* (Boston: Beacon Press, 1973), and *Communications and Cultural Domination* (White Plains, International Arts and Sciences Press, 1976).

9. The Conference Board, *Information Technology: Some Critical Implications for Decision Makers*, report no. 537 (New York: The Conference Board, 1972), p. v.

10. Ferkiss, "Technology," p. 386.

11. *Information Resources Policy: Arenas, Players and Stakes.* (Annual Report of the Program on Information Resources Policy, 1975–76, Harvard University, 1976), p. 4.

12. The hearings on the "rewrite" of the Communications Act of 1934 have taken place in the Senate Banking Committee's communications subcommittee and in a similar subcommittee of the House Committee on Interstate and Foreign Commerce. An excellent introduction to the issues debated in both committees can be found in U.S. Congress, House, Committee on Interstate and Foreign Commerce, *Option Papers: Committee Print 95–13*, 95th Cong., 1st sess. (Washington, D.C.: Government Printing Office, May 1977).

13. The excellent Japanese research on this subject is not available in English in most cases. For a useful summary of Japanese views (and American reactions), see Alex S. Edelstein and Sheldon M. Harsel, eds., *Information Societies: Comparing the Japanese and American Experiences* (Seattle: University of Washington International Communications Center, 1978). For a useful summary of Swedish views, see *New Views: Computers and New Media.* (Report by the Commission on New Information Technology, Stockholm, 1979.)

14. "People Satisfied, Says U.S. Survey," *Boston Globe*, 19 January 1981, p. 10.

15. Karl W. Deutsch, *The Nerves of Government* (New York: The Free Press of Glencoe, 1963).

16. For a summary of Bell's early perceptions of telephone use, see "Bell's Electrical Toy: What's the Use?," in *The Social Impact of the Telephone*, ed. Ithiel de Sola Pool (Cambridge, Mass.: MIT Press, 1977), pp. 19–22.

17. "One of the Great Miscalculations in IBM History." Advertisement in *New York Times Magazine*, 4, May 1980, p. 127.

18. *The Economist* (London), 23 September 1978, p. 91.

19. Colin Norman, "The Menace of Microelectronics," *New York Times*, 5 October 1980, p. G–5.

20. Richard McGahey, "High Tech, Low Hopes," *New York Times*, 15 May 1983.

21. Herbert Dordick, *The Network Marketplace* (Norwood, N.J.: Ablet Publishing Co., 1981), p. ix.

22. Ibid., p. 235.

23. Ibid., p. 242.

CHAPTER THREE

THE TECHNOLOGICAL FRAMEWORK

Communications Networks

IN HIS MASTERFUL study, *Empire and Communications*, the Canadian scholar, Harold Innis, demonstrates how all societies, from Babylon to the present, have been shaped by the production and distribution of information.[1] His emphasis is on the unsettling effects of new technologies. Innis's perceptions apply to our current transition to a new kind of information society. Here we will take a broad look at the technologies involved in this shift and their impact on our future.

Consider a fable about some fifteenth-century citizens faced with evaluating a new technology. In the city of Mainz, Germany, Master Johann Gutenberg has just developed a machine that can reproduce manuscript-like pages in many copies. News of his work has reached the local ruler, the Elector of the Rhineland Palatinate. In the spirit of Renaissance inquiry, the Elector asks a group of scholars and businessmen to assess the new machine's impact on the local economy and culture. Since bureaucracy is just beginning to assert itself as an organizational force, the group is designated the Select Committee to Evaluate Multiple Manuscript Production.

The committee visits Gutenberg's workshop, where the proud inventor demonstrates his machine. The committee is impressed, but skeptical. After considerable debate, the group submits its report to the Elector. The machine is undoubtedly a technological advance, the report concludes, but it has only limited application to Palatinate needs. The committee recommends that the government not invest research and development funds in the project. Its reasons are direct and cogent: (1) a large work force of monks copying manuscripts would lose their jobs if the Gutenberg machine were encouraged; (2) there is no heavy demand for multiple copies of manuscripts; and (3) the long-term market for printed books is doubtful due to the low literacy rate.[2]

It is easy to feel superior to the Elector's select committee and its lack of foresight, but it is wrong to do so. The same errors have consistently been made in our own supposedly enlightened times. One example of such an error is the initial reaction to the wireless radio early in this century. The United States Navy installed radio transmitters on ships of the Great White Fleet for its round-the-world voyage and then discarded them in favor of carrier pigeons. In the 1890s, a British publication, *The Electrician*, saw the telephone as a positive menace:

> It seems to us that we are getting perilously near the ideal of the modern Utopian whose life is to consist of sitting in armchairs and pressing a button. It is not a desirable prospect: we shall have no wants, no money, no ambition, no youth, no desires, no individuality, no names and nothing wise about us.[3]

In our own time, equally wrong predictions about the influence of computers, satellites, and other technologies have been commonplace.

We cannot, in any event, take refuge in the conventional wisdom that "technology is not the problem." In fact, technology is more at the core of the problem than ever before. Until recently, major communications advances could be dealt with on a linear basis. Since they were phased in gradually, there was time to make the political and economic adjustments needed to integrate them into the existing structure. The inventions of the telegraph and the telephone were separated by 40 years, another 3 decades passed before wireless radio came on the scene, and it was still another 30 years before the advent of computers. The time line has been drastically compressed in recent years, with a full range of technologies converging over the entire spectrum of the production, storage, and distribution of information.

The wild-and-wooly situation in microelectronics technology known as large-scale integration (LSI) is typical. Despite its name, LSI involves the miniaturization of electronic circuits. Using LSI techniques, a silicon chip the size of a fingernail can contain the equivalent of hundreds of thousands of circuits. Properly configured, a chip can have all the attributes of a computer; it is a microprocessor with the computational power of a 1950s wall-size machine. Microprocessor technology came out of the laboratories 15 years ago; since then it has gone through at least five technological generations, each involving major advances in capacity and efficiency.

The pace will step up in the coming decades, with the introduction of a wide array of innovations. Among them are:

- Josephson junctions, computer circuits that use superconducting metals, which lose all resistance to electricity at very low temperatures. This enables them to handle computations in trillionths of a second, a hundred times faster than existing computer circuits.

- Optical fiber communications channels, carrying the equivalent of a quarter-million telephone circuits on a light beam shot down hair-thin cables.

- Computerized storage systems, now under development, that will house as much information as is in the entire book collection of the Library of Congress in a tabletop container.

- Massive space platforms, structures assembled thousands of miles above the equator, from which will be hung communications satellites capable of beaming signals into pocket-size portable receivers.

Our understanding of the benefits and costs of these technologies is limited by our still primitive experience. But we can now see the possibilities of having a high capacity, mass access information network much earlier than anyone would have considered realistic even a few years ago. The costs — beyond the enormous economic investment required — are the dangers of building this network haphazardly without fully considering a strategy for long-term needs. Technologists can identify the physical potential of their innovations with impressive accuracy. The political, social, and economic implications are much more elusive. This uncertainty has the effect of intimidating policy makers, both public and private. As an M.I.T. study put it several years ago: "Communications technology is flooding policymakers with options they do not understand, among which they must choose, and which will have profound effects on society." The statement underlines the importance of looking at the new technologies not simply in terms of their capabilities but also in the context of a viable social strategy for their use. This calls for some understanding of the modern evolution of the science of communications and information. In this chapter, we will look at the development of communications network technology; in the next chapter, the information machines which plug into these networks will be examined.

The so-called communications revolution is, in reality, a succession of three overlapping technological stages that have taken place during the past 150 years. The first of these was the *Wire Age* (1844–1900), the second was the *Wireless Age* (1900–1970), and the third is the one we are now entering — the *Integrated Grid Age*, in which wire and wireless technologies are brought together in powerful combinations. These linkings will form the structure of the future global information utility. The technological advances that occurred between the beginning of the Wire Age and the present are awesome.[4] The early Western Union telegraph machines that opened the Wire Age could relay about 40 words a minute. Western Union's first domestic communications satellite, the successor to the old telegraph line, was placed in orbit in 1975 with a capability of transmitting eight million words a *second*. Both machines — the telegraph transmitter and the satellite — nevertheless contributed to the cumulative impact of technology on how we communicate. It is useful to take a brief look at the three evolutionary stages that brought us to where we are today.

The Wire Age was largely the creation of a group of crusty, pragmatic United States inventors, beginning with Samuel F. B. Morse and his single wire, which transmitted electrical impulses in code from Washington to Baltimore in 1844. The Morse telegraph was a major technical breakthrough, but it also involved two other innovations crucial in American communications development. The first was the federal government's decision to contribute research and development funds for the Morse invention. It involved modest sums, but set a significant precedent for the hundreds of millions of public research dollars now being invested annually in communications technology. The second innovative decision was that the telegraph system would be developed and controlled by private companies, not by the central government. This pattern distinguishes the American communications structure from that of almost every other nation, whose governments own or strictly control local communications systems. As a result, commercial revenues fueled the rapid expansion of the Morse telegraph system as well as the other major innovation of the Wire Age — the Bell telephone.

A century ago, it seemed inevitable that mass communications networking would be based on wire circuits. Nineteenth-century futurists, looking at the growth of telegraph and telephone systems, would have been safe in predicting that one day all mankind would be linked by wires. They would have forecast, correctly, that wire technology would be improved in ways that would eliminate such problems as fading, unreliable switching equipment, and high costs.

The wire networks were put to many imaginative uses in the late nineteenth century. The telephone was seen as a mass medium for the distribution of services we now associate with broadcasting — news, music, entertainment, and public affairs programming. Within a year after his first successful telephone experiments, Alexander Graham Bell transmitted musical programs by wire in Ontario. Stereophonic music transmitted over the telephone was demonstrated five years later at the 1881 Paris Electrical Exposition. The results encouraged a number of European opera houses to install telephone outlets to transmit live performances to other locations.[5]

The most extensive experiment with mass-media telephone service took place in Budapest. Beginning in 1884, the local telephone system carried a daily program of news bulletins, town happenings, sermons, music, and theater performances through a network that eventually extended 168 miles. The system operated until the late 1920s. Similar experiments on a smaller scale were carried out in other European and American cities. Service was efficient and cheap: a Budapest phone subscriber paid the equivalent of two cents each time he used the news and entertainment network.

The telephone system was not, however, destined to become the all-purpose wired network envisioned by Bell and others. This potential was undercut by another politically and economically powerful technological development — wireless communications or the transmission of radiant energy in the form of invisible waves moving through the air. The possibility of transmitting without wires had increasingly intrigued inventors during the last half of the nineteenth century: the United States Patent Office registered a number of patents for "aerial conduction" of electric signals in the 1870s. But the significant breakthrough was made by Guglielmo Marconi, who began work on the problem as a precocious teenager in the early 1890s. He had the good luck to have a mother, a well-to-do Englishwoman, who took it upon herself to convince the British Post Office that they should pay attention to her son's experiments. Marconi proceeded to demonstrate his ideas in 1896 to a group of British officials, who were intrigued but skeptical. The group may have included some of the same officials who some years earlier had dismissed the idea of large-scale use of the telephone in Britain on the grounds that there were enough little boys available to deliver messages.

More astute Britons grasped the potential benefits of wireless communications, both for business and for political links with the nation's overseas empire. They encouraged Marconi to market his invention and to lease transmitters and receiving sets on ships as a monopoly. Other governments, including the United States, quickly recognized the political dangers of such monopolistic control of communications. They convened a conference of the International Telegraph Union in 1903 that approved regulations prohibiting any nation from claiming exclusive control over wireless communications. Meanwhile, Britain and other major European powers equipped their naval ships and military installations with the new technology.

Their experience in World War I convinced governments that the wireless should be harnessed to strategic national purposes. Its value had been greatly enhanced when voice capability was added to transmission previously limited to dot-and-dash Morse code signals. The result was radio broadcasting and radio telephony. European governments moved quickly to nationalize both techniques, as they had done earlier with telephone and other wired networks. No leader at the time was more perceptive about the potential of radio broadcasting than Lenin. He recognized that radio broadcasting — what he called the "newspaper without walls" — could be a powerful instrument of political and social control. He ordered rapid development of radio stations in the Soviet Union before he died in 1924.

The American response was somewhat different. Given the well-entrenched position of the commercial communications companies, there was no doubt that wireless communications would be part of the private sector. At one point, the federal government encouraged the setting up of a "chosen instrument" company, the Radio Corporation of America, to assure a strong United States presence in the field, particularly in manufacturing the new equipment. On the domestic broadcasting front, the American Telephone and Telegraph Company tried to add radio broadcasting to its near-monopoly in telephone services. The attempt failed, and radio networking was eventually divided among a number of companies.[6]

American radio broadcasting was not brought under effective regulatory control until the Communications Act of 1934, the legislation that still defines much of national policy for both wire and wireless services. The law confirmed that both services were to remain in private hands, with regulatory controls administered by a new agency, the Federal Communications Commission. The 1934 legislation legitimized what had become, through commercial pressures, a close relationship between wire and wireless technology. As in Europe, wire services were confined by law to individual point-to-point messages — telephone calls, telegrams, telexes and the like. Wireless was also used for point-to-point messages, but its greater significance was its capability for centrally directed radio — and, later, television — broadcasting.

Wireless broadcasting was to become, in the words of British communications scholar Anthony Smith,

> the supreme cultural instrument of the nation-state...a vast socializing instrument by which all the members of a society could be contacted simultaneously. With the wireless would automatically arrive the possibility of defining cultural policy as deliberately as economic policy; it created national markets for cultural production, national arbitrage for artistic reputation and a new constituency for politics.[7]

The early advocates of controls over wireless broadcasting were sufficiently aware that *wire* transmission could be competitive and therefore had to be restricted as a mass medium. Wire is the carrier of decentralized culture, unmediated by public authorities or commercial firms. Thus, it was a threat to the centralized content control which characterized over-the-air broadcasting. This was the motivation behind the controls foreign governments imposed on broadcasting, from the relatively light-handed approaches of the state-chartered British Broadcasting Corporation to the more direct controls imposed by other governments. The United States was an exception to this general pattern. The motivation for broadcasting regulation here was essentially economic and technical, although there has always been a political factor, implicit or explicit, in the process. In any event, the wire–wireless pattern that has shaped communications practices, and a good share of our culture, for the past half-century was set by these policies and reinforced by the enormous profitability of both broadcasting and other services.[8]

This pattern is changing. The decision to separate the functions of wire and wireless technology 50 years ago was based on perceptions of how the technology of that time could be used for political and economic ends. Similar perceptions obtain as we move into a new technological era. A watershed has been reached where the capabilities of wire and wireless are coming together to form a radically different communications pattern. Despite the efforts of vested economic interests to keep them separated on the old two-track system, the distinctions between wire and wireless are being eroded. This melding of capabilities forms the base of a new information environment — the Age of the Integrated Grid — in which messages can move in any form (voice, visual, or print) through an integrated, linked network of wire or wireless channels. Wire and wireless are becoming interchangeable parts of a unitary information utility, the nervous system of post-industrial America. The political, economic, and social impact of the new utility can be understood only in terms of the way wire and wireless technologies are converging after a century of separate development.

First, the wires. Early advances in wire technology generally involved wrapping more wires in bigger cables. There was a limit to this because of the sheer bulk of the cables. In the 1940s, Bell Laboratories developed the coaxial cable, a relatively thin configuration of sheathings and wires with greatly expanded circuit capacity. The new cable could provide a large number of circuits for narrow band use, such as in telephone, telex, and so on, or a smaller number of broadband circuits for such services as television and high speed data transmissions. Coaxial cable became an important part of the AT&T long-lines network for telephone, television, and other services in the 1950s. Later, such cables provided the technical base for the cable television industry.

The new cables also made possible high capacity international communications, particularly in the North Atlantic region where telephone traffic was heavy. Although there had been oceanic cables for almost a century, these were limited to simple telegraph message services. Coaxial cable technology expanded this to other services, in particular to dependable voice–telephone links which had previously been limited to unreliable radio circuits. The first transatlantic coaxial cable began operations in 1956, with a capacity of 36 telephone circuits. Since that time, 7 more cables have been strung across the Atlantic, each more technically advanced than its predecessor. The most recent cable, known as TAT–7, has a 4000 telephone-line capacity. Because previous cables were occasionally snapped by the drag-lines of fishing trawlers, special devices for burying cables in the ocean floor were developed. One of these, SCARAB (Submerged Craft Assisting Recovery and Burial), is a remotely controlled, unmanned submarine that can dig up a cable, return it to the surface for repairs, and then bury it again on the sea bottom.[9]

High capacity cables will be an important part of the world communications grid for a long time to come, if only because of heavy investments in the present system. The next transatlantic cable, TAT–8, for example, will cost $335 million, shared among 20 European countries and 8 American firms. This figure masks the economic gains made possible over the years by more efficient cable technology. The first TAT cable in the mid-fifties cost $550 per circuit mile; in the late seventies this cost had dropped to about $10 for an advanced cable marketed by ITT. A higher technology variation of coaxial cables, known as CLOAX, with a capacity for over 4000 telephone lines has been developed at AT&T's Bell Laboratories. Defining cable capacity in terms of phone calls makes the subject somewhat more comprehensible to laymen. However, these cables can handle any form of electronic communications — voice, visual, or data — in any combination simultaneously.

This capability is shared and immensely magnified by a new type of cable technology — fiber optics — that promises to cause radical changes in the wire communications structure. In fiber optics communication, information is transmitted in optical form (that is, in light waves) along a glass fiber whose thickness is comparable to that of a human hair. The fibers have many useful attributes, the most striking of which is their information-carrying potential. Theoretically, for a given diameter of cable, optical transmission on a single wavelength can carry 30 times more traffic than a coaxial cable.

The idea of using light waves for communications had been understood for a long time. Alexander Graham Bell experimented with what he called a "photophone," a device for sending messages by sunlight reflected from mirrors. It did not work well: sunbeams are scattered by air and rain, and, in any event, the sun does not always shine. Two research breakthroughs were required before optical communications would be practical. The first was the development of a light source that could provide the concentrated, narrow band of frequencies useful for communications applications. That came in the late 1950s with the first demonstrations of the laser, a device that gives off a concentrated beam of light at a single frequency. The second major breakthrough was the development of a suitable optical transmission medium — the channel down which the laser beam travels. As Alexander Graham Bell found out, transmission of light beams through the atmosphere is severely limited. However, wires, or "lightguides," made of pure glass can trap light waves and carry them for miles with little loss in signal intensity. The technical problems of developing a glass fiber with few impurities to impede the beam have been essentially solved in the past decade by scientists at ITT, Corning Glass, Bell Labs, and other research groups. Today's fibers are so transparent that light loses more intensity passing through an ordinary windowpane than it does in hundreds of feet of glass fiber. If seawater were as transparent, one could easily see to the bottom of the deepest ocean.[10]

The information-carrying capacities of fiber optic wires are awesome. A pair of copper wires is needed for a single telephone call, but a pair of hair-thin optical fibers can carry nearly 2000 calls simultaneously. Another advantage of the fibers is their potential low cost. The basic material out of which they are made is silicon, which is universally available and cheap. Only five cubic centimeters of silicon is needed to make a fiber a kilometer long. The costs are in the refining of impurities out of the silicon. As this technology has improved and as volume production of the fibers has increased, the price of optical fibers has dropped dramatically.

Meanwhile, the fibers have many other advantages. They can be installed in tight spaces — a major factor in the new microelectronic devices. They also have high reliability. An optical fiber by itself is a fragile thing, but considerable research has gone into coatings to improve the fiber's durability. Plastic jackets, developed by Du Pont and other firms, allow the fibers to be twisted, turned, and tied in knots. The fibers are unaffected by water, varying temperatures, or corrosion. Their light source, the lasers, may be no larger than a grain of salt and may emit light continuously for a hundred years.

Fiber optic applications have been limited until recently by the short distances a signal can be efficiently transmitted. In the first practical uses, this distance was limited to a few feet inside the human body. Since the late fifties, fiber optic medical probes, known as endoscopes, have been used like tiny flashlights to examine parts of the body previously accessible only through exploratory surgery. The next step was to use optical wires as substitutes for copper wires in electronic equipment such as computers and telephone switching installations. Now, as their long distance capabilities are improved, the fibers are being used as high capacity communications circuits.

In 1983, AT&T completed the first long-distance fiber optics circuit between Washington and Boston. At the same time, a British network is being installed on 15 long-distance routes in England, Scotland, and Wales.[11] These projects are the first tentative steps toward the eventual displacement of many copper-wire networks by optical fibers.

A new era in international cable operations will open in 1988 with the inauguration of the first trans-Atlantic fiber optics cable. The cable will have a 40,000 circuit capacity, more than doubling the capacity of the 7 present North Atlantic cables. The new cable will be an important resource in meeting the expected increase in trans-Atlantic telephone and other requirements from 19,500 circuits in 1985 to 98,000 circuits in 1995.[12]

Technology is pushing these prospects into realities at a faster pace than even the most enthusiastic fiber optics boosters had imagined a few years ago. Circuit purity remains a drawback. The Japanese have taken the lead in techniques for removing such impurities as hydrogen and oxygen atoms, which impede the passage of light down an optical cable.[13] Their research, subsidized by the government, signals a strong Japanese role in the high stakes international market for fiber optics technology. Another significant research effort focuses on the replacement of the electronic components at either end of fiber optic circuits with thin-filmed optical equivalents of the electronic devices. These could even be combined on a single microelectronic chip to form a completely integrated optical circuit, performing more complex functions.[14] Even more striking — though still very much in the experimental stages — is the prospect of using laser beams in a computer to make an optical switch flip on and off at the rate of one trillionth of a second. Such a computer would calculate a thousand times faster than the fastest electronic machines now in service. In 1983, researchers at Heriot-Watt University in Scotland reported on their experimental version of an optical device analogous to a transistor which they named a transphasor. Potentially, the device could switch from one transmission state to the other in about a picosecond, or a thousandth of a billionth of a second.[15]

Still, it may be unwise to predict a fiber optics "revolution." As noted above, a number of technological restraints remain; another deterrent is the economic loss involved in writing off the billions of dollars now invested in copper cables. Nevertheless, fiber optics technology has a bright future. Arthur C. Clarke, the science writer, confidently predicts that prospecting for cast-off copper wires will be a latter-day version of the old-time gold rush.

Whether they carry their messages by copper wires or glass fibers, high capacity cables will be major links in the information age's global grid. Their new sophistication is paralleled by recent advances in *wireless* technology. This effort has focused on more effective use of the radio spectrum, the invisible physical resource which makes possible the vast network of wireless circuits. The spectrum is a figurative thing: it does not exist until it is used. Until recently, it has been regarded as an esoteric subject for engineers only. The radio spectrum, is, however, no longer an avoidable technical concern. Its efficient use is now a significant element in defining networking prospects in the information age. These prospects will be influenced as much by political, economic, and social factors as by the work of technologists. These nontechnical considerations were relatively benign only a short time ago. The spectrum was little used, and it was treated as a kind of electrical Wild West frontier with few restrictions.

Today the spectrum, like many other natural resources, is in danger of becoming degraded through overexploitation. This is so despite the fact that the spectrum is not a depletable resource. It is finite, but it is always there. The problem is to use it efficiently. At one level, users themselves create interference through their own electronic activities. Noise pollution — the familiar phenomenon of static — is a by-product of the greater general use of electrical power. (Much of this interference comes from automobile ignition systems.) The problem is compounded as more powerful transmitters are designed to punch through the noise, resulting in more noise, particularly if the transmitters are not perfectly adjusted. Most of the other difficulties with the spectrum have to do with the steadily rising number of users and types of uses, all trying to crowd into a finite physical resource. Two decades ago, probably 90% of spectrum use took place in a relatively narrow band across the Northern Hemisphere, from Tokyo east to Berlin. The heaviest users are still found within this band, but they must now consider the needs of a hundred or more developing countries, almost all of whom are expanding their use of the spectrum.

The spectrum is, therefore, a major political and economic concern, not only domestically but internationally. Since the early part of this century, it has been subject to treaty restrictions, under the supervision of the International Telecommunications Union (ITU), which is now a United Nations specialized agency. The ITU was, until a short time ago, an old boy's club composed of the Western industrial powers, the Soviet Union, and Japan. These powers gathered periodically to decide how they would allocate and manage the spectrum for their own uses. This arrangement is now finished; the rest of the world has joined the club.[16]

Under the ITU's one-vote-per-country rules, the newcomers from the Third World have considerable influence on the future patterns of spectrum use. Particular attention has been focused on their needs and demands in a series of international conferences convened for the purpose of reviewing and revising world spectrum regulations to meet changing needs. The largest of these meetings, the 1979 World Administrative Radio Conference, approved major shifts in spectrum use that will affect all communications users throughout the rest of the century. Smaller follow-up conferences have taken place since then to discuss specific spectrum problems not resolved at the 1979 meeting. In the process it is becoming clear that the radio spectrum is no longer the exclusive province of the technical experts. Given its role as the most important natural resource of the information age, it now attracts the attention of a wide range of political, economic, and social interests.[17]

It is useful, therefore, to take a closer look at the spectrum, noting some of the policy questions involved in each of its major segments. These questions will be cropping up again as we examine the political and economic issues of the information age in later chapters.

The raw material of the radio spectrum is *electromagnetic radiation* — radiant energy in the form of invisible waves moving through space and matter. This phenomenon was identified in theory in 1864 by James Clerk Maxwell, director of the Cavendish Laboratories at Cambridge University. His theories were confirmed in 1888 when a German physicist, Heinrich Hertz, produced the first man-made electromagnetic radiation by sending a strong electric charge across a spark gap and thereby causing a smaller spark — evidence of the presence of an electric field — to jump across a second gap some distance away. The history of wireless communication has been a progressive enhancement of our ability to devise equipment for generating and receiving electromagnetic radiation in the radio frequency range and to use such waves for telecommunications.

The usable part of the spectrum extends from 10 kilohertz (KHz) — roughly the lower limit of human hearing — to 275 gigahertz (GHz), a frequency which begins to approach that of light waves. A *hertz*, our permanent tribute to the redoubtable Heinrich, indicates the number of radiated "waves" that pass a given point in a second. One GHz is a thousand million cycles per second. The companion measurement is the *length* of each wave; the wavelengths for the usable spectrum run from 3000 meters — almost two miles — down to one millimeter. The spectrum is divided into eight bands, ranging from very low frequency (VLF) to extra high frequency (EHF). Each band covers a "decade" of frequencies or wavelengths. Thus the high frequency band goes from 3 megahertz (MHz) to 30 MHz, or 100 meters down to 10 meters.

Spectrum use has been tied to the development of increasingly sophisticated transmitters and receivers designed to exploit this resource. The progression has generally moved from the low frequencies to the higher ones, with one interesting exception. The United States Navy is developing uses for the very bottom (and currently unusable) end of the spectrum — below 10 KHz, which is so low it is not included in the ITU's spectrum responsibilities. The Navy is interested in the ability of these frequencies to penetrate many fathoms of ocean water and to remain relatively unaffected by upper atmosphere nuclear bursts that can blank out higher frequency communications. These attributes have important implications for communications with nuclear-missile–bearing submarines whose effectiveness depends largely on their ability to avoid detection while submerged. Very low frequency communications with the subs cannot be monitored by a potential enemy. The Navy's plan to install such a system has, however, raised difficult political problems. The system's "transmitter" involves thousands of miles of wires crisscrossing hundreds of square miles of earth. The transmitter site has to have specific geologic characteristics which, in this country, are found in the northern reaches of Minnesota and Michigan. For years, citizen groups blocked the transmitter, despite a public relations campaign by the Navy stressing the national security benefits of what was dubbed, perhaps too coyly, Project Sanguine. After considerable negotiation and compromises, the plan was approved, with completion of the full system scheduled for the late 1980s.

Just above the low frequencies are the *medium frequencies*, best known for their use in radio broadcasting. The medium wave band has many uses beyond broadcasting, such as long-range navigation devices for ships and aircraft. This part of the spectrum now serves a hodgepodge of uses. It could be better utilized for purposes other than radio broadcasting if there were not such a heavy world investment in radio transmitters and consumer receivers adapted for these frequencies.

The next step up the spectrum is the *high frequency* band (HF). This band has been described as the jewel of the spectrum because of its special capabilities, but it is beginning to look a bit antique. Unlike medium wave, whose transmitting capabilities are very limited geographically, high frequency can have a global reach. When used for this purpose, its frequencies are refracted downwards by charged layers in the ionosphere in a hopscotch pattern, bouncing between earth and sky around the world. Exploiting this capability is a neat trick, but it does not always work. HF's effectiveness varies from hour to hour, day to day, year to year, as well as by geography and the sunspot cycle. The whole band can be crammed down to a very narrow usable section during high points in the 11-year sunspot cycle.

Despite these limitations, HF channels are in high demand. Before the advent of satellites and large submarine cables, they were used for international telephone service. They are still useful for radio "hams," aircraft and maritime communications, and radar tracking. Another well-known application is shortwave broadcasting. The United States, with its Voice of America network, is only one of over 70 nations operating in this highly competitive field. The Voice of America's transmitters have a total of over 20 million watts of power — the equivalent of 400 large domestic stations. Despite this, the United States lags behind the Soviet Union, the People's Republic of China, and other countries in total transmitting hours per day.

Some of the pressure in the HF band comes from a flamboyant upstart in spectrum use — Citizen's Band (CB) radio. CB is electronic populism with its own peculiar customs, language, and folklore. In 1973, there were less than a million CB receivers in operation in this country. A conservative estimate of current operating sets would be over 30 million. CB's 40 channels are grouped in a betwixt-and-between area of the HF spectrum — a point at which receivers can be extremely cheap but where the incidence of interference is high. CB receivers interfere with television and with police radio; CBs get interference from industrial machines, medical equipment, and even washing machines. Interference is increased by certain weather conditions as well as by the practice of many CB users of installing illegal amplifiers to get greater transmitting range. This electronic free-for-all makes the job of policing this part of the spectrum very difficult; the Federal Communications Commission has long since given up any serious monitoring of CB use. The FCC's reluctance is influenced in part by the fact that CB owners represent a very large voter block who have come to regard the maintenance and expansion of their spectrum space as a natural right.

The next steps up the spectrum are the *very high frequency* (VHF) and *ultra high frequency* (UHF) bands, best known as the locations of FM radio and television channels. These bands are also the spectrum home for many so-called mobile services — police, taxi, military, and public service radio, as well as automobile telephones. Over 1.5 million two-way mobile stations are authorized by the FCC, not counting CB installations. With expanded frequencies allocated by the 1979 World Administrative Radio Conference, mobile radio will be a major area of communications expansion in the coming years. The most dramatic expansion is taking place in a new kind of mobile telephone service known as cellular radio. Using sophisticated computerized switching techniques, the service picks up portable telephone calls within small geographical "cells" and transfers them to other portable phones or to any other phone in the world. By the late 1980s, the service will be available in all major United States metropolitan areas and in many smaller towns. Within a decade, mobile services transmitted via communications satellites will be available. In 1977, NASA demonstrated a mobile radio transmitting and receiving device that fit into a small briefcase. The equipment, powered by batteries, sent and received signals from a remote area of Georgia to a Baltimore hospital via a NASA satellite in an experiment designed to test its use for emergency situations.[18] In 1983, NASA announced plans for a joint United States–Canadian mobile satellite for more advanced experiments.

At the top end of the usable spectrum are the *super high frequency* (SHF) and the *extremely high frequency* (EHF) bands. Here is where the microwaves operate, and where the most controversial advances in spectrum use have taken place. The microwave frequencies lie below the infrared region of the spectrum, with wavelength ranges from about a hundred centimeters, or 40 inches, down to a millimeter or 1/125th of an inch. (By contrast, the wavelength distance at the low-frequency end of the spectrum is almost two miles.)

The microwaves are the heavy-duty workhorses of the spectrum. They were harnessed in the 1930s when equipment was developed which could generate higher and higher frequency radio waves with proportionately greater message capacities. Microwave technology was a crucial factor in World War II, when it served as the basis for radar. Microwaves can be focused in directional beams and reflected back by such objects as airplanes. The first radar installations were limited and unreliable. As the military pressed for better definition and accuracy, technologists pushed further up the spectrum, developing equipment that allowed precision targeting by the end of the war.

The microwave revolution got underway in earnest in the late forties. A microwave system, using relay towers, was opened between Boston and New York in 1947; by 1951, a coast-to-coast network was in operation, using 107 towers. (Since microwave transmission is line-of-sight, the towers are placed on elevated points when possible.) Over a quarter of a million microwave relay towers have been built since then in this country for telephone, television, computer data, and other transmissions at increasingly high capacities. Microwaves also have noncommunications uses, such as in surgical operations, in household and industrial ovens, and in agricultural experiments to kill weeds and insects. The "death ray" weapon, favorite of Sunday-supplement editors, remains mercifully elusive, although the military is experimenting with various uses of microwaves in the increasingly sophisticated field of electronic warfare.

If the death ray remains a theory, a more immediate threat from electromagnetic radiation is just beginning to be debated publicly. This involves the concern that microwave circuitry may be responsible for new forms of environmental pollution, a kind of electronic smog that can affect human and animal well-being. In December 1971, a White House task force summed up the possible threat in these words:

The electro-magnetic radiations emanating from radar, television, communications systems, microwave ovens, industrial heat-treatment systems, medical diathermy units and many other sources permeate the modern environment, both civilian and military.... This type of man-made radiation exposure has no counterpart in man's evolutionary background...unless adequate monitoring and control based on a fundamental understanding of biological effects are instituted in the near future, in the decades ahead, man may enter an era of energy pollution comparable to the chemical pollution of today.[19]

Given political and economic stakes in microwave transmission, the general reaction to this and other warnings, until recently, has been to ignore or play down the problem. However, a number of events have directed greater public attention to the potential hazards of radiation pollution. The most publicized of these incidents occurred in the mid-seventies at the American Embassy in Moscow, where health problems among personnel were attributed to the Soviet practice of aiming electro-magnetic beams at the building. Whether or not this was true, the incident focused attention on an aspect of our post-industrial communications structure that needs more careful monitoring.[20]

In the meantime, microwaves are the aerial pathways of a major space age development — the communications satellite. The satellites are basically microwave switching stations, the space equivalent of a ground relay tower. The difference is that a satellite gives the microwave path a line-of-sight capability that stretches across one-third of the earth. Floating 22,300 miles above the equator, the satellites effectively break the boundaries of the earth's horizon. At that height, they travel at the same speed as the earth's rotation and, therefore, appear to be stationary; they are, in the engineer's phrase, "geostationary." Since the mid-sixties, the satellites have provided high quality communications circuits to nations in Asia, Africa, and Latin America that would otherwise not have had them for many more years. By 1984, over a hundred countries, accounting for over 96% of all internation-al traffic, belonged to Intelsat, the world satellite organization which runs the basic network.[21]

In less than 20 years, communications satellites have gone through six technological generations. The first "birds" were weakly powered machines, capable of providing only limited services. Later generations, relying on microelectronic technology, have had progressively more so-phisticated circuit capacity and transmitting power. The current sixth genera-tion Intelsat satellite can transmit a combination of 30,000 telephone calls and 2 television channels simultaneously. (By contrast, the first Intelsat generation had a capacity of 250 telephone circuits or 1 television channel.) Moreover, the newer satellites have a greater capacity for handling digital data, permitting use of such techniques as data packet transmissions.

The greater capabilities of the newer satellites permits the expansion of services beyond such point-to-point transmissions as telephone calls. They open the way for radio or television broadcasting from space to small earth terminals. Direct broadcasting satellites (DBS) were first tested in the mid-seventies. A NASA experimental satellite, *ATS–6*, beamed educational and other public service broadcasts to remote earth terminals in Appalachia, the Rocky Mountains, and Alaska. *ATS–6* was shifted in 1975 halfway around the world to provide educational transmissions to over 2000 remote villages in India. DBS technology has advanced rapidly in recent years; plans for space broadcast services are underway in Europe, Japan, and this country. In 1983, the Federal Communications Commission authorized eight firms to proceed with the construction of DBS networks, designed largely to provide a range of commercial entertainment, news and other services to homes. DBS technology has also stirred lively controversy in the United Nations, where developing countries are pressing for limitations on broadcasting into their territories without their prior consent. Whatever the outcome of the debate, there is little doubt that television and radio transmissions from space and into homes will become routine in the next decade.[22]

Because they involve a familiar service — television — broadcast satellites are well publicized. However, the range of satellite uses, present and potential, is considerably wider. Two dozen countries now use satellites for domestic as well as international communications. A special satellite network, *Inmarsat*, provides communications services for ships at sea. Eventually, a similar network will link aircraft to ground traffic control stations. Military satellites are an integral part of the global communications networks of the Soviet and the United States defense systems. There is also an increasing number of so-called sensing satellites, that monitor weather and earth resources, returning data to world wide networks of earth terminals.

With so many satellites floating in a narrow corridor above the equator, a unique kind of traffic jam has been created. The choicest frequencies and orbital slots — where the satellites are "parked" — are filling up fast. Given a NASA estimate that there will be a tenfold increase in international demand for satellite circuits between 1982 and the end of the century, the problem of crowded frequencies and orbital slots may soon be critical. At present, the congestion is concentrated in the high traffic areas over the Western Hemisphere and the North Atlantic region. By 1980, there were 44 satellites in the equatorial orbital arc between 4° west longitude and 150° west longitude — roughly from the mid-Atlantic to the mid-Pacific. The satellites are many miles apart in the immensity of space; adding a few more might seem to be as simple as introducing a few more cars on a lonely stretch of highway. However, unless satellites using the same frequency band are kept several degrees apart (about 250 miles), ground stations cannot discriminate between their separate signals.[23]

This has become an international issue in recent years as developing countries insist that the industrialized countries' current near-monopoly of satellite frequencies and orbital slots be ended in favor of a system assuring access to these resources for Third World countries. The issue will come to a head in an ITU conference being held in two sessions in 1985 and 1988 to develop arrangements for more equitable distribution of space communications frequencies and orbital slots.

The solution, at its simplest level, lies in the efficient use of more complex satellites. The current thrust of satellite research and development is in this direction. Whether technological advances can keep ahead of the quickly rising global demands for more circuits is an open question. So far, this has been done by providing more transmitting power in the satellites themselves and by developing techniques for more sophisticated use of frequencies. By the mid-seventies, RCA had commercially demonstrated its *Satcom* satellite's ability to send two signals on the same frequency, thereby doubling circuit capacity. The eighties have seen a new generation of hybrid satellites, capable of several different tasks. Among these is Western Union's *TDRSS* (Tracking and Data Relay Satellite System), which operates standard commercial services and also relays data to earth from other satellites operating at lower orbits as well as from NASA's space shuttle. Earth terminals can "see" the shuttle and these low-flying satellites only for a short time before they disappear over the horizon. *TDRSS* can literally look down on them from its position further out in space and track them more than 80% of the time.

The newer satellites also make greater use of digital circuitry, which is capable of moving information — in voice, visual, or data form — at much greater speeds than analog communications. This is an important consideration in the attempt to meet increasing demands for transmission between high speed computers. It takes several hours to transmit a reel of computer tape at the rate now generally available — 9600 bits per second. At digital transmission speeds of up to 1.5 megabits per second, transmittal time is reduced to 3 minutes.

Efficient use of orbital slots is complicated by the fact that most present satellites that preempt a slot have a limited purpose. The newer multipurpose satellites — the so-called hybrids — will ease this limitation somewhat, as each will be capable of doing the work of several of the older satellites. Other techniques for easing orbital and frequency congestions are being studied. One of these involves building large space platforms to orbit above the equator. Many satellites could be hung like Christmas tree ornaments from these structures, which might measure several acres in size. Moreover, the platforms would also support large solar cell arrays to supply power to all the equipment on the platform. The platforms would be assembled in space by work crews using parts delivered by the space shuttle and other transporters. Periodic maintenance checks of the platform and the satellites would be made by space-suited repairmen. The net effect would be to group a half-dozen or more satellites, each using different frequencies, in an orbital slot normally taken up by a single satellite. A prototype platform will probably be built under a NASA research program and be launched in the late eighties.

A less dramatic but possibly more practical approach has been advanced by engineer Paul Visher of Hughes Aircraft. He proposes clusters of separate satellites in an orbital slot, each transmitting its signals through a near-by master satellite. (Satellite-to-satellite communications is quite feasible, thanks to recent research breakthroughs.) A wide range of signals for various purposes could be transmitted, utilizing only one orbital slot. The value of Visher's concept is that it can be realized with currently available satellite technology. Space platform research is still in the theoretical stages; moreover, the platforms will be very expensive pieces of hardware when and if the technology proves feasible.

Other intensive research in the expansion of satellite capabilities focuses on the radio spectrum itself. Here the effort is on techniques for making more microwave frequencies available. Theoretically, there is plenty of room in the spectrum for this since, despite the research breakthroughs of recent years, less than 10% of the spectrum is being utilized for communications and other purposes. To illustrate this point, let us assume that the total radio spectrum up to 300 GHz represents an area the size of the United States. On this scale, 1 MHz — roughly the medium wave frequencies — would represent a 60-foot strip of Atlantic beach. Thirty GHz — the outer limit of most present applications — would take us 300 miles inland. Everything beyond would be largely *terra incognita*, or what the spectrum engineers call EHF for extra high frequencies. The halt at 30 GHz is equivalent to westward migration across the United States that has stopped at the Appalachians.[24]

Any further "migration" in the spectrum is liable to be slow for technical reasons. The 1979 WARC conference allocated specific frequency uses up to 275 GHz. These allocations in the EHF bands are intended largely for specialized purposes such as radio astronomy. One such proposed use is for a radio telescope to be placed on the dark side of the moon, shielded from earthly radio interference. Another involves sending signals to civilizations beyond our solar system — a favorite project of astronomer, Carl Sagan, and other enthusiasts of what is known as SETI, the search for extra-terrestrial intelligence.

Meanwhile the technological push is on to open higher reaches of the spectrum for more mundane needs such as television broadcasts and telephone calls. The most intensive research is in the 20 to 30 GHz bands — just above the present limits of practical microwave transmissions. The potential rewards of breakthroughs in this area will be vast numbers of new higher capacity microwave channels for satellites and for terrestrial use. The difficulties are formidable; not the least of them are the adverse effects of heavy rainstorms and other weather conditions on transmissions in these higher bands. The very short microwaves at these frequencies can be wiped out by rain or snow drops. One way to overcome this is to establish satellite earth stations in pairs, sufficiently separated and positioned so that such interference will not occur at both stations simultaneously. In 1978, NASA inaugurated a long-term research and development program to open up the 20−30 GHz bands for communications and other purposes.[25] If the tests are successful, overcrowding in the lower parts of the microwave frequency spectrum could be eased considerably. The Europeans, Japanese, and Soviets are also working on the problem, and all of them are as aware as the United States of the economic and political rewards of opening these bands to practical uses.

It is clear that communications satellite usage will expand dramatically during the coming decade. Counting the number of satellites in orbit is not the best way to measure this growth: the satellites come in too many sizes and varying capabilities. A more reliable measure is the number of transponders in use — a transponder being, in effect, a "package" of circuits in a satellite. Taking United States domestic satellites alone, present growth rates are impressive. In 1980, there were a total of 156 transponders on these satellites; by mid-decade this has risen to an estimated 612. Moreover, the satellites are linking a greater network of earth stations in this country. In September 1980, the FCC reported 591 stations; this is scheduled to increase to 7500 by mid-decade, and some predictions for 1990 run as high as 100,000 stations.[26]

In summary, the past 20 years have seen enormous parallel expansion in the range and capacities of both wire and wireless technology. Each mode has its distinctive capabilities. What they share is a greatly enhanced ability to handle most communication tasks interchangeably, carrying voice, visual, or data messages. Sophisticated integrated switching equipment no longer distinguishes between the type of circuitry it serves. Both wire and wireless circuitry will make up the new universal grid, providing a wide variety of high capacity channels.

Wireless communications — and microwave circuits in particular — were the fastest growth area in telecommunications during the past three decades. However, there will be greater competition in the coming years from sophisticated wire technologies. The present work horse of high capacity wire technology is the coaxial cable, the familiar phone-company cable that runs under city streets. However, the future lies with fiber optic cables and with millimeter waveguides that can send 15 billion bits of information a second down a metal pipe — strange kinds of wires indeed. These developments represent a long technological leap from Samuel F. B. Morse's experiment in transmitting a few coded words a minute over a flimsy telegraph line 150 years ago. The Wire Age started by Morse, now technologically compatible with the Wireless Age, has come full circle in the Age of the Integrated Grid.

NOTES

1. Harold A. Innis, *Empire and Communications* (Toronto: University of Toronto Press, 1972), pp. 1−11. The work was originally published in 1950.

2. The fable of the evaluation committee for the printing press was proposed by the distinguished American communications scholar, Harold Lasswell. For a comprehensive review of the initial impact of the Renaissance printing press, see Elizabeth Eisenstein, *The Printing Press as an Agent of Change* (New York: Cambridge University Press, 1980).

3. Asa Briggs, "The Pleasure Telephone: A Chapter in the Pre-history of the Media," in *The Social Impact of the Telephone*, ed. Ithiel de Sola Pool (Cambridge, Mass.: MIT Press, 1977), pp. 40–59.

4. Anthony Smith, "The Wire and the Wavelength — An Historical Study," in *Cable: An Investigation of the Social and Political Implications of Cable Television*, a report published by the Standing Conference on Broadcasting (London, 1974), p. 29.

5. Ibid., pp. 31–32.

6. Erik Barnouw, *The Sponsor* (New York: Oxford University Press, 1978), pp. 24–25.

7. Smith, "Wire and Wavelength," pp. 36–37.

8. Anthony Smith, *Shadows on the Cave* (Urbana, Ill.: University of Illinois Press, 1973), p. 351.

9. For a useful summary of international cable developments, see Arthur C. Clarke, *Voices across the Sea* (London: Luscombe Publishers, 1974).

10. Morris Edwards, "Fiber Optic Links Forge Paths for the Expected Information Explosion," *Communications News*, February 1978, p. 30.

11. "Lightwave Links Form Groundwork for U.K. Digital Network," *Data Communications*, April 1981, p. 36.

12. These figures represent projections made by American and European telecommunications carriers, and are taken from an AT&T Long Lines study, "North Atlantic Planning Process Technological Alternatives Update," November 7, 1983.

13. "Pure Is Best," *The Economist* (London), 4 October 1980, p. 93.

14. Ammon Yariv, "Guided Wave Optics," *Scientific American*, April 1980, pp. 64–72.

15. Eitan Abraham, Colin T. Seaton, and S. Desmond Smith, "The Optical Computer," *Scientific American*, February 1983, pp. 85–93.

16. For a useful description of the International Telecommunications Union, see "How the ITU Works," *Intermedia* (London), September 1979, pp. 1–2; also Delbert D. Smith, *International Telecommunications Control* (Amsterdam: A. W. Sijthoff, 1969), pp. 18–29.

17. The most extensive survey of the political and economic implications of ITU decisions can be found in ten articles on the 1979 World Administrative Radio Conference in *Journal of Communication*, 29, no. 1 (Winter 1979), pp. 143–207. For a description of the technical problems facing the ITU, see Charles Lee Jackson. "The Allocation of the Radio Spectrum," *Scientific American*, February 1980, pp. 34–39.

18. "Small Radio Could Bring Aid in a Disaster," *New York Times*, 13 November 1977, p. 61.

19. U.S. Office of Telecommunications Policy, Executive Office of the President, *Program for Control of Electromagnetic Pollution of the Environment*, Electromagnetic Radiation Management Advisory Council, December 1971, p. 12.

20. A critical view of radiation pollution is given in Paul Brodeur, *The Zapping*

of America (New York: W. W. Norton and Co., 1977). For an industry-oriented response to Brodeur's criticism, see "The Conning of America," *Microwave Journal,* October 1978, pp. 18–19.

21. Joseph N. Pelton, *Global Talk* (Amsterdam: Sijthoff and Noordhoff, 1981).

22. For a summary of the broadcast satellite controversy, see Wilson Dizard, "Direct Broadcast Satellites: The U.S. Position" in *The Cable/Broadband Communications Book,* vol. 2, 1980–81 (Washington, D.C.: Communications Press, 1980), pp. 73–86.

23. "A Traffic Jam in Outer Space," *New York Times,* 26 March 1980, p. D–3.

24. The Rand Corporation, "Radio's Last Frontier," *Rand Research Review,* 2, no. 1 (Spring 1978): 1.

25. Cutbacks in the Reagan administration threatened this and other NASA advanced research projects. See "Satellite R & D: Washington Moves to Correct a Mistake," *Satellite Communications,* April 1981, pp. 13–17.

26. The statistics on transponders are from *Satellite Week* (Washington), 9 October 1980, p. 9. The projection on earth station installations was made by Sidney Topol, president of Scientific Atlanta, Inc., a leading earth station manufacturer, in "Information Processing," *Business Week,* 6 October 1980, p. 46.

CHAPTER FOUR

THE TECHNOLOGICAL FRAMEWORK

Information Machines

HAVING LOOKED AT the technologies forming the new networks, we now turn to the information machines that plug into the grid. These are the computers, terminals, telex printers, and other devices that are the nodal points where human thoughts are transferred into electronic impulses and fed into the system. Their capabilities need to be understood as we try to measure their impact on strategies for a new information age.

We have seen how a convergence of research breakthroughs has revolutionized wire and wireless networks. This pattern of interactive new technology is, if anything, more complex when we take into account the machines that are served by these networks. There are many technological paths leading up to this convergence and many possible outcomes. There are also significant elements shared by the machines and the networks. The most important of these is their common reliance on microelectronic technology, which provides each of them with new levels of reliability and capacity and new operational functions. Microelectronic products, many of them no bigger than a fingernail, are a key resource in powering the second industrial revolution. Here I will, somewhat parochially, limit my concerns to one part of this process — the post-industrial information structure, a complicated pattern of machines linked to a growing communications grid, all made possible by the commonality of microelectronic devices.

A letter sent across the country by conventional means may involve a typewriter, a postal truck, canceling and sorting machines, an airplane, a pushcart, more trucks and sorting equipment, and finally a mailman walking his route. This is, with luck, a three-day process. A single machine — actually two terminals at either end of a satellite circuit — can deliver the contents of the letter in less than a minute. The technological advantage of this is clear. There are, however, economic, political, and social considerations where the advantages are considerably less obvious. The postal system is more than an institution potentially capable of one-minute mail delivery. It is the friendly mail carrier, Christmas cards, junk mail, and stamp collecting, all of which have to be fitted into, or discarded from, this new one-minute system. The question is relevant to any future information strategies we may devise: To what degree are we willing to modify or even dismantle comfortable ways of thinking and acting in order to accommodate the new technologies?

This accommodation is a tall order for any society. The United States is being pressed to make decisions well ahead of any other country because of its long lead in developing a mass communications system. Competitive economic pressures, in particular, will force decisions either by design or default. We will look more closely at this decision process in later chapters. Here we will survey the present state and future expectations of the new information machines.

The survey begins with microelectronics — the technological common denominator in the new integrated information grid. Its products have, of course, uses beyond communications and information equipment. However, it is probable that one-half or more of the industry's basic product, semiconductor chips, goes into such equipment. Computers alone accounted for 40% of the use of world semiconductor output by 1980. Communications and information applications have set the pace in what has come to be called "the microelectronics revolution." As in most self-proclaimed revolutions, the semantics are imprecise. A more exact, if somewhat less stirring, description would be "speeded-up evolution," with a footnote that the process has not been, nor will it be, a smooth one.[1]

Smooth or not, the evolution is impressive. The primitive era was a scant 30 years ago. At that time, interconnected radio vacuum tubes were the only device for transmitting a current of electrons between electrodes in communications and information equipment. The tubes worked, but they were bulky and fragile. In the early fifties, the process of replacing them began with *transistors*, developed by the Bell Laboratories. In a transistor, the current connecting electrodes flows through solid materials, usually silicon, known as *semiconductors*. The next step, which took place around 1960, was the development of *integrated circuits*, or many interconnected transistors on a single piece of silicon, popularly known as a *chip*. Research has since centered on the progressive sophistication of integrated circuits with larger capacities and expanded functions. The first integrated circuits had 10 transistors on a chip. This capacity has been pushed up to several hundred thousand components per chip in recent years. A million-transistor chip is being tested experimentally.

Improvements in circuit capacity have opened the way for the chips to take on new functions. The most striking change has been the incorporation of the *microprocessor*, a complex type of integrated circuit which can function as a computer. A single chip can contain the equivalent of the central processor of a small computer, which performs arithmetical and logical functions, plus some memory. It works in conjunction with *memory chips*, which store information, and with *input* and *output chips*, which are used to get information into and out of the central processor. The technological distance between the old vacuum radio tube and the present day integrated chip is formidable. The pioneering ENIAC computer, developed during World War II, weighed 30 tons, filled a large room, and had 17,000 radio tubes, which required round-the-clock replacement maintenance.[2] A present-day chip incorporating a microprocessor the size of a thumbtack can have more computational power than ENIAC. Microprocessors are still a small, specialized part of integrated circuit production, accounting for only about 10% of such production. However, this percentage is expected to double within a few years.

In Chapter 5 we will take a closer look at the industry that churns out these products. The semiconductor companies were the most dynamic industrial sector of the 1970s, expanding from $1 billion in annual sales at the beginning of the decade to $10 billion by the end. A recent survey by the Boston research firm, Arthur D. Little Inc., predicted an annual market for semiconductors of $40 billion (in 1978 dollars) by 1987 for the United States, Britain, France, and West Germany alone.[3] This growth is all the more phenomenal considering the average price of a transistor component in a chip is now less than a penny, compared to $10 twenty years ago.

Advanced chips will be, in the words of one developer, the jelly beans of the electronic age — plentiful and cheap. They are adapted so quickly to so many uses, from toys to telephones, that they have often been in chronic short supply. At one point in the early eighties, United States firms were caught up in delivery delays of up to 10 months.[4] Thanks to the competitiveness of the industry — and particularly the growing threat of Japanese competition — these shortages were made up. Another longer term problem is not so readily solved by production speed-ups. This is the inability of many chip users to get the software they need for the tiny devices. There are still too few trained *software programmers*, the technicians who write the instructions. Moreover, program writing is an expensive operation and is becoming even more so. A decade ago, two-thirds of the cost of integrated circuitry was in hardware, the rest in software. This ratio has since been reversed.

These problems will not seriously delay the shift to microelectronics, particularly in communications and information. Chips are a basic construction module in the upgrading of networks and the machines linked to them. These pea-size devices are already being used to overhaul the network most familiar to us — the telephone system. The end result will be a phone network that will eventually be called something else, since conventional voice service will be only one part of its function.

The transformation of the phone network is taking place now, mostly behind the scenes in exchanges and other system installations. Beginning in the mid-seventies, telephone companies have been replacing their old electromechanical switching gear with electronic equipment. One of the last pieces of equipment to be affected by this modernization program has been the telephone instrument itself. Telephones may be shaped like Mickey Mouse or a plastic doughnut, but the equipment inside most of them is basically the same. The telephone is a 30-year-old technology; apart from push-button dialing, the design and performance of the standard set has been unchanged since 1953. This is changing with the introduction of an all-electronic telephone, complete with chips. In one model, tested in recent years by Bell Canada, about 180 parts of the standard push-button telephone are replaced by 3 integrated circuits.[5]

The result will be not only a more efficient voice telephone as such but also an instrument better adapted, through microprocessor technology, to plug into other communications and information services, including computers. The days of the phone network's focus on POTS — Plain Old Telephone Service — are ending.

This shift is part of a larger pattern — the restructuring of United States communications and information industries. There are complex political and economic reasons for the change, as we shall see in subsequent chapters. However, the determining factor has been microelectronics technology. Given the capabilities of the new devices, it makes less sense to have a single monopoly network dedicated primarily to POTS. It was this technological imperative, more than any other single factor, that has led to the current massive transformation of the United States communications structure. The central event of this change was the 1982 decision to end AT&T's near-total monopoly over local telephone service, at the same time permitting the firm to operate competitively in the data communications market for the first time.

AT&T's reorganization removed major constraints on the application of advanced communications and information technologies in this country. For a decade before the government's decision to permit the break-up of AT&T, the company's dominant position had been eroding slowly. This was largely the result of a series of legal and administrative rulings permitting greater competition in telephone equipment and services. These limited decisions did not, however, seriously affect AT&T's dominance over the telephone network — the basic infrastructure of the information age. The 1982 decision to divest most of the local Bell companies from AT&T changed this. In the process, it opened the prospect of an era of technologically driven competition across the entire spectrum of American communications. Whether this prospect will be realized or not will be reviewed in Chapter 7 which deals with the economic and social implications of the changes. Meanwhile, many barriers to innovative application of advanced technology have been breached, from telephones to computers.

Computers are at the center of this post-industrial shift. Like the working group faced with Master Gutenberg's invention in our Renaissance fable, we have trouble getting the computer's measure. The developers of the first electronic computer in the 1940s thought that four computers, more or less, would satisfy the world's needs.[6] Given the state of computer technology at the time, their estimate seemed reasonable. But the fact is that there are now literally millions of machines that can be classified under the broad heading of "computers." After three decades of specialized use in business and government, computers are becoming a mass consumer product. The next 10 years will bring widespread use of personal home computers with their own data storage capabilities as well as links to outside data sources.[7]

At many levels, computers are integral parts of the universal information grid. They would be important even if they were only able to store vast amounts of information, like highly efficient filing cabinets, or to serve as high speed calculating machines. Their great liberating use, however, is their power to extend knowledge, particularly by simulating reality (or even simulating what seems to be unreality) in ways the human brain finds difficult to do or is incapable of doing.

Modern computers and communications circuitry both have their origins among a small group of scientists working on the East Coast and in Britain during the 1940s and 1950s. The mention of their names — Claude Shannon, Norbert Wiener, John von Neumann, Alan Turing, and others — causes few knowing nods, even among reasonably well-informed people today. It would be difficult, however, to exaggerate the contribution of these scientists to post-industrial America and, by extension, to the rest of the world. Working in the esoteric area known as "information theory," they understood that they had to define information and its characteristics accurately if their ideas about a more rational organization of information resources were to be realized. Their pursuit of this purpose in seminar rooms and laboratories and in faculty club discussions has had results that put an indelible mark on American society.

The basic orientation of the group was mathematics, and particularly the idea, advanced by Bertrand Russell and Alfred North Whitehead, that logic is the foundation of all mathematics. Russell's and Whitehead's 1910 work, *Principia Mathematica*, developed the calculus of propositions or the solving of problems in terms of statements that are either true or false. As a young M.I.T. graduate student in the late thirties, Claude Shannon demonstrated the practical applications of this calculus in improving the design of electrical circuits. Shannon's initial research, which became his master's thesis, showed that programming an electronic digital computer would be a problem not of arithmetic, but of logic. Later, at the Bell Laboratories, Shannon and his fellow researcher Warren Weaver expanded on these insights to propose a design for a general communications system.[8] They treated information input as a problem in statistics, permitting precise measurement of the amount of information delivered and the efficiency of the devices that handle it. Like computers, the theory deals with information rather than meaning. For the first time, communications and computer scientists had a definitive measure of their commodity — information.

That measure is called a *bit*, a contraction of "binary digit." The bit is the module for the input to most advanced electronic information and communications devices. It can be defined as the lowest common denominator of information, a unit resolving uncertainty or choice between two exclusive alternatives, for example, between yes and no, heads and tails, on and off, one and zero. It is the choice we exercise in choosing left or right when there are no other options, that is, when there is equal probability for each. In choosing, we resolve doubt. By putting many bits together in a computer or communications circuit, symbols (words, pictures, numbers) that transmit information take shape. Whatever form it takes, the information is transmitted onto electrical circuits digitally, that is, it is represented by two digits — 0 or 1 — in patterns that define the information. The letter A in a 6-bit binary code can be 11001, the letter *P* can be 100111, and so on. The pattern 110001 100111 100111 100011 110101 010010 110001 010100 110011 110101 stored in a computer moves through the circuits and comes out as "applesauce." Trillions and trillions of symbolic 1s and 0s move through communications systems, each a coded part of a message that may be a teenager's telephone call, a credit card transaction, a television soap opera, or a weather report from the Viking space station on Mars.

Shannon also demonstrated how to measure the capacity of a communications channel in terms of *bits per second* (BPS). The channel capacity for a telephone wire used for speech purposes is 60,000 BPS; for broadcast television, 90 million BPS, and on upward to the 15 billion BPS capacity for a millimeter wave-guide system. Shannon's contributions were only part of a convergence of concepts that made possible the new communications and information machines. Britain's Alan Turing had provided remarkable insights into the problem of digital computers in a paper written in 1937 when he was only 25 years old.[9] Another contributor was Norbert Wiener, an M.I.T. mathematics professor and an authentic genius who earned a Harvard Ph.D. in mathematical logic at the age of 19. Wiener explored the concept of self-regulating mechanisms akin to the human brain's feedback capabilities. Early work in computers spurred speculation about "thinking" machines and automation. Wiener coined a name for this field of computer control — "cybernetics" — in a book by the same name exploring the uses of such automata.[10] Meanwhile, mathematician, John von Neumann, at Princeton was developing the *stored-program* concept, the idea that a machine could control its calculating sequences by modifying its own instructions. Taken together, these concepts moved computer technology beyond storage and calculating functions to electronic, digital stored-program machines, expanding dramatically their creative capabilities as intelligence extenders.

In identifying the logical parameters of information and communications machines, von Neumann and other information theorists laid much of the base for the high technology advances that have occurred in the last 30 years. Matching their own remarkable insights was the speed with which their ideas were put to practical use. In part it was the result of close collaboration between research and development organizations, both public and private, and American industry. The Department of Defense, pressing for quick military applications of these new technologies, was an important factor in this process. There was intense pressure within the industrial sector to exploit the potentially lucrative opportunities opened up by the new electronics. A production infrastructure developed quickly, with Remington Rand producing the first production-line computer, UNIVAC I, in 1951. By the end of 1953, 13 companies were manufacturing computers, including IBM which soon became the giant of the new industry.[11]

The first electronic computers were large, free-standing information storage and calculating boxes, with no outside links. Later, computers with stored-program capabilities were developed and connected to remote terminals. These were, however, "slave" terminals, dependent on data and instructions from the main computer. By the mid-sixties, more sophisticated computer and remote terminal patterns, involving interactive networking, came on the market. These terminals could modify main computer instructions and data. More recently, they have been equipped with their own computer memory to handle "local" requirements independently of the main computer. This kind of flexibility has resulted in an explosive growth in computer-based data networks: in 1965 there were 50,000 installed computer terminals in this country; by 1975, this number had increased to over a million; over 20 million terminals are projected for 1985.[12]

A Harvard researcher, Anthony Oettinger, has suggested that the computer communications phenomenon deserves a new name — "compunications." His elision of the words "computer" and "communications" is more than a semantic trick; the computer and its communications-circuit links to other computers or to terminals constitute an integral information machine. The fact that this "machine" may stretch across continents and oceans is more or less irrelevant. "Compunications" may not make the dictionary, but it describes a reality that has long-range political, economic, and social implications for the information age.[13]

Meanwhile, computer engineers are putting more information power into smaller spaces. Many of the low capability, room-size computers of the forties and fifties are literally museum pieces. (A number of them are on display at the Smithsonian Institution's Museum of American History in Washington.) Large mainframe computers are not yet passé; they are just shrinking. ICL, the British computer company, has been developing a "giant" computer the size of three filing cabinets able to carry out five billion operations per second. At the same time, the economies of the big machines have been rapidly improving. In the early seventies, it cost $25 a month to store a million bits of information in an advanced IBM direct-access storage system. Now, 10 years later, the cost has dropped to 50¢.

Big computing jobs require a special breed of machine — the supercomputers, or "number crunchers" as they are known in the trade. The best known of the early supercomputers was the United States Defense Department's ILLIAC installation in California, developed originally in the 1970s. Like most number crunchers, ILLIAC was designed for unique tasks. One of its jobs has been to track Soviet submarines, which it does by processing data from sensing devices on the ocean floor designed to identify the subs by their acoustic "signature." ILLIAC reportedly could handle 300 million instructions per second and has a potential for expansion to handle over a billion.[14]

Supercomputer technology has advanced rapidly in the past decade to a point where a new word is used to measure the machines' capacities. The word is *flop*, defined as the ability to do a complex operation on two items of data in one second. One gigaflop is a thousand million flops. In the mid-eighties, the Control Data Corporation, a leader in supercomputers, has planned one with the capability of 10 billion calculations per second — the 10 gigaflop machine.[15] By way of comparison, the average small home computer can handle several hundred operations per second and a large main frame computer can do a million or so.

The supercomputers will continue to do big special jobs, but the general technological focus has shifted to smaller machines. The trend began in the sixties with the so-called "minicomputers" — a description that has become almost obsolete in recent years with the debut of even smaller microcomputers and microprocessors. But whatever their names, minicomputers have staked out a significant middle ground between the big number-crunching mainframes and small machines. In addition to performing specialized tasks on their own, they have become the workhorses of the fast-moving distributed data processing field. This involves linking low-cost minicomputers and terminals into communications networks instead of putting everything on a big mainframe. Today's minicomputers have computational powers well beyond the big computers of the sixties. Equally important, their price tag, usually under $40,000, makes them attractive to smaller business firms and other organizations. This adaptability to mid-level tasks is reflected in the growth of the minicomputer market. By the late seventies, worldwide sales were increasing at better than a 35% annual rate, as against a 15% growth for the larger mainframe machines.

With recent advances in microelectronic circuitry, minicomputers and their terminals are beginning to talk and to listen. They can understand spoken instructions and reply with synethetic speech. They can also store speech. One future prospect is voice mail — the storage of voice messages in digital form for delivery at a later time, either as reconstituted speech or as hard copy. In 1980, the Pennsylvania Bell Telephone Company announced a limited voice-mail system that could be the forerunner of a system-wide Bell service.[16]

Eventually, voice mail could be part of an integrated electronic mail system involving telephones, computer terminals, facsimile machines, and communicating word processors. However, it is probable that talking and listening computers will operate alone for the time being. IBM research scientists have used a computer to transcribe speech, composed of sentences drawn from a thousand-word vocabulary and read at a normal speaking pace into a printed form, with 91% accuracy. The Orator talking terminal, developed by ARTS Computer Products, can be interfaced with a computer to produce synthesized speech with a full-word capability for use by the blind.

The fastest growth area in the computer market involves smaller machines known as *microcomputers*. These are the so-called "home computers," although most of them are being used for the present by small businesses. When a full consumer computer network is developed, the microcomputer will be teamed up with the telephone in American homes. In 1983, MCI, the aggressive long-distance telephone firm, inaugurated an electronic mail service that provides, among other capabilities, direct links between home computers. Two other firms, The Source and Comp-U-Serve, had preceded MCI in supplying a similar service over phone lines.

Meanwhile, a new range of technologies is emerging that can store 100 million bits of memory per square inch on tiny magnetic regions of amorphous metal film. Josephson junctions, now being developed by IBM, use *superconducting metals* (metals that lose all resistance to electricity at very low temperatures) to do sums in billionths of a second.[18]

The chips that led the way to smaller, more efficient computers are themselves going through another change. They were originally identified as LSI (*Large Scale Integration*) technology. The new phrase is VSLI (*Very Large Scale Integration*). VSLI takes the chips up to what many scientists think may be the physical limits of miniaturization. The progression toward these limits has been swift. The problem, in simple terms, is to etch tinier and tinier circuit lines on a silicon chip. Every tenfold decrease in the width of the lines leads to a hundredfold increase in the number of circuits that can be put on the chip. Line widths have already been narrowed down to an average $2\frac{1}{2}$ to 3 *microns* — a micron being a millionth of a meter. The next goal is to narrow the gap to one micron. This would be close to what, for the present, is considered the physical limit of tiny circuit patterns — lines one-third of a micron wide. If this limit is achieved, it will be the equivalent of packing 150 lines within the width of a human hair.[19] The chip designers achieved these initial successes with silicon-based semiconductors. In their search for more efficient chips, the designers have been looking at other approaches for building integrated circuits. A long-term prospect, described above, is optical switching, using laser-generated lightwaves. An even longer term possibility is the use of bacteria, genetically engineered to produce computer switching components, in the same way that bacteria are now being engineered to turn out insulin and other chemicals.[20]

A more immediate solution has been the use of gallium arsenide as a substitute for a silicon base. Gallium is a bluish-white element obtained as a by-product of aluminum and copper smelting. Chemically, like silicon, it is neither fish nor fowl. It occupies the middle ground between conductivity and resistance which makes it a semiconductor — the raw material of integrated circuits. Gallium arsenide is more difficult to deal with in producing chips, but the rewards are worth the difficulty. Chips based on gallium arsenide technology offer circuit speeds 2 to 5 times greater than silicon. Moreover, these chips do not overheat and self-destruct at high speed, as silicon-based chips are apt to do. Gallium arsenide chips and related technological developments are bringing us closer to the most dramatic development in the computer's evolution since ENIAC, the first modern computer, was created back in the mid-forties. It involves the race to develop a totally new kind of computer in the coming decade.

These machines will be similar to the present supercomputers only in that they require extremely fast calculations. Beyond that, the similarities end. The new computers will be machines that "think," replicating (in primitive form) human brain processes. With this limited artificial intelligence capability, they will be able to understand spoken and written languages, recognize objects, and reason as an expert in specific disciplines such as medicine or engineering. In the high-tech computer buff's phrase, it is the shift from ordinary DP (dataprocessing) to KIPS (knowledge information processing systems).

The shorthand description for this undertaking is the fifth generation computer. The first four generations were largely the result of IBM research and production. The fifth generation will probably not be a uniquely IBM achievement — nor even an American one. The first nation off the mark in sponsoring a full-scale fifth generation effort was Japan in 1982. Supported in part by government research funds, Japanese manufacturers plan to spend one-half billion dollars through 1990 to develop artificial intelligence software and hardware technology for the new machines.[21]

The Japanese "computer challenge" was at least part of the reason for a stepped-up effort in advanced computer development by the United States government and by private industry in recent years. In 1983, the Defense Department's Advanced Research Projects Agency (ARPA) inaugurated an artificial intelligence project with a modest $50 million budget. More significantly, a group of leading United States computer and semiconductor makers (with the significant exception of IBM) agreed, for the first time, to pool some of their research resources to develop technologies needed for the fifth generation effort. Their limited-venture partnership, known as the Microelectronics and Computer Technology Corporation, began operations at a new research facility in Austin, Texas, in 1984. Meanwhile, IBM the prime mover behind the first four generations of computers, can be counted on to make significant technical contributions to the so-called fifth generation race in the coming decade.

European computer manufacturers have been slower to enter the race. There are indications, however, at mid-decade that they will make a stronger showing in the coming years, supported in part by research and development funds from the European Economic Community. The results of this international effort should be computers which, in the 1990s, will make the present machines look archaic.

Whether or not this goal is reached, the new generation of chips is already having its impact on computers. The computing power of the new microprocessor chips equals that of a standard minicomputer. These so-called *high-end microprocessors* are faster and easier to program than their predecessors. They completely outclass the standard small computers in price. At about $150 each, they can be produced at a fraction of the cost of the minicomputer. The implication is that the microprocessors will replace the minis. However, there is room for a full range of computers in the new information environment. What will happen is that the bigger computers will increasingly consist of arrays of microprocessors and other chips. But they will shrink even further in size as they increase in computational power.[20]

Computers are the glamor machines of the information age. They are not, however, unique solutions for storing and distributing large amounts of information. There are other methods, many of which rely on the computer and its operations. The old-fashioned book is going through a technological revolution of its own, a sort of Gutenberg revisited. Production of standard books is becoming almost completely automated, expanding production capabilities to thousands of volumes an hour. The next technical step will be direct electronic publishing, a strange new world of paperless books. The first moves in this direction were made a decade ago with improvements in microfiche readers. Existing print books and other publications have been reproduced in microfilm rolls for a long time, primarily for preservation purposes. The problem, as any one who has dealt with microfilm knows, is to eliminate the awkwardness of searching for material through the long rolls. In 1980, Kodak announced a plan for melding computers and microfilm in ways that will reduce search time to a few seconds. The trick is in coding each microfilm "page" and entering the code in a data bank. When a page is sought, its location can be readily identified and the information put onto a microfilm reader. Such devices will probably not be used for standard books but for retrieval of archival materials and for reference publications.[21]

Microfiche — the grouping of many pages on a plastic card — offers greater prospects for direct publishing. In the early seventies, the University of Toronto Press was one of the first publishers to offer all its output in both printed and microfiche form. Some scholarly magazines and publications with small circulations are now being produced only in microfiche form in an effort to cut costs. Another prospect for more efficient print storage is the *videodisc*, the LP record that "plays" pictures. Best known in its consumer version as a home entertainment device, the videodisc is also a storage bin for print and audiovisual information. One such version, developed by MCA Discovision, provides 54,000 separate "pages" of information on a single disc — the equivalent of the contents of the *Encyclopaedia Britannica*.

The next step is the "book" in a computer. In fifteenth-century Europe, Johann Gutenberg began the print revolution by printing bibles and other religious works. In twentieth-century California, a computer expert, Bill Bates, may have set off the new print revolution with a cookbook. In 1980, Bates published *The Computer Cookbook*, a work of computer data. The contents are transmitted electronically from Bates's distributor in Ohio to customer terminals without benefit of paper, printing, binding, or other traditional publishing devices. Customers call in, or "sign on," through their terminals and browse through the recipes on their cathode-ray screens at an hourly rate. They can also buy the entire text and have it transferred to a computer disk or even to an old-fashioned hard-copy printout.

Bill Bates, the electronic Gutenberg, sees his project as part of a logical progression towards a new information environment:

> Today we can see that every cost associated with traditional publishing — distribution, labor, silver, film, gas, freight, cloth—is going up, whereas every single cost involved in the electronics industry—home computers, word processors, telephone and satellite transmissions, silicon chips—is going down and will continue to go down. At some point, where these two paths cross, electronic publishing is going to become very attractive.[22]

Somewhat further down the technological road is the large-scale use of *holography* — an electronically squeezed-in information storage process that can fit the equivalent of large libraries of data into the space of a table top. Holography uses lasers to record and retrieve information. Its ability to compress prodigious amounts of data into small spaces makes it particularly useful for major archival tasks, from recording birth certificates to logging the massive data output of scientific satellites circling the earth.

These developments may seem strange and even threatening in a literate society that relies on the traditional book for information and for cultural continuity. We are still very much the heirs of Gutenberg's movable-type revolution, despite Marshall McLuhan's unilateral declarations of the end of the age of print in the 1960s. McLuhan hailed the new electronic media as liberators, freeing us from the linear, left-to-right constraints print imposed on our thoughts and culture. He reportedly characterized cultural laggards who relied on books as POBs—print-oriented bastards. McLuhan's prophecies were quickly—perhaps too quickly—rejected by the POBs who read his books. Cultural considerations aside, there is a case for looking to electronic means for moderating the continually rising tide of paper we deal with in this country.

For all our electronic progress, paper is a formidable factor in American information culture. Four out of every 10 tons of pulp and paper in the world are produced, and mostly consumed, here. Not all of this paper is used for information, of course, but that is the major use. Per capita annual paper consumption in this country in the late seventies was 600 pounds. In the Soviet Union it was 75 pounds; in India, 5 pounds. This "paper gap" is one of the little-noticed factors in the information imbalance between this country and most of the rest of the world, particularly the developing countries.[23]

The differences cannot be measured only in pounds of wood pulp. Americans have their own distinct patterns of printed information. There is some truth to the European mandarins' charge that Americans are not serious book readers. Textbooks aside, the United States book industry, whose annual revenues amount to over $8 billion, is geared largely to lightweight recreational or how-to-do-it material. How different from the sober uncut-page products that fill European bookstores or the enormous per capita production of solemn books in the Soviet Union. American scholars can, of course, match their Old World counterparts footnote for footnote; they are also disproportionate contributors to the 60,000 scientific and technical journals published throughout the world.[24]

But the fact is that long-lasting encapsulation of wisdom is not our national style, for better or for worse. Printed information is, to a considerable degree, a throw-away item. It is the product of a new kind of printing press — the photocopier and the mimeograph. The output of these machines far outweighs that of other publications or even the more than hundred billion pieces of mail that move through the postal system each year. The paper flow in this country is so pervasive that it cannot be measured with accuracy. In 1975, a Stanford Research Institute study tried to pin down the volume of formal notices and forms used in business, government, and other organizations. The survey concluded that the total may be as high as 800 billion pieces of paper annually — well over 3000 items for every man, woman, and child in this paper-choked republic.[25]

Such statistics are often viewed with dismay, which is probably a mistake. The figures suggest an uncontrollable paper glut with much waste and duplication. This is certainly a factor. On the other hand, there is a great deal to be said for a society that makes it easier for everyone to have his say through readily available paper resources and reproduction equipment. Even Marshall McLuhan, the scourge of print culture, paid his respects to photocopiers and mimeograph machines for their role in making every person his or her own publisher. This capability is being enhanced with the introduction of so-called *intelligent copiers*. Not surprisingly the lead in this area has been taken by the Xerox Corporation. Its new high technology copiers are actually electronic printing machines that can handle inputs from many sources, such as computers and word processors, store up to a thousand pages of material, arrange it in an appropriate layout, and then print it out electronically, employing up to 50 typefaces. Incidentally, it can also reproduce documents like any traditional photocopier.

Computers and associated equipment will vastly expand this populist possibility of giving everyone an updated version of the printing press. Whether this will reduce the present massive flow of paper is problematical. What is clear is that the potential exists for making a vastly expanded range of information available to more people. The computer will be the critical link; even in its present primitive stage of application, computer technology is changing work patterns and social expectations by doing the drudgery and routine tasks nobody wants to do. These jobs engage the computer at its simplest level. The more important prospect, however, is the information society's ability to exploit the coming generation of intelligent computers. As futurist Arthur C. Clarke notes:

> It's perfectly obvious that the development of such computers would restructure society completely.... And they are already doing this in many ways because our society now would collapse instantly if the computers that run it were taken away. And these are very simple, low-grade computers. This raises tremendous social and philosophical problems, not just the question of displaced people. What will the people that were only capable of low-grade computer-type work do in the future? There is the more profound question of what is the purpose of life? What do we want to live for? And that is the question which the intelligent computer will force us to pay attention to.[26]

This leads to subjects dear to science fiction writers: the possibilities of artificial intelligence beyond the limited prospects proposed in the so-called fifth generation computers. These ideas remain firmly in the realm of science fiction for the present. Dr. John McCarthy of Stanford's artificial intelligence laboratory begins his discussion of the subject with the observation that he never met a computer that was smarter than the dumbest person he knows. Nevertheless, he is careful not to dismiss the prospect of some form of machine intelligence: "One way of putting it is to say that it takes 1.7 Einsteins and .3 of a Manhattan Project, and it is important to have the Einstein first and the Manhattan project second." Even this estimate is challenged by other experts in the field, notably M.I.T.'s Joseph Weizenbaum, who dismisses such projections as "simply and utterly ridiculous."

Arthur C. Clarke, in one of his science fiction stories, puts the issue in human perspective. He tells of the computer failure in a space ship that puts the craft into a disastrous orbit. A Japanese crewman teaches the rest of the crew to make abacuses out of wire and beads which are then used to calculate a course that saves ship and crew. The expectations offered by computers are extraordinary enough without delving too deeply into fantasy. One type of computer use, however, does skirt the edges of artificial intelligence and promises to be a major area of research and application during the coming decade.

This involves robots — or, more accurately, programmable automation. The idea of machines doing human work has fascinated and frustrated engineers for ages. In the eighteenth century the royal courts of Europe were entertained by the Green Lady, a mannequin with hidden machinery under her fancy costume, though all she could do was draw a single picture. Robot research took on new dimensions after World War I with the emphasis on production-line automation. The result was the servomechanism, which could perform relatively simple automation tasks. Today's work with programmable automation is spurred by the possibilities opened by microprocessors. NASA is stepping up its robotics research, for instance, in hopes of lowering the costs of deep-space probes. Its managers think that automated decision-making technology can reduce the need for already scarce trained people to program future missions. The Voyager mission to Jupiter in 1979 required 200 people over an 18-month period to provide its pointing, navigation, power, and experiment control sequences. NASA engineers believe they can cut back on personnel for such tasks by a factor of 10, freeing these employees for work on other space missions.

The big automation push is not, however, in space, but on factory production lines. Here the advantages are more immediate and profitable. Every major industrial country is subsidizing research in this area with the aim of upgrading industrial productivity. The Japanese are the leaders: half of the industrial robots operating in the mid-eighties are in Japan, a quarter in this country, and the rest in Europe. Most of these robots still do simple mechanical tasks. The next step will be to develop robots programmed to follow optimum paths and assemble complicated products. Beyond that are the prospects for sophisticated remote-control tools, manipulated from across a room or a continent. Simple remote devices have been around for a long time; mechanical arms for handling nuclear materials are one example. However, the new remote-control devices, called *telepresence devices*, would have more humanlike sensory channels involving touch, pressure, textures, and vibration. The prospect has been imaginatively described by Dr. Marvin Minsky of M.I.T.'s artificial intelligence laboratory, a telepresence enthusiast.

> You don a comfortable jacket lined with sensors and musclelike motors.
> Each motion of your arm, hand, and fingers is reproduced in another
> place by mobile, mechanical hands. Light, dextrous, and strong, these
> hands have their own sensors through which you can see and feel what
> is happening. Using this instrument, you can "work" in another room,
> in another city, in another country, or on another planet. Your remote
> presence possesses the strength of a giant or the delicacy of a surgeon.
> Heat or pain is translated into information but tolerable sensations.
> Your dangerous job becomes safe and pleasant.[27]

Given the economic rewards it promises, programmable automation will be a major research and development area in the coming years. It is, perhaps, a paradox that the most sophisticated use of the technology to date has not been in factories but in the telepresence control of robots on the moon and on Mars.

Robots represent only one of the almost infinite ways computers and other information-related technologies can be combined. The remainder of this book will concentrate on the social dynamics involved in bringing these possibilities to full working reality. Politics and economics are critical parts of this process. The balancing factors, however, will be the deeper trends of our cultural patterns and, in particular, our continuing commitment to the American electronic myth.

The myth is still remarkably resilient. Americans moved into the eighties with many doubts about their collective future. Among other concerns, they were uneasy about the effects of helter-skelter technological development. These attitudes were interpreted by editorial-page pundits as signs of a new national maturity or, conversely, as the ending of the optimistic American dream.

Communications and information were remarkably immune from these popular doubts. We may decide not to build an SST transport or to cut back on nuclear plants. However, no one has argued for fewer computers, telephones, or newspapers or more restrictions on the rest of the apparatus of the information environment. This could reflect at least an instinctive belief that this environment is, by and large, exempt from the law of entropy that governs other physical resources, inflexibly causing energy to be degraded or, more exactly, made unavailable. Despite our recent experiences with oil and other depletable resources, we see communications and information in a hopeful light. In these areas, more is better; they seem to be immune to many of our usual doubts about the benefits of technology.

Thus, in the final analysis, technology is shaped by cultural values. In communications and information, these values are based on an equal combination of pragmatism and mythology. The reality is the concrete achievement of democratic freedoms in this society, based in large part on an open information system. The mythology involves transforming United States society through technology, moving toward the machine-in-the-garden, the technology-powered Eden. We turn now to the day-to-day realities involved in shaping the strategy of a new kind of information-rich society, beginning with a look at the economic prospects. The stakes involved in this area are critical. They were aptly summarized in a 1979 OECD report: "The electronics complex during the next quarter century will be the pole around which the productive structure of advanced industrial societies will be organized."[28]

NOTES

1. For a useful overview of microelectronics developments, see Tom Forester, ed., *The Microelectronics Revolution* (Cambridge, Mass: MIT Press, 1981).

2. Charles and Ray Eames, *A Computer Perspective* (Cambridge, Mass.: Harvard University Press, 1973), p. 132.

3. "Applications Are Chasing the Chips," *The Economist* (London), 24 March 1979, p. 119. See also a special section on microelectronics in *The Economist* (London), 1 March 1980. Much of the material in this chapter on the technical and economic aspects of microelectronics has been drawn from this survey.

4. *The Economist* (London), 1 March 1980.

5. Peter P. Luff, "The Electronic Telephone," *Scientific American*, March 1978, pp. 58–64. See also Charles G. Burck, "Getting to Know the Smart Telephone," *Fortune*, 25 February 1980, pp. 134–146.

6. Robert Noyes, "Microelectronics," *Scientific American*, September 1977, p. 64.

7. Developments in this area are summarized in Alan C. Kay, "Microelectronics and the Personal Computer," *Scientific American*, September 1977, p. 231.

8. Eames, *Computer Perspective*, p. 144. Shannon published his findings in "A Mathematical Theory of Communications," *The Bell System Technical Journal*, 22, no. 3 (July 1948): p. 379.

9. Donald Michie, "Turing and the Origins of the Computer," *New Scientist* (London), 21 February 1980, pp. 580–583.

10. For a layperson's description of cybernetics, see Norbert Weiner, *The Human Use of Human Beings: Cybernetics and Society* (New York: Avon Publishing, 1967).

11. Eames, *Computer Perspective*, p. 136.

12. George W. Sullivan, "Telecommunications Trends and Directions," *Microwave Journal*, September 1977, p. 16.

13. A useful overview of this prospect can be found in Alexander S. Douglas, "Computers and Communications in the 1980's," *Computer Networks* (Amsterdam), 5, no. 1 (February 1981): pp. 9–14.

14. "U.S. Looks for Bigger Warlike Computers," *New Scientist* (London), 21 May 1977, p. 140.

15. "In Pursuit of the 10 Gigaflop Machine," *Washington Post*, 6 November 1983.

16. "Talking Terminals and Listening Computers Overcome Toy Image," *Infosystems, September* 1980, pp. 52–56. Also "Next: Machines That Can Talk," *New York Times*, 30 October 1980, p. D–2.

17. "Information Processing," *Business Week*, 12 May 1980, p. 68.

18. "Tinier than a Nerve Fiber, Faster than a Silicon Chip," *New York Times*, 8 January 1980, p. C–2.

19. "Pushing Chip Technology Towards its Limits," *The Economist* (London), 22 February 1980, p. 83.

20. "Computers from Bacteria," *New York Times*, 18 February 1982.

21. "The Battle of the Supercomputers: Japan's All-Out Challenge to the U.S.," *Business Week*, 17 October 1983.

22. Juri Matisoo, "The Superconducting Computer," *Scientific American*, May 1980, pp. 50–65.

23. "Microfilm Linked to Computer," *Financial Times* (London), 29 September 1980, p. 10.

24. Patricia Holt, "New Ideas from the West," *Publisher's Weekly*, 2 October 1979, p. 32.

25. "The Third World's Paper Gap," *Washington Post*, 1 September 1977, p. 1.

26. For a useful survey of the future of the print media, see "Economic Trends in the Print Industry," a series of six articles on various aspects of the industry, *Journal of Communication*, 30, no. 2 (Spring 1980): pp. 59–103. Also see Anthony Smith, *Goodbye Gutenberg* (New York: Oxford University Press, 1980).

27. The study is described in Raymond Panko, "Outlook for Computer Mail Sunny, but Dark Clouds on the Horizon Also," *Communications News*, July 1977, p. 32. The SRI researchers acknowledged that their paper-flow figures might be off by as much as a half, but their basic point remains valid.

28. Transcript of Dr. Clarke's remarks on the television program, "The Mind Machines," in the Nova series, broadcast by the Public Broadcasting System in 1978.

29. Marvin Minsky, "Telepresence," *Omni*, June 1980, p. 45.

30. "Interfutures Report," Organization for Economic Cooperation and Development, Paris, 1979. Quoted in *The Economist* (London), 3 January 1981, p. 55.

CHAPTER FIVE

THE ECONOMICS
OF THE NEW AGE

ANY STRATEGY FOR the information age has to reckon with the powerful economic forces organizing and managing the resources of the new global network. This grid may be the largest construction project ever undertaken. Robert LeBlanc, a leading communications finance expert, has estimated that it will take an investment of $50 billion a year over a 30-year period for foreign countries simply to bring their communications facilities up to current United States standards.[1] Meanwhile, the United States communications grid will continue to expand both in size and in range of services. Economics will be the driving force, primarily in the form of the network market described by Herbert Dordick and others in their research on future United States information patterns.

The communications structure in this country is the result of a complex cat's cradle of uncoordinated, often overlapping decisions going back a century or more. Marketplace economics have dominated this process, with political and social influence playing a secondary role. This point is important to an understanding of the prospects for a more coherent national strategy in this area. Any such strategy will have to recognize that there is no one agency for decision making, public or private, in the United States as there is in almost every other country because of their centralized government communications agencies.

The previous chapter described how a convergence of technical innovations points to a new physical structure in communications and information. In the next chapter, we will look at a similar, if somewhat less precise, convergence of social forces that will also affect future decisions in this field. In this chapter, we examine the convergence of economic forces influencing these patterns. The economic pattern was set 150 years ago with the decision to allow the original Morse telegraph system to be built and managed by a commercial firm, Western Union. The government's regulatory touch was light until the passage of the Communications Act of 1934. This legislation created the Federal Communications Commission, the regulatory overseer of a large segment of the communications industry, in implicit exchange for a certain amount of freedom from direct governmental intervention in the industry. This arrangement has held for a half-century with some modifications, assuring that the communications sector will remain essentially in commercial hands.

"The business of America," said Calvin Coolidge, "is business." This may be a narrow view, but it explains a lot. The United States is the only society whose citizens speak unblushingly about the education business, the business of government, the culture business, and so on. The business of communications and information touches all of these, and more. As the 1977 Commerce Department study of the information economy indicated, it may be the biggest business of all — the "premier industry of our times," as *Forbes* magazine identified it at the time in a survey of long-term United States economic trends.[2] Reviewing overall economic trends in the eighties, the *New York Times* has singled out communications/information activities as one of the two most promising fields for expansion in the decade. (The other field was genetics.[3])

Impressive production statistics tell only part of the story. There is a strong case for the proposition that communications and information will determine the economic directions of the coming decade. In part, this reflects the vibrancy of these sectors themselves. The more important element may be their role in overall United States economic growth, and in particular, in the new emphasis on reindustrialization, the overhauling of the United States economy for more efficient post-industrial tasks. Communications and information are the primary focus of the products and services for this technological turnaround. The changes are already underway: By the end of the eighties, one-fourth of all jobs in this country will be dependent on computers. Present-day computers are still relatively conventional machines, isolated from most of the work force in data processing departments. During the next decade, computers will become an integral part of work activities, on assembly lines, in offices, and in other service units. They will not always be the familiar boxes lined up against a wall or on large tables. Most of them will be microelectronic devices built into machines with enormously enhanced production capabilities.

Here is where the opportunities lie for reversing the current declines in industrial productivity. In a 1979 Brookings Institution labor productivity survey of 11 industries, only 2 sectors showed gains in the 1973–1978 period. One was banking, which has turned heavily to automation in recent years. The other, significantly, was communications, achieving the highest productivity gains of any industry largely by applying microelectronic technologies. Although it is difficult to show causal connections in productivity measures, two factors predominate. One is the labor force itself, and here the hopeful element is the growing professionalization of United States labor, with its promise of an increasing capability to manage the new technologies. Professionals and managers now hold one out of four of the nation's jobs.[4]

The other factor is the upgrading of the machines themselves. Here is where doubts arise about America's ability to maintain its lead in many areas of technology. Spending on research and development as a share of gross national product (GNP) has slipped from 2.6% in 1970 to around 2.2% in the early eighties. (The Soviet Union in recent years has generally been the biggest spender on science, as percentage of GNP, followed by West Germany.) Moreover, somewhat over 60% of United States Government support for research and development — the largest single slice of the research pie — is tied to defense and space research, two areas where technology does not always translate readily into market application.[5]

Funding for communications and information research and development tends to be higher than for other sectors, primarily because the economic payoffs are usually more immediate and tangible. Innovations alone cannot sustain the reindustrialization effort; the industrial structure is too complex for such simple solutions. However, it is clear that the new productivity effort may fall well short of its goals without significant input from these sectors. Historic trends confirm this, with the telephone industry as a useful case in point. In 1910, AT&T handled 6 million telephone calls with a staff of 120 thousand; that is about 50 calls a year for each employee. In 1979, the system handled 185 billion calls with less than a million employees, or 185 thousand calls per employee. Handling current telephone traffic at the 1910 level of technology and company staff would require many times the present United States labor force.

There are other hurdles to overcome in the reindustrialization effort. Investment policy, and particularly the persistent low rates of capital formation in recent years, are critical obstacles.[6] Another is the high cost of conforming to environmental and other regulations, as well as the impact of inflation on incentive to invest in innovative (in other words, risky) projects. There is also an amorphous but powerful psychological barrier, the fear of change, particularly when it affects pocketbooks and deep-seated habits. This is reflected in the bloody-minded Ludditism with which people resist the introduction of new techniques through encrusted corporate practices, union rules, or special interest laws. There will be a heavy social cost in the reindustrialization cycle, most of it falling on those who are undereducated or otherwise disadvantaged. An important part of any strategy for the information age is to find effective ways of easing social disruption without losing the advantages of technologies that improve productivity and raise overall job prospects.

As noted earlier, the underdeveloped nations of the next century will be those which choose to ignore the implications of microelectronics and other information technologies. There is a curious, and potentially harmful, tendency in this country to suggest that it cannot happen here. Recent events forcing us to lower our expectations as undisputed world leader should make us realize that we are not — if we ever were — insulated from the consequences of such changes. Our industrial partners in Europe and Japan are beginning to respond to the microelectronic challenge. Moreover, a significant group of Third World countries — India, Brazil, and Korea, among others — have made it clear that they will not restrict themselves to making the shirts, shoes, and bicycles that the industrialized West can no longer produce economically. There is no reason why they cannot begin to challenge the West in some areas of high technology. The proof is that they have already begun, with small electronics industries that produce an impressive range of communications and information products. These fledgling efforts are useful training grounds for more advanced production projects and a challenge to any complacency we may have about our long-term economic position.

In summary, the communications and information industries need to be considered not only as strong elements in economic productivity, but also as instruments for shaping the overall pattern of post-industrial society. Accepting these premises as true, one might assume that United States economists are engaged in a massive effort to identify the dimensions of the new information-based economy. But this is not the case. Two decades ago, University of Chicago economist, George Stigler, noted that the study of information resources occupied a slum dwelling in the town of economics.[7] Fortunately the subject has been gradually gaining more respectability in recent years. Since Professor Stigler made his analogy, information studies have moved up from the slums at least to middle-class status, largely as the result of the work of younger economists.

Two pioneering studies identify information factors in the new post-industrial environment. The first of these, conducted by economist, Fritz Machlup, was a book, *The Production and Distribution of Knowledge in the United States*, written in 1962.[8] Machlup looked at information activities, which he called "the knowledge industries," and concluded that 29% of gross national product and 31% of the nonfarm labor force were involved in such activities during his base year, 1958. Moreover, he added, the overall annual rate of growth for such activities was considerably higher than the industrial growth rate. His conclusion was logical and direct: information-related activities would eventually outdistance industrial production as the major element in the economy.

Machlup's research had a useful impact on scholars' attempts to define the new post-industrial environment. Information and communications activities were classified under the "service sector" rubric in economic analysis until Professor Machlup extricated them from this catch-all category. In documenting their unique, growing role in the economy, he supplied important insights on the shape and content of the new information environment. His approach was broadbrush and did not attempt to analyze the common characteristics of the many "knowledge industry" sectors he identified. It was another 15 years before a precise analysis of the information and communications sector was carried out, making clear their full impact on the United States economy.

This was done in a United States Department of Commerce research project the results of which were published in *The Information Economy*, issued in 1977.[9] Primarily the work of a young Stanford-trained sociologist, Marc Uri Porat, the study is a massive, nine-volume look at information activities in the United States economy. It confirms and expands on Machlup's thesis. It also provides a more sophisticated analysis of the characteristics of the new information economy. The report concludes that overall information activities accounted for 46% of gross national production in 1967, the base year for the study. In the same year, half the labor force, earning 52% of total income, held some type of information-related job.

These conclusions are both dramatic and debatable. In Porat's words, "Information is the data that has been organized and communicated. The information *activity* includes all the resources consumed in producing, processing and distributing information goods and services."[10] Having set up this standard, the study looked at the characteristics of information capital and information workers. Information capital, in Porat's analysis, included the machines, buildings, and other goods and services, from computers to mimeograph machines, that go into the information economy. Somewhat to his surprise, he found the division between information and noninformation activity relatively easy to define: "Most goods are not ambiguous. A tractor is obviously a member of the food activity, and a seismograph is a member of the information activity."[11]

Information workers cannot be divided as readily. All work involves some component of information processing. Porat approached the problem by looking at each of the 422 occupations reported by the United States Census and the Bureau of Labor Statistics. He asked: Does income from this work category originate primarily in the manipulation of symbols and information? In many cases, Porat found the answer came easily. In other occupations there were complications. Doctors presented a problem: To what degree were they in the information business? After considerable investigation, Porat concluded that a doctor's schedule broke down to about half-time in information activity and half-time in noninformation work.

Whether the information-related activities of doctors can be so accurately determined is, however, peripheral to the Commerce Department study's overall analysis of the information economy. The report is most valuable in providing a more accurate picture of the role of information activities. While the Machlup study lumped these activities together in apples-and-oranges fashion, the Commerce study made some important distinctions. It suggested that the information economy is best understood when it is divided into primary and secondary sectors. The distinction between the two can be determined by asking whether information goods and services are exchanged in the marketplace. The organizations and individuals involved in such exchanges are in the primary information sector. The secondary sector includes all the information services produced by public and private organizations for their own internal consumption.

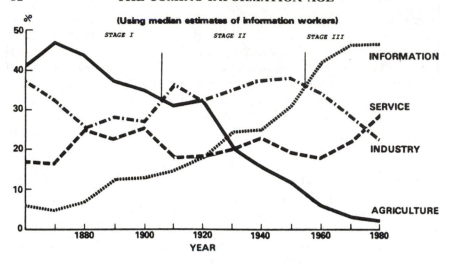

FIGURE 5.1.   Four sector aggregation of the United States work force by percent (1860–1980). (*From the United States Department of Commerce,* The Information Economy, *9 vols., Office of Telecommunications Special Publication 77–12, Washington, D.C.: Government Printing Office, 1977).*

FIGURE 5.2.   Time series of United States labor force (1860–1980). Two sector aggregate by percent. (*From United States Department of Commerce,* The Information Economy, *9 vols., Office of Telecommunications Special Publication 77–12, Washington, D.C.: Government Printing Office, 1977. Except for 1980 projections which are supplied by the Bureau of Labor Statistics, unpublished data).*

These bureaucracies are the repositories of the planning, decision-making, and control apparatus in the economy. By Porat's reckoning, activities in the secondary sector accounted for 21% of total gross national production in 1967, almost as much as the 25% accounted for by the primary sector.

The long-term evolution of the new information economy is shown in Figures 5.1 and 5.2 which were reproduced from the Department of Commerce study. The relationship between the agricultural, industrial and information economies clearly indicates the long-term shift toward the primacy of information-related activities. The other chart, tracing the relative standings of the information and noninformation work forces, indicates that the two groups are roughly in balance at the beginning of the 1980s. The significant element to note here is that information-sector employment has leveled off since the beginning of the seventies.

There are important implications here for the United States economy during the coming decade. The new information economy has, in a sense, already reached a level of maturity. The time may have passed when the addition of information resources, both people and machines, would automatically have resulted in large productivity gains. Gains may be harder to come by from here on, resulting in a more cautious approach by managers in increasing their information resources. Moreover, there are indications that expansion is slower within the primary information sector — the market sector — than within the secondary sector, the bureaucracy which, whatever its value, does not directly add to the national product. The result may be to reduce the overall efficiency of the information sector, as more resources are siphoned to its bureaucratic component at the expense of more productive elements.

Inevitably, there have been criticisms of the Commerce Department study's methods and conclusions. Some critics have argued that its interpretation of information is overly broad, embracing too many disparate activities. Others have questioned whether information is a commodity that can be as precisely defined as the report suggests. Nevertheless, the study has performed a service in rescuing information factors in the economy from their obscurity in the traditional service industries category. Questions remain, but there is no doubt that the information sector is different from the operation of hotels, dry cleaning establishments, funeral homes, and other businesses lumped together as services.

There will undoubtedly be more rigorous analysis and revision of the Commerce Department study in the coming years. One such revisionist approach has been undertaken by Dr. John Bermuth, a University of Chicago educator studying what he calls "literacy activities." Defining "literacy" as the exchange of information through the written word, Bermuth goes well beyond the traditional stress on language skills. Literacy, he suggests, is a major economic activity, amounting in 1972 to more than one-fourth of the gross national product, taking up about 29% of the average worker's time on the job and about 17% of the average adult's waking hours. Whether or not Bermuth's literacy format takes hold as a model for clarifying information activities, it and similar new research attest to the continued quest for a more accurate definition of the information economy.[12]

While the academicians debate the meaning and extent of the new economy, its superstructure is being built around them by the communications and information industries. As the 1977 Commerce Department report has shown, these industries are part of the largest single segment of the United States industrial economy. Their range extends from AT&T down to the latest hopeful one-room firm, banking on a new piece of electronic technology that may or may not catch on.

The communications industry is complex, profitable, and currently in splendid disarray. After decades of relative stability, communications and information firms are being reshaped by economics and technology. New companies with cryptic names like ITEL, MCI, UTEC, Racal, and T-Bar are challenging the established giants and the giants themselves are changing. The Bell System may have been, as one wag has suggested, the closest approach to immortality on earth, but it too was losing some of its eternal aura before it was split up in 1984. Semi-immortal or not, the telephone system will be quite a different institution in the coming years. The long-term impact of the Bell break-up will be crucial in shaping post-industrial patterns in this country. AT&T and other communications firms pass the American pragmatic test — they make things work in exchange for profit. And the profit-oriented market system, battered and berated as it may be, is still a very useful mechanism for dealing with social costs. Despite long-term attempts to wrap itself in the security blanket of government regulatory protection, the United States communications industry is being exposed to the winds of competition and change, as technological innovation is forcing massive shifts in its ways of doing business, and even changing the business it does.

This contrasts with the industry's relative stability of only a few years ago. Then it was stabilized around the voice-telephone network, the first interactive mass communications grid. The network's ability to provide nearly universal service was essentially a political achievement, the result of a decision (incorporated into the 1934 Communications Act) to give AT&T a quasi-monopoly in exchange for the development of a full network. This promise was largely fulfilled. In 1934, only 31% of the nation's households had phones; today the figure is well over 90%. As sociologist, Sidney Aronson, notes, the telephone's ring became as "ubiquitous...as the ever-present tolling of church bells in a medieval village."

Whatever the corporate faults and failings of the American Telephone & Telegraph Company (and 1600 smaller systems) over the past half-century, this record of supplying what the engineers call POTS — Plain Old Telephone Service — to such a geographically diverse, economically varied population is unique. Canada aside, no other nation has begun to match it until recent years.

Beyond the telephone grid, the next largest of the old-line telecommunications networks carried data, or "record," traffic — essentially telegram and telex messages. This grid was designed primarily for business use, and it was dominated by the Western Union Company in this country and by a group of "record carriers" internationally — International Telephone and Telegraph (ITT), Radio Corporation of America (RCA), and several smaller firms. The third group of basic grids was the television and radio networks, reaching into almost every home with popular entertainment and news programming. The 1934 Communications Act gave a strong measure of political and economic stability first to radio and, in the postwar years, to television by assuring them government-granted broadcasting licenses that were, for all intents and purposes, permanent. Although the legislation lays down clear public service responsibilities in exchange for renewal of licenses, the Federal Communications Commission, which grants the licenses, has seldom lifted one for a broadcaster's failure to serve the public interest. As one critic of the licensing system, former California Congressman, Lionel Van Deerlin, notes, "If a licensee has managed to stay out of jail, he is renewed."[13] Given this kind of stability, the New York-based networks and their local affiliates developed both radio and television into highly profitable merchandising devices for delivering mass audiences to advertisers.

This was the situation with broadcasting and the other major communications networks through the 1960s. Each network was in its own groove, applying technological improvements as necessary without changing its basic operational format. Advanced computers and other high technology machines based in microelectronics were in the early stages of influencing communications and information patterns. Future historians studying our particular part of the twentieth century will be able to pinpoint more accurately the significance of the technological shift that took place sometime around 1960 in this country, establishing the physical parameters of the new information society. They will see, more clearly than we can at this short distance, a series of converging scientific developments affecting the entire spectrum of communications and information activities. This was quite different from developments in the previous 100 years, when major technical innovations like the telegraph, telephone, and radio appeared one at a time, allowing a cushion of several decades' time in which to sort out their political and economic implications.

For the first time, this adaptation process began to occur all at once. Moreover, the shift involved technologies that provided a quantum increase in quality and capacity of services, as opposed to the slower advances of earlier years. Included among the innovations that came to the forefront during this shift were satellites, high capacity cables, lasers, advanced, microwave techniques, computers, and electronic miniaturization of all manner of technology, from the 1950s transistor to large-scale integration (LSI) technology.

This rush of innovations from the laboratories to production lines two decades ago set the pace for the economic upheaval that has occurred in the communications and information industries since then. The changes are still going on, and no one seems to have a clear view of how a vastly changed industry will look in the future. Indeed, this pace has increased in recent years, creating unsettling implications for decisions on "freezing" the technologies to be used in the industry's hardware. The other ambiguous factor is the effect of a lack of political and social decision-making on the overall pattern of the new information society, a situation that also inhibits economic decision-making. We will examine these problems in decision making, particularly as they relate to changes in the three key networks — telephone, data, and broadcasting.

We begin with the phone system, and specifically AT&T. Although the company gave up its most familiar activity — local phone service — in the massive restructuring of its activities at the end of 1983, it remains the standard against which United States telecommunications is measured. The events around the divestiture of the local Bell phone companies set the ground rules — and the opportunities — for a new communications framework in this country. I will examine the future impact of this divestiture in the next chapter. Here I will look at the events leading up to it.

In her telephone operator skits, comedienne Lily Tomlin could tweak AT&T's corporate nose by telling her imaginery customers: "We're the phone company. We can do no wrong. We serve everyone from kings to presidents down to the scum of the earth." Most Americans are prepared to accept the Bell System's oft-repeated claim that it provided the best phone service in the world. (In defending its corporate actions during a 1981 court case, a Bell attoney referred to AT&T unblushingly as "the greatest enterprise on earth."[14]) It is probably true that if a decision had been made 20 years ago to entrust the construction of a full-service information utility in this country to AT&T, the system would be completed by now.

A good part of the technology for such a system has come, over the years, from AT&T's own research arm, the Bell Laboratories, certainly the most productive communications research facility on earth. AT&T was never shy in claiming jurisdiction in areas other than traditional voice-telephone service. In the 1920s, it actively sought to become a major developer of radio broadcasting in this country.[15] The company was prepared to move into commercial cable television networking in the 1950s until checked by the FCC.

In each of these instances a political decision has prevented or limited AT&T's expansion into areas beyond its traditional service. Meanwhile, technology, economics, and politics were combining to create a new set of operational conditions for the vast Bell System and for a host of new competitors. On the one hand, traditional Bell control of long-distance circuits and the right of the company to install its own equipment was being eroded by government regulatory decisions designed to increase competition in these areas. The Justice Department brought a suit against AT&T in the early seventies over alleged antitrust violations, particularly in connection with the company's manufacturing affiliate, Western Electric. On the other hand, in the seventies, the company took the first steps to develop a strategy for increasing its share of the data communications market, the newest and fastest growing area in the industry. At the time, AT&T president, Frederick Kappel, declared that the company's revenues from data communications would eventually be greater than those from its traditional voice-telephone traffic. This seemed to many observers a long-shot prediction, but it is now well within the realm of possibility.[16]

In any event, the seventies marked the end of almost a half-century in which Bell's dominance over telephone services was the law of the land. The near-monopoly was raised to the status of dogma by Bell executives and their many supporters. The Bell argument was simple: The telephone system is a natural monopoly, since there has to be a centralized system for connecting phones with each other. Moreover, economics dictate a monopoly since a universal system cannot be built without cross-subsidization between high density profitable and low density unprofitable services.

Given the Bell System's generally commendable record in providing telephone services, it could be forgiven its sentimental boasts, usually spoken with a catch in the corporate throat, about getting a phone line up to the last house on the remotest mountain in the nation. AT&T claimed, several years before the divestiture, that it lost about seven dollars a month on its average telephone customer, a figure disputed by outside observers who suggested that it all depends on who's counting and what's being counted. The facts about telephone economics are very much in the eye of the beholder, an observation raised to high art by the platoons of phone company lawyers, government regulators, and public interest advocates in the interminable rounds of arguments about AT&T's rate structure. Beyond all the graphs and statistics, Bell's primary argument on behalf of its dominant position was that it worked. The claim was incorporated in a corporate slogan, "The system is the solution," widely advertised by Bell companies in the early eighties.

Whatever its virtues, Bell's case in favor of its quasi-monopoly was being passed up by events. A curious but revealing episode in the history of the company's defense of its position took place in 1976 with the introduction of Congressional legislation designed to affirm (or as far as Bell was concerned, reaffirm) the company's telecommunications primacy. Known as the Consumer Communications Reform Act, the legislation proposed standards designed to avoid "unnecessary and wasteful duplication" in telecommunications. It specifically required Bell's competitors in long-distance services to prove that they would meet these standards. In other words, they had to prove, before introducing a new service in competition with Bell, that they could do better, a regulatory process that would be expensive and time consuming. It is a tribute to the political clout of AT&T and the independent phone companies that the legislation was cosponsored by 175 representatives and 17 senators. The bill never came up for a vote, which was, in turn, a tribute to the collective ability of the rest of the telecommunications industry to stymie it. The subject eventually moved into legislative limbo, following the introduction of more comprehensive proposals to revise the Communications Act of 1934 — a subject that will be examined in the next chapter.

AT&T was looking for political relief from a technological and economic reality whose time had come. The assault on its near-monopoly began in the late sixties with a series of relatively minor Federal Communications Commission decisions which set the tone for what happened since. In the first of these decisions, the so-called "Carterphone case" in 1968, the FCC determined that AT&T could no longer bar the use of telephone equipment of which it did not approve or in effect, any equipment not made by its Western Electric affiliate. The Carterphone was just such a piece of banned equipment, used for mobile telephone units. (With imperial *hauteur*, AT&T referred to such equipment as "foreign attachments.") The Commission ruled that customers could use such attachments, provided they did not harm the network technically. For the first time, suppliers could compete with AT&T's manufacturing arm, Western Electric — a major breakthrough that opened the equipment industry to a new range of products and services.

A year later, the Commission allowed a new firm, MCI Telecommunications, to build and operate specialized microwave facilities offering private-line telephone service between Chicago and St. Louis and gave it the right to connect with the local phone company network within these cities. The service was directly competitive with (and cheaper than) AT&T's long-distance service. The FCC later authorized other specialized common carriers to operate similar networks. AT&T protested that these decisions violated its legal rights and, in particular, threatened the economics of consumer telephone service by skimming revenues from its intercity traffic. In the corporate battles that ensued, MCI brought a suit against AT&T charging it with attempting to undermine MCI services by blocking access to Bell System local phones. In a 1980 verdict that rocked the industry, MCI was awarded $1.5 billion in damages by a federal district court. AT&T's appeal of the verdict will probably take years to settle.[17]

MCI and the other challengers have since pressed hard to expand their services in competition with Bell, but the going has not been easy. At least one company which started off with high hopes, Datran Corporation, went into bankruptcy after several years. Most of the firms challenging Bell were corporate upstarts, new to the business. However, in January 1979, the Federal Communications Commission authorized an industry giant, ITT, to operate a national long-distance phone network linking eleven major cities from Boston to Los Angeles.

The new competition represented a very small threat to the Bell System's revenues at the time. The odds against the new firms' capturing a significant share of AT&T's long-distance traffic were still limited. For example, in 1979, MCI's revenues were $144 million as against AT&T's $23.4 billion for long-distance services.

Nevertheless, the age of competition in telecommunications was plainly at hand. It began with old telephone service, but it is rapidly expanding into data networking. The stakes were massive, affecting the shape and size of the United States information utility well into the next century. Given their importance in any strategy for the new information environment, the economic factors deserve a closer look.

The look begins with a quick review of the steps leading to the technological marriage of computers and communications. In simpler days, 20 years ago, most computers were "stand alone" machines; computation and communications were separate operations with no electronic links. In the sixties, they began to merge, with computers that were linked to outside terminals. The result was the rapid growth of *time sharing*, computer power dispersed to multiple users however remote they may be from the mainframe machines. This was the beginning of computer networks, with terminals interacting with a central computational base. However, computation and communications technologies were still essentially separate and distinct.[18]

These distinctions have been steadily eroding in the past decade. Computers are being used to switch both voice and digital messages. Data processing services are moving rapidly toward *distributive networks*, in which the terminals possess memory and logic of their own, placing greater intelligence capability in the terminal rather than concentrating it in the computer mainframe. Thus, telephone equipment can be programmed to monitor toll usage and to perform billing and accounting functions.

In other words, computer capabilities are being built into the entire communications system. Microprocessors with memory capabilities are now commonplace in telephone exchange and private branch exchange (PBX) equipment. Digital data transmissions services are oriented toward computer uses without requiring *modems* — the attachments to telephones that permit connections to computers. In these and many other ways, the distinction between computation and communications are being blurred to the point that data communications are done by computers and network circuits that are, in effect, a single computational/communications machine.

Communiputers? Computercations? Compunication? Whatever this hybrid is called, it will upset most of the old ways of storing and transmitting information. A new kind of business emerged in the seventies, and the rush was on to exploit its possibilities. Conspicuously absent from the initial rush was the Bell System. Critics cited this as another example of AT&T reluctance to shift to more efficient technologies, though many of these technologies were developed in its own Bell Labs. In Bell's defense, it is fair to note that the company was sitting on top of a massive communications network whose upgrading involved complex operational and financial problems. The equipment had to be amortized over a relatively long period of time. Writing it off early could have resulted in higher rates for all services. The arguments and counter-arguments are not simply corporate fiscal games, however. The problem of continually outmoded technologies is a consideration in any information age strategy.

Whatever its reasons, Bell moved carefully into the high technology data network competition. From the mid-seventies on, however, the pace quickened. Bell Labs unveiled the so-called *transaction phone*, a credit card verification unit, among other things, that could be viewed as a type of computation device. AT&T also produced a new generation of telephone-connected data display terminals, beginning with "dumb" terminals and moving toward a sophisticated type called Dataspeed 40-4, which has enhanced computational capabilities. Following a series of legal challenges by other firms, Dataspeed was authorized by the FCC as a legitimate — and regulated — part of AT&T's operations.

The company also began promoting "network processing services," its euphemism for a store-and-forward message switch that IBM and other computer firms claimed was part of the data processing services and equipment market. Continuing their euphemistic course, AT&T executives spoke of a dial-up service (for instance, a voice answer-back service for reading bank balances) that, they said, was just delivering a message. Not so, retorted the computer firms. Such a service, they argued, is processing information, which is their bailiwick. Finally, AT&T moved into the satellite communications area, where there was the promise of access to high speed circuits for data communications. This access turned out to be somewhat less than immediate, however. The FCC delayed AT&T's use of satellites for data networks for several years in order to give other firms a chance to establish their own satellite operations without Bell's overwhelming presence. By mid-1979, the restrictions were lifted and Bell was ready to compete for what it regarded as its destined large share of business in the evolving integrated information utility. With classic simplicity, AT&T christened its project ACS — for Advanced Communications System.[19]

The technology to create the utility was available, but the political and economic means for bringing it about were considerably less clear. The 1982 divestiture agreement between AT&T and the Department of Justice was a critical, necessary step in clarifying the future pattern of United States telecommunications.

We will take a closer look at this new pattern in the following chapter. Here we will focus on a related subject — the changes in the electronic information business where technology is erasing the distinctions between telecommunications and computer processing. The decade of the centralized mainframe computer is giving way to a decade of distributed computing networks. The emphasis is on flexible, lower cost processing of information at the point where it is to be used rather than in a distant computer center. The mainframe data business, providing centralized storage and data bank services, is still very much alive. General Electric was one of the pioneers in this profitable business, and sophisticated variations on networking from centralized data bases will continue to develop during the eighties. One prospect, already well advanced abroad, is a videotex service, providing business firms and homes with access, via telephone, to many sources of data material displayed on a modified television set. Such systems are now being offered experimentally to the public in Britain, France, Canada, and Japan. The British system provides access to over a hundred "information providers" or operators of specialized data banks.[20]

These systems will be common in this country by the late eighties. Meanwhile, the industry is concentrating on the immediate prospect of expanding distributed processing networks and services for business. Its goal is the automated workplace, the so-called "office of the future." For all of its oversold future, the integrated electronic office system is on the way. Office-of-the-future enthusiasts are fond of declaring that, while industrial productivity rose nearly 90% during the seventies, office productivity went up only 4%. Further, they add, average capital expenditure per office worker was only $2000 compared with $25,000 for the factory worker. The figures are slightly suspect, as well as the apples-and-oranges comparison. It is true, nevertheless, that productivity has declined steadily in offices, which are a major part of the secondary, or bureaucratic, sector in the Department of Commerce's study of the information economy described earlier in this chapter. Whether machines can turn around, or even modify, the bureaucracies' devotion to Parkinson's Law on programmed inefficiency remains to be seen.[21] What is certain is that a $15-billion-a-year industry is expanding, with its market focused on sophisticated office word-processing machines, terminals, long-distance facsimile equipment, phototypesetting machines, high-speed printers, and related communications gear. The business is dominated by such old-line equipment manufacturers as IBM, Xerox, and Burroughs, although there are many newcomers, including Exxon.

This equipment, much of it linked to networks outside the office, is largely an electronic mail and storage system. In fact, over 85% of all first class postal service mail can be handled electronically. This includes bills and other business forms that now form the largest share of postal volume. The prospects for an electronic postal service are reinforced every time a piece of the new high technology office equipment is installed. Whether this network will be run by the postal service, by private firms, or by a combination of both is an important issue that has yet to be resolved.

In summary, the economics of the information and communications hardware industry are being transformed by technology. Even IBM, the rock on which the computer industry was built, has not been spared. The firm's share of United States-based companies' shipments of computer hardware dropped from 61% in 1974 to 50% in 1980. The statistics reflect the general shift to smaller minicomputers and away from mainframe products, where IBM has been traditionally strong. The initial minicomputer market was dominated by such innovative upstarts as Digital Equipment, Hewlett-Packard, and Data General. However, at the beginning of the eighties, IBM was clearly not to be counted out as overall industry leader. Following a 3-year period in which it invested $4 billion in cash (and another billion from its first bond offering ever), the company came on strong with a new line of small computers and associated distributed data processing equipment that reinforced its position as the major competitor in the field. The changeover was not without cost: In 1979, the firm suffered its first decline in net profits since the early fifties. Nevertheless, it strengthened its hold on the big mainframe market in 1980 with a new product line that included machines twice as powerful as the company's previous large computers.[22]

The strategic industrial focus of the eighties will, however, be on semiconductors, the tiny chips that are the power modules of the new computers and most other information and communications hardware. They are, one industry expert declares, the crude oil of the 1980s: "From a strategic point of view, this industry is sitting on the reserves that are necessary for the future growth of the economy." Semiconductor production began in the late sixties with a small group of innovative companies playing technological leapfrog with one another in the race to develop more efficient products. By the early eighties, the industry had moved into early middle age and many of the pioneering firms were being absorbed into larger corporations dependent on their products. Only 7 of the 36 semiconductor firms that began operations in the late sixties were still independently owned by 1980.[23]

Foreign competition, threatening to cause a significant loss of United States leadership in semiconductor research and production, was an important factor in this shift. Japanese and European firms, supported by government resources, are mounting a serious effort to displace United States research leadership and to erode the two-thirds share of world markets held by American firms in 1980. The stakes are awesome. The electronics industry, increasingly dependent on chips, is now among the leading sectors of the global economy. By 1990, it is expected to rival automobile production as the world's largest manufacturing industry.[24] With their easier access to sources of capital investments, the large firms now beginning to dominate semiconductor production should be in a better position to assure continued United States leadership.[25] Significantly, however, the most advanced new semiconductor plant to be built in the

United States in the early eighties is owned by Japan's Nippon Electric Corporation.

Despite worries about foreign competition, the United States semiconductor industry weathered the economic recession of the early eighties with confidence that it could maintain its technological and marketing edge. "American creativity is still the source of major innovations in microchips," the London *Economist* pointed out, adding however that it would be a mistake to rule out continuing Japanese capabilities in this area.[26]

The American chip industry came roaring back in 1983 from its recession-induced slowdown. By the end of the year, it had an estimated $6 billion backlog in orders — roughly equal to the entire United States market in 1979. Manufacturing capacity appeared to be the only obstacle to greater growth at the time. The American industry was confident, moreover, that it could win back the share of the market it had lost to the Japanese earlier in the decade.[27]

One area in which United States dominance will be maintained for some time is in the collection and storage of specialized information — the so-called "data banks." The reason for this is simple: American firms began to gather up and store such information, as well as to distribute it, usually for a profit, earlier than anyone else. The result has been to make this country the information bank of the world. No one knows how many data banks there are, since the industry's definitions are vague. The banks come in all sizes and purposes. The Medlars bank at the National Institute of Health provides doctors with summaries of the latest medical research, abstracted from over 2000 journals. Congress has a data bank to track the progress, or lack of it, for every bill introduced into the House or Senate. The National Technical Information Service in Springfield, Virginia, supplies material on over a million items of research funded by the federal government in recent years. A Canadian researcher has catalogued every known performance of Shakespeare's plays. The list goes on.

The data bank industry is increasingly dominated by a group of old-line publishing companies who have in recent years realized that they are really information handlers. These firms are beginning to put their print products into computers and to sell them as data. The *New York Times* took the lead with its "Information Bank," a computerized version of a newspaper morgue, containing all the information that has appeared in the paper since the late sixties, when the bank began.[28] The Information Bank has been expanded to include the contents of 60 other newspapers and magazines, which are also made available on terminals to customers throughout the country. And in 1981, the *Times* added a special Middle East data section to the bank. Other publishing firms that are moving into data bank operations are Dow Jones, McGraw-Hill, Dun & Bradstreet, and the *Reader's Digest*. Meanwhile, other firms not usually associated with information services are moving into the field. One of these, Mead Data General, is part of a paper products company. It operates the Nexis network, an on-line service supplying business firms with a range of full-text material from major United States and foreign news agencies, magazines, newsletters, newspapers, and government publications.

The great unanswered question as these and other services proliferate is how, and when, they will be able to expand beyond the business market into the potentially lucrative home market. The basic technology, in the form of telephones, television sets, and cable systems, is already in place. However, the economic target, namely specific consumer needs, remains elusive. There was a rash of home teletext experiments in the early eighties, each supplying data services aimed to test potential interest. The tests were inconclusive at best. Despite this, Time, Inc. took the lead in sponsoring an extensive national teletext network, banking on its earlier success in supplying cable television programs through its Home Box Office affiliate.[29] After substantial experimentation and a reported expenditure of $30 million, the project was abandoned at the end of 1983. Undaunted by this turn of events, the Knight-Ridder newspaper chain has moved ahead with plans for Viewtron, a videotex system which allows subscribers to receive news and information, shop, and bank through their television sets. Other systems are also in the wings, encouraged by the interest of bankers, retailers, and others in expanding their merchandising reach electronically to the consumer at home.[30]

In the absence of a full-fledged home videotex network, they are turning to a simpler and more available technology — audiotex. This system provides information services by telephone, using electronic voices. It differs from ordinary dial-up information services in that it allows a computer to respond vocally to requests made by punching buttons on a touch-tone telephone keypad. In 1983, Dun & Bradstreet introduced a system that gives credit ratings of companies over the phone. United Press International began offering audiotex stock quotes to the general public in 1984.[31]

Data banks and other sectors of the information industry will expand rapidly during the eighties. There will be numerous shake-outs as technology and economics combine to challenge the competitive standings of both the old-line firms and the upstarts. The bulk of their business, and profits, will come from sales to other industries engaged in the massive reindustrialization process now underway. A still open question about the future of the information industry is whether there will be a *consumerization* of the market, in which goods and services will be supplied to the home. The answer will have an important effect on a third major telecommunications area — radio and television broadcasting.

Until recently, radio and television were secure in their dominant positions, supplying news and entertainment to a mass consumer market. Protected from the shocks of outside competition by benevolent government licensing and regulatory arrangements, the broadcasters prospered on their ability to provide advertisers with a range of audiences readily identified by age, sex, and income level in their programming tastes.

The debate on television's beneficent or baleful influences on American life will go on for a long time without conclusive results. What is clear is that the unchallenged dominance of commercial television and radio is coming to an end.[32] Between 1977 and 1983, the 3 major networks' share of the nation's television viewers slipped from a commanding 91% to 77%. Television will continue to be a powerful influence in its present form for a long time, but at a slowly decreasing level. The reasons for the shift are complex. Contrary to the self-fulfilling prophecies of television's critics, there are few indications that people are getting bored with television or that their tastes are improving. There are other reasons why they are beginning to spend more time away from the television screen. One significant element, at least for daytime television, is that more women are working outside the home than ever before. Another is that competition for audience attention is being challenged by a range of new communications channels and services.

The big three networks face growing competition from a range of specialized "fourth networks" that rely on satellite distribution of their programs. The most extensive of these grids is operated by the Public Broadcasting System (PBS) and National Public Radio (NPR). Both have used satellites since 1978 to provide their member stations with a broad mix of national and regional programs. The result has been to give local PBS and NPR stations more control over their programming choices, a major objective of public broadcasting. Another specialized network using satellites and microwave relays is the Spanish International Network (SIN), serving what will be by the end of the decade the largest ethnic minority in the nation. SIN began feeding Hispanic programming to nine stations in 1977; part of its offerings come from Mexico's national network by direct relay from Mexico City. Another satellite network, the Christian Broadcasting Network (CBN), offers fundamentalist gospel programming from its headquarters in Virginia Beach, Virginia, to hundreds of cable systems throughout the country.

A highly successful "fourth network" servicing cable systems by satellite was developed in the late seventies by Ted Turner, a flamboyant Georgian, who controls, among other enterprises, television station WTCG in Atlanta. Turner has transformed WTCG into a "super station" through satellite transmission of its programs to cable systems throughout the country. Within months after he announced his plan in 1977, over 500 cable systems in 27 states applied to carry the WTCG signal.[33] By the end of 1980, the network had been extended to over 800 cable systems. Cable viewers got a new entertainment channel — mostly old films and TV reruns — while Turner's station extended its audience to several million additional households, with appropriate advertising revenue benefits. In 1980, Turner added the first cable news network to his operation. His success led to a number of other "super station" operations throughout the country.

The most dramatic proposal for new national networking involves direct-to-the-home satellite broadcasting. In 1981, Satellite Television Corporation, an affiliate of the Communications Satellite Corporation, was given approval by the FCC to plan such a service, with entertainment and other programming beamed directly to roof-top antennas. At the same time, eight other companies were given permission to develop similar services. The first satellite broadcast service went into operation in November 1983 in the Indianapolis area, with several others authorized during 1984.

A more earthbound threat to the television networks' ability to attract a mass audience is the range of new machines that can provide alternative news and entertainment facilities in the home. As consumer items, most of these are still in the early developmental stages, but they each represent an alternative to regular television viewing. The concept of an "electronic newspaper," challenging commercial television's strong hold on news delivery to homes, was given its first practical experiment in 1980, when an Ohio newspaper, the *Columbus Dispatch* began transmitting its entire editorial content to 3000 home terminals around the country on a computer network.[34] At the same time, the Knight-Ridder newspaper chain was experimenting with a system to provide news, advertising, and other consumer services to homes in Coral Gables, Florida. More advanced systems, similar to those already in use in Britain, France, and Japan, are in the planning stages now and should be put into operation soon.

After years of big promises and false starts, two other technologies — videotape and videodisc — moved into commercial markets in the early eighties. The early lead for the vast consumer market was taken by videotape machines, which permitted recording of television programs for later viewing and for showings of the expanding catalogue of old Hollywood movies being recycled once again. With a dozen major electronic companies vying for the business, prices for the recording machines have fallen below the $500 mark, opening the prospects for mass market appeal, the results of which could revolutionize television and other home entertainment patterns as well as the film industry.[35] With over 12 million United States homes equipped with videorecorders at the end of 1984, industry analysts predict that the total will rise above 40 million soon. One result is the increase in sales of blank videotapes used for copying movies. In 1983, Americans bought about 50 million tapes, while the film and television industries fretted about loss of control over their products.

The most important potential challenge to network television has been around, in a different form, for some time. It is cable television — originally known as CATV, for Cable Antenna Television. CATV dates back to the early fifties when hundreds of small systems were installed in suburban and rural areas to provide improved reception of over-the-air television programs from nearby cities. The equipment was simple: a tall antenna to catch the signal and a cable to relay it to subscriber homes. Broadcasters welcomed CATV, since it extended their audience range and, therefore, their advertising-revenue base. However, this CATV bonus has turned into a threat as cable operators begin to supply other programming services.

After years of delayed promises of cable programming abundance, cable television services finally became a significant factor in the mid-seventies. The first successful national cable programmer was Home Box Office (HBO). A subsidiary of Time Inc., HBO began distributing current Hollywood films and sports events in 1973 to cable systems. It took the firm five years to turn its first profit, but by 1977 it had 800,000 subscribers on more than 370 cable systems across the country. Its success coincided with its inspired decision to distribute its programs by satellite, cutting its transmission costs significantly and allowing it to reach every cable system in the nation.[36] The pay-television rush was on as other big media conglomerates elbowed their way to sign up cable systems for their films. The boom has propelled the industry into an expansion that would have seemed visionary a decade ago. By 1981, there were over 3000 cable systems with almost 20 million home "hook-ups." This represents a 25% penetration of all United States homes, with the prospect that over half will be cable-connected by the end of the decade. In the competitive scramble for cable franchises and home customers, cable companies will expand their program offerings beyond pay television Hollywood films to other programs and services.

The first large demonstration of a full range of cable services was inaugurated in Columbus, Ohio, late in 1977 by the Warner Cable Corporation, one of the largest national cable firms. The project has been a test of cable's ability to merchandise its services in urban areas. Its basic product — retransmission of regular television signals — had not been a big selling point in cities where television signals are generally satisfactory.

Warner's Columbus system, known as Qube, offered a Chinese menu of services on 30 channels. These included transmission of 9 regular TV station signals (5 of them imported from other cities), a variety of locally produced community programs, and several "premium" channels providing new movies, sports events, arts programs, and educational courses. The system is interactive; 5 response buttons on each Qube home terminal allow subscribers to participate in local game shows, vote on referenda, take quizzes, and purchase products from local stores. There is a "home security option" providing fire, burglary, and emergency service connections. The original basic cost to a subscriber was about $11 a month, with extra charges for first-run films and other premium services.

By the end of 1979, after 2 years of operation, Qube had 26,000 home subscribers and had begun to turn a modest profit for Warner. It also provided the firm with other benefits that could not be measured in bookkeeping terms. Qube indicated that there was an urban market for sophisticated cable services. As the first company to demonstrate this, Warner was the frontrunner in the early eighties in the competition for cable franchises in large cities. Within a few months in 1980 it had won franchises in Dallas, Pittsburgh, and Cincinnati, largely on the strength of its Qube experience.[37] By mid-decade, however, Warner and other large cable companies which had won big-city franchises were having financial problems as a result of their commitments to build the expensive systems.

Competition for building urban systems nevertheless continues to be fierce. Competitors include large communications conglomerates such as Time Inc., Cox Communications, the Westinghouse Corporation, the Times Mirror Company, and the Storer Broadcasting Company. Since cables must be installed underground (rather than on telephone poles) in many urban areas, the cost of cabling city neighborhoods is very high. In the intense jockeying for position, the cable industry has witnessed a bewildering pattern of mergers and amalgamations in recent years, prompted largely by the need for greater financial resources to play the urban cable game. In 1980, Warner Cable, a subsidiary of Warner Communications, Inc., strengthened its financial base by selling 50% interest to American Express and changing its name to Warner Amex.

The significance of infusing major financial resources into urban cable projects goes well beyond merchandising Hollywood films or major league sports. The new urban networks can provide the missing links for the development of a full-service consumer-oriented information utility, the network marketplace envisioned by researcher Herbert Dordick and his colleagues in their studies of the economics of information services that we discussed in Chapter 2. The ability to get high-capacity cable facilities in urban areas is critical to the development of an economically viable national network. Such a network could be a reality by the end of the decade as cable facilities are installed in a significant number of large United States cities. It will involve massive funding that will be possible only if the cable industry can continue to attract large investors, in deals like the Warner–American Express agreement described above. American Express not only brought financial resources to Warner, but also its broad merchandising expertise, a key element in the potential success of the new cable-based network marketplace.

Most of these plans for expanding information services to the mass consumer level are still in their early stages. Many of them will fall by the wayside, victims of poor management, financial anemia, or both. However, others will succeed, with high-capacity cable systems offering the greatest hope for realizing the benefits of a full information utility.

Success will depend primarily on economic decisions about the viability of such a system. A new communications and information infrastructure is being built. The strategies for assuring that it will provide a full range of consumer services are still to be worked out. How does a society make wise decisions in this critical area? The answers are not clear. However, as war is too important to leave to the generals, so the future of the information society is too important to leave to IBM, AT&T, ITT, CBS, and the other private communications powers.

NOTES

1. Robert LeBlanc et al., "Changes and Opportunities in Telecommunications," *Telecommunications Industry Monthly*, issued by Salomon Brothers, New York, 1 February 1978, p. 1.

2. "Communications," *Forbes*, 15 September 1977, p. 139.

3. "Technology — Elixir for U.S. Industry," *New York Times*, 28 September 1980, sect. 3, p. 1.

4. Eli Ginzburg, "The Professionalization of the U.S. Labor Force," *Scientific American*, March 1979, pp. 48–53.

5. "America Tries to Cure Its Innovation Blues." *The Economist* (London), 6 September 1980, p. 83.

6. John Dizard, "The Revolution in Telecommunications Finance," *Institutional Investor*, September 1979, p. 143.

7. George J. Stigler, "The Economics of Information," *Journal of Political Economy*, June 1961, p. 213.

8. Fritz Machlup, *The Production and Distribution of Knowledge in the United States* (Princeton, N.J.: Princeton University Press, 1962).

9. U.S. Department of Commerce, *The Information Economy*, 9 vols. Office of Telecommunications, Special Publication 77–12, May 1977.

10. Ibid., vol. 1, p. 2.

11. Ibid., vol. 1, p. 3.

12. John R. Bermuth, "Value and Volume of Literacy," *Visible Language*, 12, no. 2 (Spring 1978): pp. 118–161.

13. Quoted in Gerald D. Rosen, "Communications Dog Fight," *Dun's Review*, June 1977, p. 18.

14. "Government, AT&T Fire First Salvos at Trial," *New York Times*, 16 January 1981, p. D–3.

15. Erik Barnouw, *Tube of Plenty* (New York: Oxford University Press, 1975), pp. 43–50.

16. Mr. Kappel's prediction was reported in "On the Head of a Pin," *Forbes*, 15 September 1976, p. 32.

17. "High Stakes in Bell-MCI Case," *New York Times*, 13 June 1980, p. D–1.

18. Manley R. Irwin, "Where Do Computers Leave Off and Communications Begin?", *Telephone Engineering and Management*, 15 January 1976, p. 30.

19. "Innovation: Key to Bell's Plans," *New York Times*, 16 July 1979, p. D–1. For a history of the Bell System's research activities, see Prescott C. Mabon, *Mission Communications: The Story of the Bell Laboratories*, published by Bell Laboratories in 1975.

20. The problem of technical compatibility between the systems was resolved largely in May 1981 when AT&T announced that it would adopt a standard compatible with the Canadian and French systems. Given the Bell System's economic and technological influence, its standard will probably be adopted worldwide.

21. Jon Stewart, "Computer Shock," *Saturday Review*, 23 June 1979, p. 14.

22. For an estimate of IBM's long-term plans, see "No. 1's Awesome Strategy," *Business Week*, 8 June 1981, pp. 84–90.

23. "Can Semi-conductors Survive Big Business," *Business Week*, 3 December 1979, p. 66.

24. Ibid.

25. Colin Norman, "The International Stake in Microelectronics," *Technology Review*, January 1981, p. 40.

26. "Setting the Pace in Microchip Technology," *The Economist* (London), 13 March 1982, p. 83.

27. "Capacity is the Only Limit for Chipmakers," *Business Week*, 9 January 1984, p. 72.

28. Anthony Smith, "All the News That Fits in the Databank," *Saturday Review*, 23 June 1979, pp. 18–19.

29. "Time Inc. Drops Teletext Experiment," *New York Times*, 22 November 1983.

30. "Electronic Publishing Moves off the Drawing Boards," *Business Week*, 8 August 1983.

31. "Audiotex: Data by Telephone," *New York Times*, January 5, 1984.

32. An interesting projection of long-term shifts in television and other mass media can be found in Richard Maisel. "The Decline of the Mass Media." *Public Opinion Quarterly*, Summer 1973, pp. 159–170. See also "Television's Fragmented Future," *Business Week*, 17 December 1979, pp. 60–66.

33. "Superstation Breakthrough," *Broadcasting*, 30 October 1978, p. 25.

34. "First U.S. Experiments in Electronic News," *New York Times*, 7 July 1980, p. B–13.

35. "How a Video Revolution Is Shaping the Future of Film," *New York Times*, 23 November 1980, p. D–1.

36. "Home Truths for Hollywood," *The Economist* (London), 30 July 1983, p. 72.

CHAPTER SIX

THE DAY ALL BELL BROKE LOOSE

FUTURE HISTORIANS TRYING to date the symbolic beginning of the American post-industrial era will likely do no better than to pick January 8, 1982. On that day, a large part of the pattern of the evolving United States information age was suddenly put in place.

The central event was undramatic, consisting of two announcements from the Department of Justice in Washington. Each one described the disposition of an anti-trust suit, the first involving AT&T, the second IBM. Those two far-reaching decisions will influence the form and direction of United States communications and information development for at least the next decade and probably into the next century.

Until that cold January morning, AT&T and IBM clearly predominated among the expanding forces of communications technology in the United States economy. They will undoubtedly continue to stand out for a long time to come. However, the two anti-trust decisions announced that day have created a new environment for both AT&T and IBM, one in which a wider array of competitive forces will challenge their leadership.

Of the two firms, AT&T was more noticeably affected. The company had built and operated the basic national telecommunications system during the twentieth century, benefiting from the Communications Act of 1934 which had given legal status to its monopoly position. The 1982 decision ended this particular protection along with the era to which it belonged.

The decision was sweeping. It entailed an agreement (technically, a consent decree) with AT&T on a plan for reorganizing the company. The firm was to be divested of all of its local telephone operations. In exchange, it was allowed to compete in communications and information activities previously closed to it. Moreover, the Justice Department dropped an expensive, long-running anti-trust suit against the company. As one wag put it at the time, it was "the day all Bell broke loose."[1]

In a separate but parallel action, the Justice Department dealt with another long-standing anti-trust case, the one against IBM. For a generation, Big Blue had been recognized, here and abroad, as the front runner in the computer industry. Indeed, the anti-trust suit against IBM was intended to test whether the company so dominated the industry as to unfairly stifle competition. In the jargon of the times, was IBM a "good monopoly" or not? In its January 1982 decision, the Department of Justice came down on the side of goodness, actually dismissing its own case as being "without merit." In effect, the decision removed the threat that IBM might be split into component parts, ending the integrated operational pattern that had been the key to its success.

At first glance, the two decisions appeared to be countervailing. One broke up the largest company on earth; the other affirmed that an equally dominant firm should remain in one piece. Yet, the decisions were, in fact, compatible and coherent. Taken together, they have given shape to the national framework within which an advanced information utility would be built.

Changing technology forced the two decisions. For years, the nation's political and economic institutions had been straining to cope with the new communications and information technologies, attempting to channel them to meet social needs. But the new communications capabilities were so vast that they did not fit into familiar channels of the policy process. Old ways of dealing with contending political issues did not work. Economic issues arising from the new technologies also made old procedures obsolete. Economically, the future of the communications and information sectors was clouded by the lack of policy decision and direction.

In the case of AT&T, the January 1982 divestiture decision represented the culmination of decades of contention over the balancing of public interest concerns with the complex organizational needs of the company. For a short period during World War I, the firm had been nationalized. However, even in those early years, AT&T had sufficient political power to support its claim that it could operate more efficiently as a private firm. It also promised better service of public interests as a privileged firm. This promise was well kept, largely because of the vision of one of the company's early presidents, Theodore Vail. Vail saw the importance of developing the phone network as an integrated national service. He directed the consolidation of hundreds of smaller companies into the Bell System and the development of efficient long-distance service. Alexander Graham Bell may have invented the telephone, but Theodore Vail laid out the telephone network.

The price of avoiding nationalization was the acceptance of federal and local regulation, together with almost constant probing into phone company operations. During the 1930s, New Deal investigators carried out extensive studies of Western Electric, the Bell System's captive equipment supplier. In 1949, the Department of Justice instituted the first suit to break up the company. The outcome, after years of legal wrangling, was a 1956 consent decree allowing the company to remain in one piece, but stipulating that its operations be limited to essential telephone business. At the time, this decision seemed to favor the company, no one foresaw the later growth of the computer-based data communications sector.

Meanwhile, the Bell system flourished with the post-war economic boom, aided by an impressive range of technological breakthroughs. Most of these research developments came from the Bell Laboratories, the firm's in-house research arm. The labs were responsible in whole or in part for the transistor, communications satellites, silicon chips, fiber optic cable, and advanced small computers, among other innovations. Despite occasional complaints from government regulators and consumer groups, AT&T's future as *the* phone company remained secure. Throughout this era, AT&T could boast that it provided the best telephone service in the world.[2]

However, events were to modify this placid optimism. First came a series of government regulations curtailing the firm's near monopoly in two major areas, equipment supply and long-distance service. Western Electric, AT&T's equipment manufacturing subsidiary, took the initial blow. In 1968, the Federal Communications Commission decided to permit the use of a piece of non-Western Electric equipment known as the Carterphone in the Bell network. This was a move toward ending the AT&T rule that only Western Electric equipment could be used in the Bell network. A second assault on AT&T's monopoly position came in the area of long-distance operations. In 1970, the FCC voted to permit other companies to compete with AT&T in inter-city long-distance service.

These newly competitive intrusions actually had little impact on the Bell System stronghold at the time. Although the Carterphone decision spawned a new set of competitors, Western Electric maintained its position as the largest producer of telecommunications products in the world. In the long-distance field, competition did not seriously undermine AT&T revenues, despite the aggressive efforts of MCI and the other firms moving into the market.

Gradually, however, subtle modifications in regulations and the gathering momentum in technology changed the climate of operations in information and communications. The change was obvious by the mid-seventies when the corporate perceptions of AT&T and IBM about the new environment began to merge. A couple of decades earlier, the two firms operated in quite separate spheres and each clearly held control within its own. IBM made large computers and dominated two-thirds of the market, leaving the remainder to be divided among a number of smaller manufacturers. (In the industry, this group was known as "Snow White and the Seven Dwarfs.") At the same time, in a distinctly different market, AT&T and its local operating companies were engaged in the business of voice telephone service. Here, the Bell System (and some independent local phone companies) were responsible for over 90% of domestic communications revenues. When IBM wanted communications lines to link its computers, it went to AT&T. When AT&T wanted a computer, it went to IBM or one of the Seven Dwarfs.

What changed the picture was not primarily the result of modifying rules or growing competition. Rather, advancing technologies, largely promoted by the two master firms, themselves, broke through the bounds of old organizational structures. In the seventies, AT&T and IBM each looked down their respective corporate roads and both saw the need for new strategies to match the changed reality. Bell viewed the prospects for computer-based data networking in its future. IBM, looking in the same direction, saw the need to move into the telecommunications networking business as a requirement for protecting its overall hardware and software marketing interests.

Even before the January 1982 Department of Justice decisions, the two firms began to adapt their strategies to these new perceptions. The decisions reinforced these strategies.

Attempting to head off the threat of a government-ordered breakup in the late seventies, AT&T reorganized its operations into two separate entities — one for its older regulated telecommunications business and a new one for its ventures in unregulated data communications. The latter would operate without subsidies from the firm's regulated business.

"We are going to draw a bead on the information business," AT&T chairman Charles Brown declared in 1980.[3] The strategy was designed to allow the company to break out of the constraints imposed on it by the consent decree of 1956. The decree had effectively prohibited the firm from dealing in the growing business of "smart" computer terminals or in the data processing field.

The objective was to found a "new Bell," designed by the company itself. However, the proposed reorganization was taking place in the shadow of an anti-trust suit filed by the Department of Justice in 1974. Like its 1949 predecessor, the suit threatened to split up the company. Only this time, the company faced a significantly different opposition. In 1949, Bell was up against the government. This opponent was formidable enough, but given the company's rich heritage of political connections and its battalions of lawyers, it was able to avoid dismemberment.

By 1974, conditions had changed. The enthusiasm of the Justice Department's anti-trust lawyers for splitting up the company remained undiminished. Now, it was abetted by a steadily increasing number of companies that were, or wanted to be, competitors in the expanding telecommunications equipment and services markets. The lobbying efforts of these ambitious new firms, added to the persistence of the Justice Department, proved overwhelming even for the largest private organization in the world. The final result of the contest was the 1982 divestiture of AT&T, which broke up the company.[4]

Meanwhile, IBM spent the seventies implementing its strategy of moving into the telecommunications business, which it saw as a natural extension of its computer and data processing operations. Big Blue announced its plan for a national data communications network in 1977. Partners in the venture were Comsat General (an affiliate of the Communications Satellite Corporation) and the Aetna Life Insurance Company.

Comsat General's participation was based on the network's special use of a new technology: It was the first extensive grid to rely solely on satellite links. Called Satellite Business Systems (SBS), the new venture had an initial capital investment of over $400 million. Its network, inaugurated in 1981, has linked small earth station terminals throughout the United States via its own satellites.

Originally, it was expected that SBS's first customers could be big corporations from among the Fortune 500 group, those large enough to make use of the system to facilitate their own internal communications. SBS could give both financial and technical advantages to such corporations in expediting their internal operations. With its all-digital format, SBS is capable of providing transmission of voice, high speed data, facsimile and video on an integrated basis. By bundling a wide variety of these services and, pointedly, bypassing both local and long-distance telephone networks, SBS is able to considerably reduce operating costs.

This strategy of concentrating on large customers, initially at least, proved to be a miscalculation. The Fortune 500 group did not come flocking to SBS in the numbers expected. Marketing strategy was, therefore, changed, and the network's services were adapted to attract smaller business customers. More recently, even home customers were being sought through a separate consumer telephone service.

Under sponsorship by any group with lesser resources than IBM and its two partners, the SBS project would have been an enormous gamble. For IBM, participation in the project was within the guidelines of its corporate philosophy. Swallowing a natural aversion to government regulation, IBM recognized the need to operate as a regulated common carrier (via SBS) rather than run the risk of losing control over an essential element of its long-range computer market by being dependent on AT&T and other carriers. This reflected the hallowed IBM principle of maintaining total end-to-end control over its operations.

Even while stretching to claim its place in the new network technologies, IBM was wrestling with changes inside the computer business. IBM's traditional strength in large main-frame machines remained essentially unchallenged, despite inroads by foreign and domestic competitors. The new threat came from the small machines — the personal computers. This was a market that IBM had not aggressively pursued even when signs showed that low price small machines could begin to replace IBM products at the lower end of its line and also create a new market for small office, school, and home uses.

Was Big Blue too big and unwieldy to make the turnaround to mass marketing consumer products and services? The answer was complicated by the Department of Justice antitrust suit, which had been working its way through the court system since the early seventies. IBM faced a possible dismantling of its vertically integrated operations. Competitors argued in favor of breaking up the company, on the grounds that its research, production, and marketing practices inhibited competitive growth in the industry. IBM replied that it would be penalized for success if such a break-up should be mandated. The court case dragged on, employing platoons of lawyers and producing literally tons of documents.

Then, on the morning of January 8, 1982, the Justice Department made two separate announcements which decided the future of IBM and AT&T, and, by extension, the United States information-based economy. For IBM, the decision was simply to drop the case as being without merit. For AT&T, the decision was considerably more complicated.

Years will pass before any balanced judgment can be made on the wisdom of the 1982 decisions. Already, a range of contentious opinions are being expressed. Were the decisions a Reaganite concession to big business, selling out consumer interest? Or did they herald the opening of a golden age, a push-button paradise, as promised in corporate advertising? Whatever the final judgment on them, the decisions are in effect. American society is in for a long period of sorting out implications at many different levels. The sorting out will take place in political arenas like Congress, as well as the courts and regulatory agencies like the FCC, the Federal Trade Commission and the Securities & Exchange Commission. It will occur, too, in the financial community, with enormous sums of money going toward expanding the telecommunications and information utility now in the making.

Meanwhile, technology and economics have brought about a convergence of the corporate sightlines of IBM and AT&T. The two firms will become increasingly competitive with one another as each moves on toward more fully integrated communications/information operations. Both are entering uncharted areas of sophisticated equipment and services for automated workplaces — offices, factories, schools, and laboratories. They are also looking at the household market, keenly aware that the average person uses the telephone only 15 minutes a day — a striking under-utilization.[5] They and their competitors are developing strategies for filling the hours of unused capacity with new and potentially lucrative services.

It is useful to look more closely at the ways in which the 1982 Department of Justice decisions have affected IBM, AT&T, the former Bell System local companies, and the rising number of competing firms.

AT&T. When the divestiture agreement was announced in 1982, the company was faced with the formidable problem of a transition from a monopoly of imperial proportions to a new kind of competitive business. By court order, the divestiture had to take place within two years. There were no precedents to serve as guides. The closest parallel was the break-up of the Standard Oil Company early in the century, but the circumstances were not comparable in size or complexity. AT&T's revenues in 1983, its last year as an integrated company, were over $65 billion — more than the individual gross national products of over a hundred nations. The process of breaking up the Bell System underscored the myriad ways in which the system affected every life in this country.

Millions of words have been written about the AT&T reorganization, touching on financial, technical, managerial, political, and social aspects of the event. Each of these aspects is important, but the critical element for AT&T has been the psychological turnaround the company has had to undergo.[6] The Bell System was a service organization with a well-honed tradition of solid reliability. The rumblings of competition preceding the divestiture had the effect of slowly forcing the firm to reconsider its service-oriented philosophy. Although AT&T maintained its overall dominance in most telecommunications areas, new competitors made inroads in particular sectors. The most notable example of this during the seventies was the lucrative market for PABX office telephone equipment. From a position of almost total monopoly of this market, Bell's manufacturing affiliate, Western Electric, fell to hardly a half market share by the end of the decade.

As the brisk breeze of the new competition began to be felt, AT&T and the local phone companies discovered marketing. Before 1970, the local companies did not have a sales force in the accepted sense of the term. They had "service representatives" who dealt with the public too often with a friendly but firm "Ma Bell knows best" attitude.[7]

The 1982 diverstiture decision gave AT&T what it said it wanted — a chance to compete fully in the expanding telecommunications and information markets. However, its new marketing organization had not advanced quickly enough to match the formidable task of moving the world's largest communications operation into the rough-and-ready competitive environment. Almost every realistic estimate of AT&T's future cites the firm's ability to make a full competitive turnaround as the critical factor. "The toughest thing to change is corporate culture, and AT&T's corporate culture was not designed for competition," said one former Bell executive in 1983. But there were those who echoed the feelings of another watcher: "Anyone who discounts AT&T and Western Electric is crazy."[8]

By January 1984, when the divestiture agreement came into full force, AT&T had reorganized itself into several basic units.

- *AT&T Communications* The largest of the new units, handles the traditional long-distance phone business.

- *AT&T Information Systems* Charged with moving the company into data-related equipment and services.

- *Western Electric* and the *Bell Laboratories* Each retains its public identity; this speeds product development and facilitates marketing, both directly and through third parties. (Sears Roebuck, for instance, has become an important outlet for Western Electric consumer products.)

- *AT&T International* Handles global marketing of products and services — an area in which the company had not been active for over fifty years.

Each of these units is organized to be as self-contained as possible with as much research, manufacturing, and marketing strength as it needs. In order to understand how the "new AT&T" functions, it is necessary to be familiar with each of its five basic units.

AT&T Communications — the long-distance phone business — is the most solid pillar in the new corporate structure. In the early years of the reorganized company, it is expected to provide nearly two-thirds of AT&T's revenues and most of its profits. In large part, this is because long distance is a booming business. A generation of Americans has grown up in a communications environment in which long-distane phone calls are taken for granted as a preferred means of casual, daily communication. Long-distance calling is now only a push-button away. And for most people, long-distance means AT&T, still the Old Reliable standing tall above a flourishing undergrowth of young competitors. This traditional image of dependability was the theme of the company's post-divestiture long-distance advertising. Hollywood actors in television ads were seen affectionately patting their phones, and reminding viewers that AT&T was the phone company they could count on to get the message to Aunt Matilda out there in Red Oak, Iowa.

The argument was very persuasive. None of AT&T's competitors in the long-distance business could promise to reach every phone in the country until 1986 at the earliest. Nevertheless, this disadvantage did not inhibit the competition from full-fledged campaigns to expand their share of the market, the overwhelming bulk of which involved traffic between cities and towns somewhat larger and more easily served than Red Oak.

The divestiture agreement did, in fact, open up important new advantages for AT&T's competitors. Their customers, for example, were no longer required to use the cumbersomely long codes formerly needed to get into special long-distance systems. With pre-divestiture uncertainties behind them, MCI, GTE Sprint, and the other challengers announced new services, many of them anticipating AT&T post-divestiture strategy. These younger firms are confident they can continue to outcompete AT&T in price, despite some initial confusion over government-mandated access charges designed to provide continued subsidies for local service from long-distance revenues.[9]

The rewards for challenging AT&T's long-distance dominance will be substantial. From roughly $45 billion at the time of divestiture, long-distance revenues are expected to rise to $100 billion by the end of the decade. In 1984, AT&T's competitors had about 8% of long-distance traffic. Eventually, their share may stabilize at about 25%. Their gain will result partly from aggressive competition, but it will also be, in part, the consequence of curious twists in the United States anti-trust law. In effect, AT&T will have to permit a decrease in its share of the market as an earnest of its willingness to adjust to a significant level of competition. If the expected decrease should fail to take place, the company could be dragged back into court, charged with violation of the conditions of the divestiture.

No matter how the market stabilizes, no one expects that AT&T will give up more of its traditional telephone business than is necessary to avoid a repetition of the legal battles of the past decade. Despite the inroads made by other firms in long-distance markets, AT&T remains a formidable competitor. No other telecommunications organization approaches the research capabilities of the Bell Labs or the manufacturing range of Western Electric. For all its conservatism, AT&T has experimented with almost every technical prospect available in the field.[10]

AT&T's long-term health will depend on how it expands beyond its plain-old-telephone base into high tech communications and information operations. This will take in a wide scope of activities, but the focus will be the company's ability to move in two highly competitive areas — computers and integrated office communications. In the latter field, AT&T's inability to maintain its traditional lead in PABX development was an ominous sign, according to industry observers. However, in recent years, the company has developed advanced office products based on a PABX telephone switch, including word processing, building maintenance controls, and local area networks to link computer systems.

In these networks, the computers, themselves, will in many cases be AT&T products. Only IBM has more research and development experience with the evolution of computer technology than has AT&T. The inclusion of computer production in its strategic plans signalled, more than any other single decision, that AT&T was challenging the entire information industry, IBM included. AT&T's minicomputer, introduced in 1984, operates on UNIX, the company's well-tested and versatile software operating system. The prospect of an AT&T minicomputer led IBM to announce that it was adapting its own computer line to accommodate UNIX — and, hopefully, if less outspokenly, to preempt AT&T computer sales. In addition to these business-related activities, AT&T has moved quickly in the post-divestiture period to explore other services. In 1983, for instance, it set up a joint venture with Coleco Industries to develop a home video game service to be delivered by telephone.[11]

All this activity has left unanswered the question of AT&T's ability to compete effectively in new fields. For generations, the firm's reputation rested on equipment designed with all kinds of safeguards against failure. It was an expensive strategy, that could only be indulged in a protected monopoly assured of its profits. In the new market, most equipment is designed with less concern for long-term stolidity than for short-term consumer appeal. Evidence of this market trend is to be seen in the stripped-down telephones, mostly from the Far East, which have flooded the United States consumer outlets in recent years. Over 20 million telephone receivers were imported in 1983 alone. They are a far cry from AT&T standards, but they are cheap and, after a fashion, they work. Although AT&T has made significant strides in responding to changing consumer demands, it is relying on its reputation for equipment and service reliability to meet the new competition in the coming years.

Another major initiative by AT&T is its decision to move into international markets. The company has set its sights high: "We aim to be among the three largest suppliers anywhere we go," AT&T International's vice chairman, James Olson, declared in 1984.[12] There is an element of bravado in the statement since the international telecommunications and services markets play by different rules than those at home. In most countries, telecommunications is a protected sector, with the government operating a network whose equipment needs are met by local industry as much as feasible. Consequently, most American equipment companies have not competed vigorously for this business in the past, concentrating instead on the large and lucrative North American market. The exception was ITT, most of whose operations have been located abroad since early in the century.

Although protectionism is still a strong factor in telecommunications abroad, the situation is changing. The United States government is putting pressure on its industrial allies to open their markets to American products and services. Japan — the largest single telecommunications market abroad — has been a target for these efforts, with some initial success. Governments in less-developed countries will need advanced equipment from American firms to upgrade their communications and information facilities. Hence, the overseas market is now of vital interest to the Americans eager for their share of the $1.5 trillion that will be spent on expanding the world network in the next decade. At the same time, American companies are facing increasing competition in this country as foreign telecommunications firms move into the North American market, which is still the largest in the world. Competing in the international market has become a necessary counter-strategy for American companies.

AT&T is the newest major player in this game. Until it set up its overseas affiliate, AT&T International, it had not operated directly in foreign countries for over 50 years. Such is the global mystique surrounding the company that its entry into the market has had the effect of defining a new era in the way in which the world communications grid will be assembled. For most foreign observers, the puzzling question was why AT&T had not gone into overseas operations earlier. Its Bell Laboratories research strength, Western Electric's production capacity, and the firm's unrivalled financial resources have always made it a strong potential international force. Moreover, the company has had business connections with telecommunications organizations throughout the world as a result of its long-distance telephone operations.[13]

Despite its potential, AT&T's overseas push did not make a strong initial impression. In these early years, AT&T has remained well behind the established leaders — ITT, L. M. Ericsson of Sweden, CIT-Alcatel of France, West Germany's Siemans, and the ubiquitous Japanese. This rather slow start reflects the difficulties of breaking into a strongly-entrenched marketing pattern which is not susceptible to easy assault by newcomers, even one with AT&T's resources.

In developing its overseas marketing organization, AT&T started from scratch. To compensate for this initial handicap, the company established links with foreign telecommunications firms that already had global marketing capabilities. The most important of these arrangements was completed in 1983 when the firm announced a joint venture with Philips, the Dutch electronics multinational. A few months later, AT&T Interntional bought a 25% interest in Italy's Olivetti Company in order to strengthen its entry into the European office electronics and computer markets.[14] AT&T has also linked up with East Asian manufacturers, notably in Japan and Korea, to strengthen its prospects in that region.

In the coming years, AT&T's international strategy will focus on the advanced office equipment market. It is the fastest growing electronic market, one in which American firms have taken a strong global lead in both technology and marketing. With its new overseas partners, AT&T brings powerful resources to the competition. This strategy also has another intriguing aspect: It puts the firm in direct global competition with IBM, the dominant international player in this field.

Meanwhile, in this country, the 22 local Bell telephone companies have been adapting to the opportunities — and uncertainties — of life beyond the old AT&T monopoly. In 1983, they organized themselves into seven regional holding companies. Even regionally divided as such, each of the seven was large enough in itself to be included in the top 10% of the Fortune 500 companies.

Getting ever larger, local telephone operations will continue to expand rapidly in the coming decade as home consumer demand continues to increase and, more spectacularly, as business data communications experience a spurt in growth. A new high was marked in 1984 when the New York Telephone Company found it necessary to divide New York City into two area codes, with Brooklyn, Queens, and Staten Island becoming a "long-distance" call from Manhattan and the Bronx. An overload on local circuits had been felt due mainly to heavier business computer traffic over telephone lines. In the Manhattan financial district in 1983, the phone company found that for every person calling another person, there were 5 computers calling 5 other computers.[15]

While the regional Bell companies find themselves in a rapidly expanding market, they also find themselves facing new types of competition. The 1982 divestiture agreement, together with other recent government actions, has effectively unwrapped telephone operations from their protective cocoon. Specifically, the FCC, for example, authorized a series of alternative systems competitive with the traditional local telephone network. One is a technological innovation called multi-point distribution (MDS), a commercial microwave system which bypasses local phone circuits and offers a range of other services. Another is cellular mobile telephone networks. By FCC decree, the 300 largest metropolitan areas in the country have each been allowed two such mobile phone systems — one operated by the local phone company and the other operated by a competitor. Also, several domestic satellite communications systems are now authorized to transmit directly to offices and factories as long-distance networks, bypassing the local phone networks. Cable television operators are exploring ways of providing home and business services formerly handled exclusively by telephone companies. Finally, many large business firms are setting up their own private communications networks, linking offices and other installations by satellite, microwave circuits or cables which they own or lease.[16]

The primary target of both the local phone companies and their new competitors is the business market. However, the companies each keep a corporate eye on the potentially vast home communications market with a view to supplying data networking to the much heralded "electronic cottage" for shopping, banking, information retrieval, and electronic mail. In 1983, MCI announced the inauguration of the first national consumer electronic mail network, servicing both office and home terminals.

At-home electronic shopping and banking services are developing more slowly due to consumer resistance against changing personal business habits. Consumers could gain significantly from these innovative services. In banking, for instance, a transaction costing $1.27 through a teller at a bank can be effected through an automated teller machine for 55¢ according to an estimate by Citibank of New York. Transactions from home terminals directly to the bank, linked by telephone or cable lines to a computer, will eventually cost much less than even the teller machine.

The telephone companies are looking at prospects for these service possibilities — and beyond them. They are actively considering the replacement of bulky (and lucrative) Yellow Page directories by an expanded electronic directory to be made available through terminals in homes and business locations. The seven Bell holding companies have also begun to move outside their local geographic areas. In 1984, Bell Atlantic Corporation acquired a 40% interest in a national radio paging ("beeper") company. On the West Coast, Pacific Telesis Group announced plans in the same year to set up an international subsidiary. Its purpose is to sell its expertise in designing, building, and operating telephone systems abroad, particularly in East Asia.[17]

The main business of the reorganized Bell companies and their competitors, however, will continue to be POTS, plain-old-telephone-service, for a long time to come. Americans make three-quarters of a billion phone calls a day. The telephone has long ceased to be a luxury; its low-cost universal availability is considered a public right. This comfortable assumption was severely tested in the early post-divestiture period, when the tradition of relatively low telephone rates was brought into doubt. Historically, AT&T long-distance toll rates were set to include a built-in subsidy for local service. With the divestiture, the arcane but practical old formulas for distributing costs between local and long-distance operations were no longer applicable.

The in-house subsidy gone, local phone companies proceeded to seek substantial rate increases. Applications for over $6.7 billion in such increases were filed with the regulating government agencies in early 1984. There were dire predictions that phone rates would triple over the course of a few years.[18]

At issue was more than an economic question of relief for telephone companies deprived of their former internal subsidies. An important political question was involved, namely the basic concept of universal phone service and, by extension, the matter of equal access to advanced information services. In wired-up America, the personal telephone is an economic and social necessity. But universal access to the network had been achieved only through a highly complex set of formulas that had suddenly been made obsolete.

The search for alternatives to obsolete rate schedules led down thorny paths. At both federal and state levels, politicians and regulatory officials hunted for solutions. The FCC proposed a monthly levy on all telephones to make up for the lost subsidy. Congressional committees put forth counter-proposals. None of the new formulas was immediately acceptable. Meanwhile, long-distance rates were free to drop as they no longer had to be set by subsidy-producing schedules. Lower long-distance rates are a welcome relief to AT&T as the company meets the challenge of new competitors in the expanding market. One way or another, however, customers will have to pay the price for separated local phone costs. The ultimate threat is an erosion of universal personal phone service, with lower income families and geographically isolated users in danger of losing easy access. In the new information-based economy, the danger is critical.

Meanwhile, the former Bell System companies have moved, at varying speeds, into the bracing new competitive environment. It will take years to sort out their role in post-industrial America. One thing is certain: they will no longer be just "the phone company." With their technical and management experience, they will expand well beyond their traditional business into a wide range of new services.

We turn now to IBM — the other company whose future status, along with that of AT&T, was clarified in the January 1982 Justice Department decisions. For IBM, the end of the anti-trust case meant that it would continue to operate as an integrated research, production, and marketing organization. The alternative was to have been split up into smaller units. No IBM-watcher doubted that a fragmented company would have survived and thrived. However, most of them agreed that the dynamism which had made the firm a world leader in computers and business machines for most of this century would have suffered in the process.

The anti-trust case had, in fact, cast a shadow over the company's future throughout the seventies. Although it was a decade of technical advances and rising profits, computer developments generally appeared to be moving at a faster pace than IBM's ability to innovate, particularly in marketing. The company trailed its competitors in the two biggest changes in the industry since the introduction of large-scale production of main-frame machines in the 1950s. In minicomputers, the small mainframe machines, Digital Equipment Corporation (DEC) set the pace in the early seventies. The other innovation, microcomputers, was introduced by small start-up companies like Apple Computers in the late seventies. The peren-nial Cassandras among IBM-watchers revived their claim that the company had run its course, that it was fixated on big computers at a time when technology and economics were combining to give smaller machines the largest share of the market.[19]

However, the Cassandras were wrong again. Its future confirmed by the Justice Department's 1982 decision, IBM moved ahead smartly. The company had, in fact, been gearing up for the change for years. From 1976 to 1983, it had invested $25 billion into new plant and equipment. The shift also involved some important intangibles. Fortune magazine, in a 1983 analysis of the new IBM, described it as a cultural change: "To its old motto, 'Think,' IBM seems to have appended the word 'differently.'" Whatever transitional problems it may have had in the seventies, the company demonstrated in the eighties its corporate ability to encourage innovation and to act on its consequences.[20]

In doing so, IBM challenged the thesis, beloved of business-school case study exercises, that large corporations cannot innovate as quickly as smaller ones. IBM's approach has been to set up its own independent small venture firms within the company. These are known, in its corporate jargon, as special business units. In the early eighties, IBM created 14 such units to explore opportunities outside its current business. The result was to lead the company into such areas as industrial robots, electrocardiographs, and directory-assistance equipment for telephone companies.

The most dramatic example of an IBM company-within-a-company was the unit set up to design and develop a small personal computer. In the late seventies, this was the biggest gap in its product line, and the gap was becoming more apparent as Apple, Radio Shack, and other firms moved in to fill it. In 1980, the small computer venture was set up with unusual freedom to bypass the IBM corporate bureaucracy. It was, as one observer noted, the firm's answer to the question: "How do you make an elephant tap dance?" The first IBM personal computer, intended primarily for business use, was put on the market in August 1981. Two years later, a less expensive version was introduced, with the educational and home market in mind. The initial results were stunning. IBM's little machines took the lead almost immediately in an explosive new kind of computer market. In 1984, the value of desk-top computers — machines that were virtually unheard of a decade before — overtook sales of the traditional large mainframe machines in the United States market.[21]

It was the coming-of-age of the American computer industry. From now on, the computer will be a mass-market product. By 1987, there will be roughly 60 million terminals installed throughout the country. The closest comparable event in United States industrial history was Henry Ford's decision to develop assembly-line production of automobiles early in the century. As with Ford, IBM's achievement was not so much in producing a mass-market product as in setting a standard around which a significant part of American economic and social development would take place.[22]

IBM matched its new product line with changes in its traditional marketing pattern. In previous years, the company had a rather condescending attitude towards its customers. Most of its equipment was leased, with the implication that customers should consider themselves honored by the association. This attitude began to change during the seventies, but it was the introduction of the small computers that marked the full corporate turnaround. Gone were the dignified formal advertising approaches. They were replaced by a promotional campaign centered around a Charlie Chaplin look-alike, spreading the word that even a lovable old tramp could use a computer. There was also a suggestion that owning an IBM machine could be fun as well as profitable. It was a long leap from the firm's traditional starched white-collar image.

In other marketing moves, IBM adopted sophisticated pricing policies, along with new patterns of consumer retailing. In addition to opening its own retail stores, the company struck deals with Sears Roebuck and other large chains to carry its products. Again the walls of corporate tradition were breached, with stunning effect. Sales of the small computers broke the million unit mark in 1984, from a standing start only three years earlier. For the long term, however, IBM's most important marketing strategy has been to encourage independent software companies to develop programs for its computers. The net result has been to encourage the widest range of software compatible with its machines.

The personal computer is the most visible example of the company's new look. However, the little machines have never been regarded by company planners as a stand-alone product. The small terminals are intended to link into a national network for which IBM will supply a full range of machines and services. Large mainframe computers will still be an important part of this pattern. The difference is that they will have shrunk in size. Midsize mainframes in the mid-eighties represent about 4 out of every 5 mainframe sales. The sales curve for these machines is beginning to flatten out as more powerful smaller computers are introduced. Nevertheless, the big-computer market is a significant one, with IBM having a three-quarters share at the middle of the decade. Industry estimates are that, as late as

1982, almost 30% of the firm's sales, and an even larger share of its profits, came from mainframes.[23]

Given the displacement of many mainframe machines by smaller computers, the shift is most directly felt by IBM's mainframe competitors — Sperry, Burroughs, NCR, Control Data and Honeywell. Unable to compete individually with IBM's research and production resources, several of these firms are turning to the small-computer market. Here they are latecomers, facing such aggressive competitors as Apple, Wang, Digital Equipment and, of course, their old nemisis, IBM. At least two firms, Sperry and Honeywell, have established production links with Japanese computer manufacturers in an effort to hold on to their share of the mainframe market.[24]

The immediate target of IBM and its competitors is to share in the electronification of American business. Communications and information technologies are merging in the office at an ever-increasing pace. Internal as well as external needs of business firms can now be dealt with through integrated networks. There may be as many as 19 million computer terminals installed in United States business organizations by 1987, more than triple the 1984 figure. By that time, most of these machines will be linked to outside electronic networks via telephone lines or other circuits.[25]

With its longtime experience in business machines, IBM is a primary contender in this market. Its goal is end-to-end equipment and service, including (via the Satellite Business Systems network) the telecommunications that will link its machines to each other and to a wide array of IBM-compatible equipment across the country. In 1983, the firm strengthened its telecommunications equipment resources by buying nearly 20% interest in the Rolm Corporation, a major manufacturer of advanced office private branch exchange (PABX) equipment and other telecommunications products. Once just the hub of office telephone communications, PABX machines have been digitized and computerized to handle data as well as voice. IBM's arrangement with Rolm will make it more competitive in a market crowded with rival advanced systems.

AT&T will be one of these competitors. The company brings to the market its experience as the basic provider of office electronic communications for over a century. This experience has largely been limited, however, to providing voice communications. AT&T will have to expand quickly beyond this if it is to challenge effectively IBM and other firms, many of whom have a considerable head start in developing and marketing integrated voice, data, and visual systems.

Beyond the office automation market, both IBM and AT&T have active projects designed to bring advanced communications and information services to Americans. Of the roughly 60 million terminals of all kinds installed by the end of 1987, 37 million will be in homes (i.e., almost half the households in the country).[26] AT&T is experimenting with a range of videotex services for homes — shopping, banking, community information, general news, and the like. Not to be left behind, IBM announced in

February 1984 plans to develop a national videotex network service, offering a full range of information and transactional services for homes and other locations, in partnership with CBS Inc. and Sears Roebuck.

As noted above, AT&T and IBM will not be the only firms reaching out for these potentially lucrative markets. Xerox, General Telephone & Electronics, Wang, Digital Equipment, ITT and dozens of other companies are also converging on these new opportunities. Over the horizon, Japanese and European firms have been positioning themselves for a share of the business in this country. In 1984, there were over 50 Japanese companies producing personal computers, all with an eye on potential markets in the United States and other countries. The coming years will see a strong marketing push by the Japanese in this area, reminiscent of their earlier successes in exporting television sets, pocket calculators, and hi-fi equipment. Similar efforts can be expected from Korean and other Asian firms.

This prospect raises the critical question of United States international competitiveness in the electronics field. It is an issue that tends to produce more heat than light, as advocates of tighter protectionist controls press their case against the dwindling group of trade-liberalization supporters. The reality is that the United States retains a comparative advantage in high tech electronic products. The difficulty comes in translating this lead into export sales. The reasons for this are often unrelated to technology. The inflated value of the United States dollar during the early eighties played a major role in reducing the international price competitiveness of American products. Even if this difficulty is reduced, the competitiveness issue will remain. A 1983 Congressional Office of Technology Assessment report noted that there has been a steady 20-year decline in international competitiveness within the United States electronics industry, particularly in consumer electronics.

The issue goes beyond trade statistics to the overall position of the United States as a high tech leader in the new global economy. For 25 years after World War II, roughly 75% of high tech innovation came from this country. The figure is closer to 50% now, with the prospect of a drop to 30% or 35% later in the decade. The shift was, of course, inevitable as Japan and Europe developed independent high tech capabilities. Nevertheless, there is a strong case for understanding the implications of the shift, and for taking steps to strengthen policies and programs which encourage high tech innovation.

IBM and AT&T will each have a unique role to play in this global high tech competition. They are still the pacemakers at home and abroad. IBM's position is well established. Despite the steady pressure of foreign competition, the company has held its own in most overseas markets, the source of about half of its annual profits. The new aggressiveness it has shown in the United States market in recent years is also reflected abroad. It has, for instance, marketed its small computers overseas with the same zeal and success demonstrated in this country.

AT&T's international role is, in the mid-eighties, somewhat less clear. Its initial entry into overseas markets after the 1982 divestiture decision was not particularly strong. In part, this reflected the company's priorities at the time, which were focussed on the complex job of sorting out its domestic reorganization problems. It would be wrong, however, to underestimate AT&T's long-term impact on overseas markets, and in particular on its role in sustaining United States high tech leadership worldwide. The firm's lack of overseas marketing experience will be balanced by partnerships it has formed with such experienced multinational marketers as Philips of Holland and Italy's Olivetti.

AT&T's strongest overseas opportunities initially will be in the industrialized countries. Its prospects as an international competitor also include the so-called Third World. Latin America, Africa, and Asia (outside of Japan) have only 10% of the world's telephones. The pressure is on to change this imbalance, for both economic and political reasons. Eventually, these developing regions should be able to produce and service a large part of their own telecommunications and information equipment. Until that time, AT&T will be available as the world's unique expert in building and maintaining a mass telecommunications system. The experience will not be totally new for the company. During World War II, its managers and technicians moved all over the globe, setting up communications systems for the United States military. The Third World's transition to adequate communications will occur in fits and starts, but the momentum is already there. AT&T can be an important factor in maintaining it.

IBM and AT&T are, by no means, the end-all and be-all of the newly integrated American communications and information sector. There are thousands of other firms, big and little, ready to compete with them and with each other. One or two of these smaller companies may become the AT&Ts and IBMs of the early twenty-first century through a combination of technological breakthroughs and managerial skills of the type that have characterized the two leaders over the years. For the present, however, AT&T and IBM are the bellwether organizations against which a good share of the opportunities for a new kind of advanced United States information society has to be measured.

NOTES

1. The best overall account of the divestiture and its implications can be found in "Breaking Up the Phone Company," *Fortune*, 27 June 1983, pp. 60–67.

2. In defending its corporate actions during a 1981 court case, a Bell attorney referred to AT&T unblushingly as "the greatest enterprise on earth." See "Government, AT&T Fire First Salvos at Trial," *New York Times*, 16 January 1981, p. D–3.

3. The goal has been in AT&T's plans since the mid-seventies. In 1976, the then-president of the company, Frederick Kappel, predicted that the firm's revenues

from data communications would eventually be greater than those from traditional voice telephone traffic. See "On the Head of a Pin," *Forbes*, 15 September 1976, p. 32.

4. The best description of the complex situation leading up to the divestiture is contained in a Congressional study, *Options Papers*, issued by the House Subcommittee on Communications, Committee on Interstate and Foreign Commerce, 95th Congress, 1st session, committee print 95–13, May 1977.

5. "A Strategy for the Telephone," *New York Times*, 18 May 1980, p. D–3.

6. For a useful summary of these psychological factors, see "Cultural Shock is Shaking the Bell System," *Business Week*, 26 September, 1983, pp. 112–114.

7. "The New World of Telecommunications," *Computer Decisions*, 15 September 1983, pp. 95–118.

8. "Changing Phone Habits," *Business Week*, 5 August 1983, p. 71.

9. The problems that AT&T's competitors will have in the early post-divestiture years are summarized in "MCI Loses Some Sparkle," *New York Times*, 12 February 1984, p. D–1.

10. "Why Western Electric Has to Hustle," *New York Times*, 17 January 1982, p. D–1.

11. "AT&T and Coleco in Video Game Venture," *New York Times*, 8 September 1983, p. D–2.

12. "Can the New AT&T Compete in World Markets?," *Business Week*, 30 January 1984, p. 32.

13. "AT & T's Impact Abroad," *Data Communications*, February 1982, p. 36.

14. "Can AT&T Compete in World Markets?", *op. cit.* Also "Crafting a High-Tech Renaissance at Olivetti," *New York Times*, 19 February 1984, p. D–3.

15. "New York to Get a Second Area Code by Middle of 1984," *New York Times*, 9 February 1983, p. B–1.

16. "Spotlights on the Data Battles Between Cable and the BOC's," *Data Communications*, December 1983, p. 45–50.

17. "Some Bell Offspring Look beyond Telephones," *Business Week*, 27 February 1984, p. 112.

18. For a good description of the controversy, see "The AT&T Breakup: A World of Confusion," *Washington Post*, 11 December 1983, p. A–14.

19. "The Big Boys Counterattack," *The Economist* (London), 24 December 1983, p. 69.

20. "Meet the Lean Mean New IBM," *Fortune*, 3 June 1983, p. 69.

21. "Bailing Out the Mainframe Industry," *New York Times*, 5 February 1984, p. D–1.

22. "The Colossus That Works," *Time*, 11 June 1983, p. 44

23. "Gene Amdahl Bets the Big Chip," *The Economist* (London), 11 February 1984, p. 70.

24. "Bailing Out the Mainframe Industry," *op. cit.*

25. These estimates were made by Link Resources Corporation in a survey, "The Personal Information Revolution," published in *Information Times*, Information Industry Association, Washington, November 1983, pp. 11–20.

26. "The Personal Information Revolution," *op. cit.*, p. 14.

27. "International Competition in Electronics," *OTA Report Brief*, Office of Technology Assessment, U.S. Congress, Washington, November 1983.

CHAPTER SEVEN

THE POLITICS OF CHANGE

HOW DOES A SOCIETY make wise decisions? How do we determine who we are and what we want to become? How do we organize ourselves and our resources to match these perceptions? These questions are particularly relevant to information and communications policy. A fast-changing society needs access to greater knowledge resources to handle the uncertainties and disruptions that change brings.

Until now our examination of information age strategies has concentrated on technological and economic developments. The United States has already crossed the technological divide into the new age. There are no longer any serious physical barriers to the creation of a full-scale information network utility. We are now crossing the economic divide, as shown in the 1977 Department of Commerce study on the information economy and in more recent research. The major unresolved issues are in the political arena, involving basic decisions on the form and purpose of the new information environment.

This is the most sensitive point in the entire transition. Technology and economics deal largely with immediate problems, focused on particular outcomes in terms of their specific success or failure. As influences on the United States information environment, they are powered by their own internal dynamics. Left to themselves, they could create a post-industrial information structure that would be difficult to modify with public policies in the future, if we should wish to do so. On the other hand, reaching consensus in any area of public policy is difficult, especially in communications and information matters. There are strong contending interests involved, together with a healthy First Amendment tradition against government interference in these areas.

Nevertheless we have arrived at a point at which public decisions are becoming imperative. Technical and economic developments are converging in ways that require a clearer definition of their relationships to overall social goals. Until recently, the pace of technical and economic changes has been a linear progression, spread across many years. The transitions from telegraph to telephone, from radio and television to computers and satellites were marked by relatively long pauses, allowing time for us to sort out their economic and social consequences. Today this time-frame is compressed, marked by a convergence of technologies with overlapping decision complexities. As a result, communications and information are being regarded as general political issues, instead of, as in the past, the concerns solely of the industry and a few government agencies.[1]

Public involvement in these policy subjects is still fragmentary, but it is there and it is growing. There is a general recognition of the need for a new information resources design that assures all of us the advantages these resources offer. This goal seemed easier 20 years ago, when many of the early prophets of the information age painted a rosy-hued picture of its prospects. This occurred during what might be called the "first computer decade," roughly from 1960 to 1970. Then, the electronic mythos was in full flower, based on the unfolding promise of computers and high-speed communications circuits. There were visions of a new order of data richness and computer-assisted decision making, a more efficient social competence replacing the old disorderly ways of managing issues and events.

It was a heady goal, spurred by the rhetoric of Kennedy's New Frontier and Johnson's Great Society, together with almost uninterrupted economic prosperity. The literature inspired by this vision evoked memories of the earlier technocracy movement of the 1930s with its engineered solutions to social problems. In the thirties, the great dams of the Tennessee Valley Authority were the prototype for future technocratic success. In the sixties, the model was the Apollo space program and its systems-analysis path to the moon. The new computer-based age would bring similar analytic efficiency to such earthbound problems as education, poverty, foreign policy, transportation, and the cities. Writing in March 1967, a team of researchers studying inner city problems in Detroit declared, "We feel that, in a very real sense, the age of the computer has ushered in a new age of urban planning."[2]

Four months later, Detroit went up in flames, urban renewal projects included. The smoky pall that hung over the city for days was a pungent reminder that stubborn social problems were not amenable to computer printout solutions. Civil disorder was followed by escalation in Vietnam, economic setbacks, and the public scandals that culminated in Watergate. The experience with the new information technologies during the first computer decade, however overblown, had its usefulness in defining the limits of computerized shortcuts. The result has been a more realistic view of the role of communications and information — as important but not cure-all resources in reducing economic and social problems.

If there is now a better understanding of what can be done practically, it is also true that we are still only at the beginning of a consensus on how to go about it. The prospect is still a promising one: providing everyone access to a full range of information resources, allowing every person, as Emerson urged, to produce that peculiar fruit each was born to bear. But this objective forces us to face some fundamental questions. Having reached the point where it is technically possible, is full access to information one of our basic rights in a post-industrial democratic society? Or is it simply a desirable long-range goal, whose attainment will be left to the play of economic and social forces, a linear extension — with some technological flourishes — of what we are now doing, with benefits trickling down largely through the workings of the market?

Choices between these options will reflect our contemporary view of the democratic tradition of open information, which supports our need to know, our right to challenge. We have made many public commitments to these ideals in the past two centuries. Those most relevant to our present situation were the decisions favoring universal free public education over a century ago. Our forebears agreed that this was a necessary democratic entitlement, and so, with some lapses, saw that it was provided. Public education moved from one-room schoolhouses to consolidated schools to our present variegated patterns of learning opportunities. In the post-industrial era, computers and related information devices can be an effective part of a new lifelong learning cycle quite different in style from traditional classroom practices. To what degree will we extend our concept of education to include greater access to these information resources? The response to this question will signal, to a considerable degree, our willingness to evolve to higher forms of democracy in the new era.

The alternative — restricted access — may push us towards a controlled, perhaps even benevolent, authoritarianism in which an elite has effective control over key information resources and uses this power to manipulate a complacent *lumpenproletariat*. An amusing, if somewhat chilling, illustration of this possibility was provided several years ago by a Columbia University professor, Alan Westin. It takes place in the early years of the next century, when an authoritarian information elite, working out of National Databank Headquarters in Philadelphia, controls the rest of society. Their plan is temporarily set back by an assault on their computers by a terrorist group known as the Fold, Staple, Spindle, and Mutilate movement. The elite leaders defeat the terrorists, and take the ultimate step of programming every event in each citizen's life to prevent further disruption. Professor Westin's scenario ends with a surprise twist that suggests that human freedom may prevail. We may never have to contend with such a dire situation, but we do have to face up to the future consequences of present trends pushing us towards an information environment where questions of access, control, and privacy are still unresolved.

These are political questions, and the answers will come from the untidy, often frustrating give-and-take of political action. The basic issue is the control and distribution of power, enhanced by the ability of the new technologies to permit massive centralization and manipulation of a wider range of information resources than ever before. This issue was identified by Karl Deutsch in his masterful work, *The Nerves of Government*, published in 1963, in which he argued that control of information resources and communications channels was displacing traditional forces — the military and the police — as the measure of power.[3] This has always been true to some extent, but the new technologies vastly enhance the prospect. This fact argues powerfully against our present inclination to leave major decisions in communications and information to the economic and technological sectors. It is putting a burden on those sectors that they are not equipped to handle, and that may be harmful to their orderly development over the long run.

This point was stressed by a former AT&T board chairman, John deButts, several years ago when he said, "It is not technology that will shape the future of telecommunications in this country. Nor is it the market. It is policy."[4] Mr. deButts made his remarks in the course of presenting his company's ideas on what national telecommunications policy should be. Whatever the details of his advocacy (a unique one, as befits AT&T's special status), he acknowledged — as many of his shortsighted industry counterparts did not — the need for public debate and decision on the future of American communications.

Participatory democracy, an informed citizenry, a strong economy, technologies that serve human needs — these are the stakes in our consideration of the prospects for viable communications and information policies in post-industrial America. It is well to dismiss at the start any fantasies we may have about a tidy master plan for the new information environment. Such an approach would be unacceptable to almost everyone concerned, since no one would be prepared to suspend his or her negotiating rights in the rough-and-tumble of political negotiation of sensitive issues in the interests of a neat, orderly, and probably unworkable system. A more realistic approach is to define minimum guidelines and goals for the near-term, say the next decade. This will be difficult enough, given the obstacles involved.

Any agreed-upon policies will, for instance, have to be grafted onto complex existing structures, controlled largely by organizations that are generally unwilling to trade the promise of long-term gains for present advantages. The changes will have to be nudged, coddled, and cajoled through a political process heavily influenced by interest groups who settle their differences through complex compromises.

Serious consideration of communications and information issues is hindered by the fact that political leaders generally do not regard them as critical. The issues involved seem too abstruse, too wrapped up in technological and economic complexities to attract sustained popular attention. As noted earlier, this attitude is changing as communications and information impinge more directly on people's lives and interests.

Nevertheless, the present lack of any clear-cut public consensus inhibits the development of strategies for dealing with information age issues. Political scientist Harold Lasswell once suggested that an annual balance sheet of "gross enlightenment outcome" of the nation be drawn up so that there would be a measure for necessary knowledge resources. As yet, however, there are no firm indicators of public needs in this area — a handicap to intelligent planning.

The result is a kind of tinker-toy approach; we are trying to piece together bits and parts of a complex structure without knowing quite what we want it to do for us. The results will inevitably be disappointing unless we can agree on a blueprint that combines economic and technological resources with social goals in a workable fashion.

What are the prospects for such a blueprint? The answer begins with the Constitution, that very flexible document which set down the basic guidelines, in law and in practice, for American approaches to communications and information. The Constitution alludes directly to communications in only one passage, which deals with the powers of Congress "to establish Post Offices and post roads." The document's most abiding influence in this area, however, comes from the First Amendment prohibition against laws abridging freedom of speech and the press. Any discussion of policy on communications or information begins with, and returns to, this fact. These strictures against government involvement explain why the United States is unique in not having a centralized bureaucracy to directly control or heavily regulate communications.

As a result, communications policy is defined and carried out by a large number of public entities at the federal, state, and local levels. The pattern is confusing, often overlapping, and frequently contradictory. Whatever the faults of this system, it reflects a common agreement to limit government intervention in the communications and information field, particularly in those areas affecting First Amendment rights. The pattern has also been shaped by pressures from the private sector against excessive regulations, that is, over and above the numerous laws and regulations designed to protect its own interests.

The limitation of government activities in the communications field was set early in the telecommunications age. The first federal involvement was to provide financial support for the initial demonstration of Samuel Morse's telegraph system between Washington and Baltimore in 1844, although this support was withdrawn the following year. In the following decades, the telegraph and telephone systems developed under private auspices, with government playing a generally benign supportive role.

The same pattern applied internationally. The United States refused to join the new International Telegraph Union, founded in 1865 to provide needed international standards for the new telegraph networks. The United States' refusal was based in part on the fact that it had few international communications links at the time, but more pointedly on a general suspicion about foreign interference in United States communications affairs. It was not until the turn of the century, when the British-controlled Marconi Wireless Company attempted to establish a global monopoly over radio communications, that the United States joined the Telegraph Union to protect its interests and, in particular, to thwart the British monopoly.

Technological developments after the First World War forced a stepping-up of government involvement in communications. The Federal Radio Commission was established in 1927 to sort out the chaotic frequency situation caused by an influx of hundreds of new stations. Before the Commission began its work, radio stations gained "authorization" by sending a letter to the Department of Commerce simply notifying it that they were on the air.[5] The Communications Act of 1934 set out more comprehensive legislative standards, including the establishment of the Federal Communications Commission (FCC). The creation of the FCC was an important step in providing a mechanism for sorting out many of the pragmatic problems brought on by the new technologies. However, its authority has been limited to regulating the telecommunications industry. Fast-moving technological developments make it increasingly difficult to define the boundaries of its jurisdiction. A 50-year-old communications act, designed to cope with telephones and radios, does not provide much help.

The bureaucratic process for dealing with communications and information has developed gradually over the years. Until World War II, government communications matters were handled as a part-time concern of the military. The Navy took the lead in the 1920s in helping create the Radio Corporation of America (now RCA) as a United States "chosen instrument" for challenging foreign competition in international communications. The need to set up a worldwide communications network during World War II focused official attention on communications policy matters for the first time. President Truman later appointed a special assistant for telecommunications to deal with the issue. The office and its duties were expanded in a series or reorganizations under presidents Eisenhower, Kennedy, and Johnson. But these changes still left communications policy as a small-fry concern in the bureaucratic fishpond.

The Kennedy administration became more deeply involved in communications policy in 1962 as the result of a technological breakthrough. The technology was the communications satellite, whose capabilities were demonstrated in July of that year when NASA launched AT&T's *Telstar*, the first active repeater satellite capable of switching incoming and outgoing messages in space. (Previous experiments involved passive satellites, with signals bounced off a balloon.) It was a major technical achievement that immediately raised political and economic questions.

The politics involved problems of organizing a system, both domestically and internationally, for exploiting the new technology. Intelligence reports at the time indicated that the Soviet Union was actively engaged in similar satellite research. In that post-*Sputnik* era, the thought of another Soviet space success, and the prospect that the Soviets might take the lead in organizing a global satellite network, was a sharp goad causing Kennedy administration officials and Congressional leaders to move quickly. The result, decided upon in record time for major legislation, was the Communications Satellite Act of 1962, which set up the Communications Satellite Corporation (Comsat) and detailed a plan for organizing an American-sponsored international satellite system. Comsat would be the government's "chosen instrument" for organizing the system and representing the United States in its management.

It was an innovative solution, combining both public and private sector elements, which provided the basic framework for the development of the highly successful Intelsat global system, owned by over a hundred nations. The 1962 legislation was a critical event in focusing American attention on communications policy matters, even though it dealt with only one, albeit an important, aspect of the problem.[6]

A hopeful step toward the development of a coherent policy was taken in the late sixties when the Johnson administration appointed a Presidential commission to study the subject. The commission, headed by Yale law professor Eugene Rostow, made a thoughtful and controversial attempt at the first national overview of communications issues. It defined communications as a critical issue in United States society and proposed a series of specific actions for strengthening its role in economic and social development.[7]

Along the way, the commission's report also challenged longstanding government and corporate interests. Given the complex nature of these interests, this was perhaps inevitable, as was the fact that the report was quietly relegated to that special Washington limbo for controversial advisory commission reports. Nevertheless, the Rostow study was important because it did attempt to present a coherent view of the future implications of technological, economic, and social developments in communications. It set a basic agenda which is still valid — no mean achievement.

The Rostow study also influenced the Nixon administration, in 1969, to take a more serious look at the way in which communications policy matters were organized. The result was a decision to upgrade the subject in an enlarged White House unit known as the Office of Telecommunications Policy (OTP) with a charter for coordinating overall government policy and planning on the subject. Setting up OTP was a significant step toward a more rational national approach to communications, but its effectiveness was almost immediately compromised by political controversy. The new office became the Nixon White House's stalking horse for an attack on the alleged liberal biases of the major television networks. Its charges reinforced the fears of the industry and of Congress that the administration intended to use the new office to gain political control over the media in the United States. This, together with the general distrust of OTP by old-line government agencies concerned with communications matters, effectively ended the hope that OTP would bring a fresh approach to national communications planning. The fact that the office performed some valuable services, particularly in funding policy research projects, was hidden in the black political clouds that surrounded most of its history.

In 1977 it was inevitable that the new Carter administration would abolish the unit. With an eye on the political sensitivities involved, the Carter planners rejected suggestions for a replacement that would have a stronger charter for coordinating policy and planning matters. Instead, they redistributed OTP's functions, assigning the bulk of them to a new agency, the National Telecommunications and Information Administration (NTIA), in the Department of Commerce. NTIA was immediately perceived as weaker than the OTP, particularly because it had no direct bureaucratic entrée to the White House, as did the OTP. However, it is a well-established Washington rule that proximity, bureaucratic or otherwise, to the White House can be an elusive benefit.

OTP's effectiveness was destroyed by the political connotations of its direct White House connection. (On a day-to-day basis, the connection was not all that strong.) In its early years, NTIA demonstrated that a lower political profile was, on balance, a help rather than a hindrance in its work. Like OTP, its most important assignment was to provide a coordinating point for the federal government's own communications and information activities. It is also charged with advising the President on overall national policy in these areas. Significantly, for the first time telecommunications and information were newly paired as common policy concerns in one agency, a welcome recognition of the technological and economic realities of the information age. With the advent of the Reagan administration, there has been an attempt by some of Reagan's more conservative advisers to eliminate NTIA, primarily on the theory that any such federal policy involvement in these areas is undesirable. After some confusion, the administration retained the NTIA structure while at the same time cutting back on its budget, personnel and policy responsibilities.

If coordination has been the key word in NTIA's mission, it has also been its most difficult task. The image is of a tidy system meant to bring coherence and order to the federal establishment's far-flung involvement in communications and information matters. The reality is considerably more complex, and less neat.[8] The federal government's involvement is a tangle of facilities and operations — from the White House office that instantaneously provides circuits for the President wherever he may be, to Voice of America transmitters in the Thailand jungles, to the dogsleds used by the postal service to deliver mail in Alaska.

By one estimate, federal communications facilities were capitalized at $67 billion in 1977 and were expected to rise to $100 billion by the mid-eighties.[9] The federal government controls over half of all the radio frequencies assigned to this country under international agreements. It is also by far the world's largest owner and user of computers, though no one is quite sure how many it has.

The agency most heavily involved in telecommunications and information operations is the Defense Department, which uses half of all the frequencies assigned to the government. Although the military has extensive telecommunications facilities of its own, it is heavily dependent on civilian communications. The problems of meshing the two systems came to a head during the 1962 Cuban missile crisis, when serious coordination gaps emerged. This led to the first attempt to develop a strategic-communications plan, centered around the establishment of a National Communications System with the Secretary of Defense as executive agent. The case for such a policy was made at the time by Dr. Harold Brown, then Defense Department Director of Research:

> It is...important to recognize that our domestic and international telecommunications systems are critical factors both in our military posture and in our cold war struggle and, indeed, throughout the whole spectrum of conflict. We cannot today consider our communications systems solely as civil activities merely to be regulated as such, but we must consider them as essential instruments of national policy in our struggle for survival and establish policy and organizations consistent with our situation.[10]

The National Communications System charter is limited to assuring government communications "under all conditions from a normal situation to national emergencies and international crises, including nuclear attack." The Secretary of Defense is responsible for the daily operations of the system under White House policy direction. Several attempts have been made to expand the system's scope since it was set up, but these have been resisted by other elements in the government's communications establishment.

There are, conservatively, two dozen civilian government agencies with major communications and information responsibilities. The largest of these is the postal service, a hybrid organization operating in a bureaucratic no-man's-land, heavily dependent on government subsidies. The postal service is, for all its faults, a major element in the national information and communications network. Moreover, its future is the subject of considerable debate, particularly concerning its antiquated methods of using high-priced hand labor to carry pieces of paper to tens of millions of homes and offices every working day.

Besides the postal service, there is a conglomeration of other agencies with major communications and information responsibilities. These include the Department of Transportation, which handles air and maritime communications; the State Department, which handles negotiation of international agreements; the United States Information Agency, operating the Voice of America overseas radio network and other media facilities; the National Aeronautics and Space Administration, handling communications satellite experimentation; the Central Intelligence Agency, seeing to analysis of telecommunications developments abroad; and the National Security

Agency, a highly classified operation monitoring foreign communications. Other agencies are also involved, though less obviously. The Federal Bureau of Investigation operates extensive files on American citizens and electronic links to local police authorities. Its capabilities, however, fall short of the computerized national crime information network it and many local police departments have pressed for, despite so far successful resistance by civil liberties advocates who claim that such a system could lead to abuses. Another agency with extensive information responsibilities is the Internal Revenue Service, with its extensive files on what Americans earn and spend. In 1978, as a result of congressional and other pressures, the Carter administration halted the development of an $850 million computer network designed to provide IRS agents with immediate access to the detailed records of taxpayers and corporations.[11] Another government-controlled information base affecting most citizens is operated by the Social Security Administration and contains millions of separate files on almost anyone who has ever had a job in this country since the mid-thirties.

Less known examples of federal information activities are the scientific and professional services provided by the government both for its internal and for general public use. The medical profession relies heavily on MEDLARS and MEDLINE, the National Library of Medicine's computerized compilation of articles published in medical journals throughout the world. Industry and research institutes make extensive use of the Department of Commerce's National Technical Information Service (NTIS), a computer-based source of technical research done by federal agencies. Educators turn to ERIC, the data base operated by the Department of Education, for information in their field. The Smithsonian Institution's Science Information Exchange indexes about 10,000 research projects a month as part of an effort to keep track of research the federal government pays for.

The overall issue of government-held computerized information has been the subject of intense debate in recent years. The technological prospect that previously independent data banks can be interconnected means that information collected by one agency can be made available to many. This led to recommendations that government-held computerized information be centralized in an interconnected data system. The arguments of those stressing the efficiency of such a system have so far been successfully challenged by those who fear its misuse.

The proliferating and jealously guarded division of responsibility over communications and information among so many agencies has at least lessened the threat of Big Brother centralism. But it has also inhibited the development of a workable coordinated policy approach to the problems of the new information age.

The National Telecommunications and Information Administration may eventually be able to play a significant role in improving policy coherence, but it has not yet proved its ability to do so. At present, the most important federal influence on communications and information development is the Federal Communications Commission (FCC). The Commission dates from the technologically innocent days of Franklin D. Roosevelt's first administration, at which time its principal duties were to regulate radio stations and telephone companies. The agency quickly took on the usual bias of such commissions, namely a protective attitude toward the industries it was assigned to regulate. For decades it operated in near anonymity in the gray background of Washington bureaucracy.

This situation changed slowly at first, then rapidly toward the end of the 1960s, for several reasons. New technologies began to intrude on long-standing regulations based on the older techniques. The combination of advanced technologies and more aggressive economic pressures to expand the industry brought communications and information more into the orbit of political controversy. This situation was exacerbated by an increase in public awareness, particularly in the consumer reform movement, about communications and information matters, from childrens' TV programming to telephone company rates. (After decades of being accorded almost reverential treatment by the public, the phone company found itself facing protestors with bell-shaped buttons labeled "Public Enemy No. 1.")

With its restricted mandate, the FCC was in a difficult situation, straining against the limits of outdated legislation (the Communications Act of 1934) that did not anticipate the regulatory problems raised by satellites, computers, high-capacity cable systems, and other new technologies. For many reasons, most of them having to do with the difficulties of appeasing conflicting economic interests, neither the White House nor the Congress was prepared to make controversial policy choices to resolve the conflicts in ways that would benefit the national communications and information structure.

The task has fallen largely to the FCC, which has proved to be an unwieldy agent of change. As an independent regulatory agency, it is not directly accountable to Congress or to the President, although it clearly must take into account signals from both these sources. In the absence of legislated policy, the Commission is a policymaker by default on a wide range of issues. Its failings do not necessarily lie with the Commission or its staff.

The FCC's problem is in coping with the bits and pieces of important communications and information matters in the absence of a clearly articulated national policy. The Commission is less a regulator in the traffic cop sense than a referee without an up-to-date rulebook or even a clear whistle.

Despite these handicaps, the FCC has moved to act on a number of pressing issues in recent years. A good part of this momentum was generated by activist Commission chairman, Richard Wiley, in the early seventies. A lawyer with little previous communications experience (as he once confessed, "I thought digital communications described something you didn't do in polite society"), Wiley took initiatives over a wide range of Commission matters, adding considerable prestige and authority to the agency. However, his activism — which also had its controversial side — could not make up for the absence of overall national decisions by the White House and Congress on the shape and direction of the new information age. Uncertainty continued to hamper the Commission during the Carter years, although important decisions were made to deregulate many telecommunications services and open them up to the fresh winds of new competition. Given the conservation make-up of the Commission as a result of Reagan administration appointments, this trend can be expected to continue under the agency's chairman, Washington lawyer Mark Fowler. In particular, the Fowler Commission stepped up the deregulatory pace set in previous years, often with the useful result of eliminating outdated regulatory practices. At times, however, the Commission's actions showed a naive faith in the efficacy of allegedly objective market forces at the expense of legitimate social interests.

A less known but still significant influence on the formation of national communications policies are the hundreds of federal advisory committees, commissions, boards, councils, and other groups that provide, with varying degrees of effectiveness, outside expertise to federal agencies. They are a particularly strong factor in the communications area, where their membership is drawn largely from industry. One survey indicated that, in 1976, eight of the eleven corporations who contributed the most personnel to all federal advisory groups were in the communications field. In part, this reflects the fact that a considerable amount of expertise — particularly in technical matters — is concentrated in the private sector. It is also an indicator of the outsized role that the industry plays in influencing small parts of a fragmented government policy-planning mechanism, sometimes deterring more effective broader based planning. Although the Carter administration made considerable progress in cutting back the number of advisory groups, the membership of most groups still tended to come from industry. A 1978 survey of advisory group membership showed that AT&T filled 120 positions on such groups.[12]

The absence of overall policy direction in communications and information does not reflect a failure to study the problems in these areas. They have been examined in numbing detail for years. As already noted, the first major study was the Rostow Commission's, reviewing a broad range of policy matters in the late sixties. This was followed by a series of competent research studies sponsored by the Nixon administration's Office of Telecommunications Policy. Also, the independent, congressionally funded National Academy of Engineering and the National Science Foundation sponsored useful studies on the social applications of new communications and information technologies.

Other projects examined the government's role in developing effective technical information networks — a priority concern for the scientific establishment as well as for American industry in its attempt to maintain a technological lead against increasing foreign competition. Important work in setting standards and recommending actions in this field was done by the Federal Council for Science and Technology in the 1960s. One result of this initiative was the setting up of a central source for all research results produced by federal agencies — the National Technical Information Service.

However useful these studies and the actions resulting from them, they have tended to focus on relatively small parts of the total communications and information problem. None of them recommend a general strategy for public policy in these areas. An exception was a 1976 report to President Ford entitled *National Information Policy*, prepared by the Domestic Council's committee on the right of privacy, headed by Vice-President Nelson Rockefeller. The report's major recommendation was that "the United States set as a goal the development of a coordinated National Information Policy."[13]

Although the document stressed problems of access and privacy, it touched on most of the other major political concerns involved in developing a democratically based information environment. Despite its controversial recommendations, the report had little influence, in part because it was issued in the last, lame-duck months of the Ford administration. Nevertheless, the Rockefeller committee's initiative in proposing an overall national information policy provided an important base from which other studies of this subject can be made.

Any moves toward a new approach to communications and information policy will have to consider the role of Congress. The subject is a sensitive one for Congress, involving constitutional issues as well as the relation of Congress with the executive branch and with important constituencies. This sensitivity explains why Congress has not passed a major piece of communications legislation in half a century, since the Communications Act of 1934. Nevertheless, the subject is intruding more frequently on congressional agendas. By and large, Congress shares the long-time executive branch predilection for dealing with communications and information matters in a fragmentary manner.

The exception to this practice in recent years has been the effort, inspired largely by former California Congressman Lionel Van Deerlin, to revise the 1934 Communications Act. Van Deerlin, a former San Diego newsman, headed the House subcommittee on communications until he was defeated in the 1980 elections. He suggested that the committee take a hard look at the 1934 legislation with a view to making it reflect current technological and economic realities.

Van Deerlin's proposal grew out of an effort by the Bell System in 1976 on behalf of legislation known as the Consumer Communications Reform Act. This bill, quickly dubbed "the Bell Bill," was an artful attempt to strengthen AT&T's preeminent position in the telecommunications industry. The legislation in effect reaffirmed the Bell System's monopoly and proposed severe restrictions on the ability of other communications firms to compete with Bell service. The bill was opposed by most of the rest of the industry, particularly by firms whose interests would be affected by any extension of AT&T's quasi-monopoly power. Their lobbying campaign was a well-directed and, as it turned out, effective effort to kill the legislation.

The way was open for Mr. Van Deerlin and his mild-mannered suggestion that it might be better to look at all the issues in the telecommunications field, not just those directly affecting the Bell System, and to determine what changes should be made in the 1934 Communications Act. The result was the most extensive review ever made of national communications policy by Congress. Beginning in 1976, scores of witnesses appeared before Congressman Van Deerlin's subcommittee to present their views. The committee staff prepared a massive "options papers" document, outlining all the issues involved in adjusting the 1934 legislation to current economic and technological realities.[14]

The committee's hearings were a classic interest-group exercise, with all the affected parties bringing different perceptions and pressures to bear on the attempt to review and rewrite the old legislation. The communications industry was split between those arguing for the status quo and those who saw the benefits of a legislative imprimatur for the new economic and technological forces. Government agencies were generally suspicious of legislation that would affect their prerogatives. Public service groups came to the hearings with expectations of a more consumer-oriented approach to communications problems. The conflicting pressures were strong enough to stretch out the process for years, with renewed attempts in the early eighties to develop a comprehensive bill updating the 1934 legislation by the House subcommittee's chairman, Representative Timothy Wirth, a Colorado Democrat. At the same time, Congress had to take a number of actions to bring the Communications Act and other legislation into conformity with the 1982 divestiture agreement between AT&T and the Justice Department.

Nevertheless, the House (and related Senate) hearings had their effect. They have helped sort out the problems involved and focus them in unique and constructive ways in a forum — the U.S. Congress — that counted. In particular, the hearings identified many of the very real policy issues involved in adjusting economic and technological factors to new information and communications needs. The process was limited in that it addressed itself primarily to the narrow framework of telecommunications. House and Senate committees have been reluctant to address directly the larger issues of the information society, although they heard considerable testimony on this subject. Telecommunications were regarded as a big enough subject, with enough prickly issues to engage the full attention of the committees. Despite these limitations, the committee hearings have performed the singular service of putting national communications issues on the public agenda and providing a unique forum for airing them.[15]

In the absence of definitive legislation, the courts have played a significant role in defining legal aspects of the new communications and information environment and expanding First Amendment interpretations of privacy and other civil rights implications of the new technologies. The Supreme Court's ruling on the Nixon Watergate tapes in 1974 was the most publicized example of this. Other cases have dealt with data protection, wiretapping, and the limits of electronic surveillance. Outstanding instances of the influence of the Courts on telecommunications policy are the AT&T anti-trust suit of the seventies and the complex legal decisions involved in the 1982 divestiture agreement.

Any review of communications policy has to take into consideration the parts played by states and localities. States have had a regulatory role in telecommunications through public utility commissions for many years. Many states and cities are now beginning to see telecommunications and information issues in the wider context of their relationships to such local services as education, law enforcement, library systems, and the like. A number of them have organized special units for this purpose: Virginia has had an integrated telecommunications planning unit for public service purposes since the early seventies. Many large cities are following suit: Los Angeles, Portland (Oregon), Boston, and New York City all have commissioned studies on the role of local public telecommunications in recent years.

In summary, policy questions dealing with the new information environment are moving into the public agenda in a variety of ways and at different political levels. The effort is fragmented, discursive, and complex, reflecting the division of power in a sensitive area of national policy. Meanwhile, the communications and information structure is expanding rapidly, largely as a result of incremental decisions and actions based primarily on their immediate utility to commercial interests. The argument favoring a continuation of this approach is that, by and large, it works. The question is whether this time-tested process can continue to cope with the communications and information requirements of a more complex post-industrial environment. The present lack of answers to this question suggests the need for a more accurate guide to where we are going and what policy options and actions are available in developing a workable strategy in this area.

This strategy must deal with the relationship among public needs, available technology, and economic resources. In part, this involves a more precise allocation of responsibilities between the private and public sectors. In the public sector, more definitive guidelines are needed for meeting overall national requirements in the new environment. In the private sector, industry requires reasonable conditions for meeting communications needs in a period of growing demands for increasingly diverse services.

The allocation of tasks between the public and private sectors is clearly a difficult, sensitive job. Kurt Borchardt has suggested a private/public coordination model based on the Atomic Industrial Forum, which is essentially a systems approach for joint government/industry study and evaluation of the allocations of tasks.[16] There is good reason to question whether this solution would work in the communications sector. It tends to assume that the problem is between bureaucratic policymakers and the industry. There has been relatively little citizen input into the decision making of the Atomic Industrial Forum. This might have been explained — unsatisfactorily, in the view of many — by the esoteric technical nature of nuclear problems. However, a case can be made that more citizen input earlier on in the process might have prevented or modified some of the faulty assumptions made by nuclear planners over the years.

Communications and information policy, by its very nature, requires broad public input. It is a subject that touches everyone at every level. A weakness of our current approach to the new information environment is that decisions are being made, and options closed, every day that should be open to public scrutiny. Despite the advances in consumer rights practices in recent years, decisions on the consumption of communications and information still tend to be the exclusive province of the bureaucracies — public and private — involved. At a time when we need to take actions to strengthen communications and information patterns in this country through the end of the century, an important element in the decision process is often missing — the views of individual consumers.

A good example of the stakes involved is the future of the postal system. This lumbering giant is currently wandering in the limbo between a respectable past and a highly uncertain future. By any slide rule calculation, there is no question about its future: a drastic cutback in its present mode of operations, including daily mail delivery. The old Norman Rockwell image of the friendly postman, slogging his way through snow, sleet, and rain to deliver Valentine messages will fade into folklore. The reason is that 80% of all first class mail deliveries is routine business correspondence, mostly bills being delivered or being paid, which could be handled electronically through the telephone system or cable networks at considerably lower cost, according to most experts.

The trouble with this alternative, as we mentioned before, is that the postal system is not just a business, it is a social institution whose value is not totally measurable in terms of profit and loss. The shift to electronic mail delivery already underway may be both logical and acceptable, but the public deserves to have considerably more involvement in the decision-making process than it has had to date. The alternatives need to be presented clearly, including the crucial question of who should pay for maintaining traditional mail services.

The future of the postal system is, however, only a part of the problem of organizing public and private resources for the new information age. Until very recently, the subject was relegated to seminar discussions in a few universities and research institutes. This is changing as more individuals and groups see how their interests are tied to a resolution of the larger public issues involved. For the present, it is largely a sensitizing process, a slow realization that a radically different information environment is taking shape in ways that call for review, and redefinition, of long-standing national goals and purposes.

The need for a broad-based policy debate goes beyond particularistic decisions about computer access, cable television, broadcasting satellites, or the many other issues that have to be resolved. The essential issue is preserving and expanding the sum of two centuries of freedom in increasingly complex circumstances.

In 1787, Thomas Jefferson summed up the case for an open information society in a letter to Edward Carrington during the debates leading up to the adoption of the Constitution:

> The basis of our government being the opinion of the people, the very first object should be to keep that right; and were it left to me to decide whether we should have a government without newspapers, or newspapers without a government, I should not hesitate a moment to prefer the latter.

If Jefferson were debating the principles of a new Constitution today, it is probable that he would have expanded his views on the importance of a free press to include the electronic media and perhaps even open-access computer networks. The principle is the same, whether the technologies involved are eighteenth century flat-bed presses or modern computers that can print out thousands of words a second.

How do we organize ourselves to match Jeffersonian ideals with the opportunities opened by modern communications and information technologies? Given the complexity and sensitivity of the subject, the answer does not lie in any master plan but in a range of general approaches, each of which advances the prospect for making adjustments to the new information environment within a democratic framework. The factor they have in common is the need to establish a workable balance between public and private sector responsibilities.

The facile approach is simply to do more of what we have been doing. This assumes that the public sector will neither take the lead in setting comprehensive national goals nor play an activist role in assuring the orderly expansion of communications and information resources over and above its traditional responsibilities for formal education, library services, and the like. The federal government would continue to act as a regulatory balance, brokering between the major economic interests involved and buffering the present communications structure against the instabilities of too rapid change. Given the hundreds of billions of dollars invested in the present structure and the need to amortize these costs over a long period of time this approach is clearly favored by most of the present managers of the system, as well as by that large segment of the public bureaucracy that has a stake in preserving the status quo. The public argument for continuing the present system is a compelling one, namely, that the system works. A second argument is also compelling, that it would be politically impossible to make any major adjustments in the system, no matter what the theoretical benefits might be, given the political and economic power of its present managers.

Despite the realism of these arguments, they are less and less convincing. There are weaknesses in our present approach, particularly in its heavy reliance on economic cost-benefit standards in determining both the form and pace of communications and information development. We are inclined to be impressed by the very real achievements and to miss the gaps. The assumption is that the gaps will be filled in by a trickle-down process. The question, from a social viewpoint, is whether we can continue to rely on this haphazard approach, given the pressure to bring formerly disadvantaged groups fully into the system.

The second, and more radical, approach is to make the public sector a more active participant in developing and managing an expanded communications and information network. The few proponents of this idea argue that only direct public intervention can create an integrated, full-service network, operated as a publicly owned utility. This would be a major reversal in our national style. The fact that other industrial democracies — those of the Japanese and the British, for instance — have thrived with considerable government involvement at this level would have little weight. There are, in fact, interesting examples closer to home of the workability of publicly managed communications utilities. These involve a handful of cities which in recent years have decided to develop their own coaxial-cable utility networks, providing a mix of commercial and public services to homes. Despite the determined opposition of the cable television industry to public ownership, these systems have been well managed and have generally been much more responsive to public service needs than most of their commercial counterparts.[17]

The problem with this alternative is that it is politically impractical. Comparisons with the experiences of the British or Japanese are irrelevant in considerations of the day-to-day performance of a preponderantly commercial system. Justified or not, the idea raises the specter of domination by government in an area where it has up to now largely been excluded, both by law and custom.

There is a third approach, one that tends to get lost in conflicting rhetoric about the virtues of private enterprise against the evils of socialistic centralized government. It is based on establishing, as public policy, a firm commitment to the evolution of a full-service national information grid, augmenting the present fragmentary system in stages. This would require a more clearly articulated division of responsibilities between the public and private sectors. The basic construction and management of the completed system would be the responsibility of the private sector, which would develop the grid in as many competitive modes as technology and economic considerations would justify. Its performance would be judged by agreed-upon social goals which would be reviewed to reflect the changing communications and information needs of the post-industrial age.

The public sector's role would be limited largely to providing, where necessary, fiscal and other incentives for encouraging the application of innovative technology. The case for such an approach was made several years ago by Dr. Simon Ramo, then Vice-Chairman of TRW Inc., the electronics firm:

> The modifications of the structure of business and the pattern of all other activities needed to exploit the new information technology will involve massive start-up costs.... Despite the potential of economic and social gain inherent in the productivity increase and greater flexibility the technology will provide, the speed with which this kind of technology can come into being is greatly contingent on a new organizational teaming of corporations and government. The government may need to sponsor large-scale experiments to develop the basic ideas, perhaps seeking improved information flow in government operations as the first proving ground, and be willing to allow, even encourage, the setting up of private industry teams to share risk.[18]

Another expanded public sector role would be to assure the availability to individuals and groups of essential communications and information services that might be uneconomic and require public subsidizing. The experience of the Rural Electrification Administration in bringing power and telephone service to the countryside is a classic case in point. A critical element in this process would be cutting back government regulatory restraints whose effect, if not intent, is to inhibit the efficient development of a full-service national information utility. It would foster competitive conditions that would stimulate innovation, flexibility, and responsiveness to overall consumer needs. As John Eger, a communications attorney, has noted, "A regulatory commission can do a pretty fair job of curtailing undue monopoly profits, but it cannot issue an enforceable decree mandating alertness to changing market requirements."[19]

The present regulatory system is based largely on three assumptions, one of them valid and two of them increasingly less so. The valid assumption is that there is a need for public regulation and monitoring of technical standards so that the total system is technologically sound. The second assumption, which has eroded over the years, is that regulation is necessary for the orderly economic development of the system. Originally justified largely by the need to amortize the high capital investment needed for communications, regulation became increasingly an excuse for protecting old technologies from new ones. If any lesson in communications regulations has been learned in the past decade, it is that the admirable, if somewhat tentative, FCC decisions allowing more competition in the industry have brought new vitality to the industry, not caused its predicted collapse.

The third assumption, which also is losing some of its validity, is that there is need for public controls over the radio spectrum, a valuable but limited resource. For a long time, government's role in mediating industry demands on spectrum resources was essential, given the steady expansion of spectrum use. The difference now is that the scarcity argument is increasingly less convincing, because of technical advances in efficient use of the spectrum and also because of the increased availability of cost-effective, high-capacity systems such as cable and fiber optic circuits that can conserve radio frequencies. Spectrum scarcity has become a considerably less important barrier to the play of market forces in determining which technology, and which segments of the private sector, can supply the most efficient services in developing a full-scale information grid.

In short, many of the old reasons for government regulation of the communications system are disappearing. Given the economic and political stakes involved, the regulatory structure cannot be phased out immediately. But there is no reason why a national commitment, based on a new pattern of public- and private-sector cooperation, could not be made now to carry us through the transitional phase to a full-service information grid providing low-cost, high-capacity services to every sector of American society.

Conditioned by the onward-and-upward rhetoric of the American electronic mythos, we can easily miss the full significance of this commitment. Certainly the most important outcome can be the fulfillment of First Amendment purposes — the right (*and* the capability) to hear and be heard, to see and be seen, to write and be written about, with due allowance for libel and privacy restrictions. For all our gains, we are still well short of this goal. The late critic of the American press, A. J. Liebling, once noted that there is freedom of the press for anyone with $5 million to buy his own newspaper. (The price is considerably higher these days.) Marshall McLuhan has correctly identified the most revolutionary characteristic of the Xerox and other low-cost copying machines: they make everyone his own publisher, if only on a limited basis. The ubiquitous new electronic circuits can expand our information rights in ways we find difficult to imagine, hemmed in as we are by the present limited range of available communications channels and information sources.

The new circuit-rich environment can be dramatically different. Much of our communication will continue to be private and personal, as in the telephone call and its extension to videophone or data communications, either as two-way or as round-robin conference calls among friends and associates. The major changes, however, will come in the way that wider information services are transmitted and received. This new phenomenon might be called "open electronics publishing." It is the logical outcome of the technological prospects opened up by the new high-capacity communications networks and by computers. With the evolution toward channel abundance, supplying a wider range of visual, audio, or print information, competitive electronics publishing will allow any individual or group to offer messages on the new universal information grid. The grid would be a vastly expanded common carrier open to all, no longer restrained by radio spectrum restraints or other circuit limitations.

This approach would represent a giant step toward the realization of Justice Oliver Wendell Holmes's marketplace of ideas. It would be an *open* market, with high-capacity channels available to all comers, big and small, seeking out consumers willing to pay for access to whatever information or services they want for themselves or what they determine, as a social good, should be made available as a general service subsidized by public revenues.

Electronic publishing would be a competitive enterprise on both a large and small scale. Information producers and consumers would be linked in a network operated as an information utility by commercial common carriers. No general laws would be required other than those already governing publishing such as copyright and libel. Public intervention would be limited to circuit rate regulation and to the setting of technical standards for the utility. Meanwhile, much of the present regulatory structure dealing with telecommunications could be dismantled so as to eliminate most of the present restrictions on information access.[20]

There are many reasons — political, economic, and social — why electronic publishing of the type described above is not an immediate prospect. However, there is no reason the concept of an open market in electronic publishing should not be set as a desirable national goal for implementation by the end of the century. The opening up of the information marketplace is beginning to happen already, with the growth of cable television and independent satellite networks and the beginnings of consumer computer grids. The old-line controllers of limited access, centralized news, entertainment, and other information resources are being challenged and this is all for the better. Their instinctive reaction is to seek government protection for their privileged position, drawing on a wide range of self-serving arguments. Media critic Edwin Diamond has neatly summed up some of the more prevalent myths supporting continued government regulation:

The myth of spectrum scarcity. Since the wavelengths are limited, government has to ration their use to ensure that everyone is heard. Cable television will spell the end of that notion, though it hasn't held up very well in recent years in any case. Newspapers also have limited resources — newsprint, delivery trucks, distribution points — but the private market is allowed to operate without Government control.

The myth that, without government, only the monied interest would be heard. Who's kidding whom? With government now, the richest people in town — the bankers, insurance-company owners, real-estate operators, what Kansas editor William Allen White called the "country-club set" — own both newspapers and broadcast stations (if the even wealthier chains haven't yet taken over).

> *The myth that government rules ensure diversity of ideas, the airing of controversy, and the chance for "both sides" to be heard on television.* In practice, many broadcasters worry about broadcasting *anything* that might interfere with the nice sounds of their ringing cash registers. They don't like controversy because it gets in the way of profits. Also, where is it written that all issues have two sides, and two sides only? There may be more than two sides, or there may be only one.[21]

Although he does not use the phrase, Diamond is defending the concept of "open electronic publishing." His target is the television pattern in this country, our most visible centralized, limited-ownership information arrangement. It is the medium that could be most radically altered in an open electronic publishing environment. In fact, television's period of automatic onward-and-upward influence is already ending, after a profitable 30 year run (1949–1979). The reason is that a new pattern of competitive services — new forms of electronic publishing — are cutting into the television networks' hitherto unchallenged ability to attract huge audiences. Increasingly, the audience is looking at and listening to a new range of attractive alternatives, such as feature films and information services on cable systems and specialized over-the-air television networks. No one of these new electronic publishers is yet a strong challenger to the three big networks. Collectively, however, they are eroding the network audience base, and every indication is that the trend will accelerate in the coming years.

There is enough residual snobbism about television among intellectuals, pseudo and otherwise, to encourage and expand on all reports, however premature, about network television's demise. Their enthusiasm may be somewhat misplaced. Media critic, Douglass Cater, has noted that, for all its faults, network television and its large audiences have been an important element in maintaining social stability during a particularly rocky passage in the American experience:

> Is the fractionalization of audiences a net social gain? . . . What happens when each minority group can tune in to its own prophets? When there are no more Walter Cronkites each evening to reassure us that despite all its afflictions the nation still stands?[22]

The real problem may be that television, because of its pervasive influence, has been overburdened by too many expectations. Its natural bent is as a news and entertainment medium, yet it has been charged, under the dubious rubric of balanced programming, with being the electronic surrogate for school, church, town meeting, and other specialized institutions. Television cannot, in fact, serve as the equivalent of these institutions, and it would be wise for us to curtail these unrealizable expectations. By sharing its functions more widely with other electronic publishing channels, network television could be freed up very effectively (and very profitably) to carry out its more natural news and entertainment functions, instead of trying to be the electronic Elmer's Glue binding all our interests.

However, the argument for a new pattern of electronic publishing goes well beyond television and other mass media. Its greatest impact will be in the consumerization of electronic networks, providing a full range of text, voice, and visual information services for the general public. Because of costs and technical limitations, such networking has been the province of big business and big government up until recently. A current trend, however, is toward the steady expansion of information networking for smaller organizations and individuals. Two important components of the grid — telephones and television sets — are already in place in over 90% of United States home, as well as in schools and other institutions.

High-capacity coaxial-cable lines are already installed in over 40 million homes and this number will rise to over 50 million by 1990. Until a few years ago, there seem to have been few prospects that another vital element — a low-cost electronic information terminal — would be soon available. However, microprocessor technology makes this possible, either as "black box" attachments to television sets or as separate home terminals connected to telephone and cable lines.

This leaves one significant missing link in the universal grid. It is the consumer-oriented data bases and other services whose product will be useful to the mass audience needed to support a universal grid providing text, voice, and visual services. The grid's full development may hinge on the resolution of a difficult public policy question. A significant group of consumers is clearly identified as a market for any specialized educational and information services. They are the natural information seekers, who are the basic marketing target for commercial electronic information services directed to their homes or workplaces. However, it is a very selective market, one that probably cannot sustain a universal grid. A full network will probably not evolve until there is a clearer definition of responsibilities for educational and information services between the private and public sectors. As long as the grid is limited to commercially saleable information, it will have a limited reach. Its full use may depend on public decisions to develop (or, in some cases, expand) public electronic information services, either as direct government services or through subsidies.

Though limited, experience with such public services on cable systems to date has underlined the difficulties involved. Cable system operators and other potential information network entrepreneurs are no more or less altruistic than the rest of us. They are developing the basic circuitry, and the data bases to serve commercially viable markets. Their circuits will be the infrastructures of what can become a universal electronic publishing network in the coming years. The services provided by the network will depend on economics, and the providing of a *full* range of services will depend on social decisions determining that they are a civic necessity. In the seventies, Edwin Parker and Donald Dunn of Stanford University's Communications Research Institute suggested that the public sector sponsor pilot projects within an overall plan for the long-term development of a national information utility:

> Since most of the funds for this utility will come from the private sector, the principal needs for Federal action are in the areas of coordination, policy analysis and assessment, and the funding of pilot projects and demonstrations designed to stimulate the development of new public-sector education and information services.[23]

Such a proposal is part of a long-standing tradition of public involvement in information resources. The public library system is, of course, the most familiar example. Public organizations are the largest single source of both specialized and general information materials in the country, ranging from the products of the Government Printing Office to the Medlars medical data bank and the National Technical Information Service.

There have been some federally sponsored experiments for public information services on cable systems, along the lines suggested above by Professors Parker and Dunn. Most of these have been funded by the National Science Foundation. One of the most successful was an interactive cable television information service for the elderly in Reading, Pennsylvania, which demonstrated the social, and emotional, importance of direct access to information for older people, and particularly for those who were homebound. Simple information on Social Security and Medicaid procedures proved to be a critically important part of the services provided. In general, however, government efforts to provide electronic data services have been limited to science and technology subjects, supporting business and professional needs. Such services are, of course, necessary, but they are far removed from ordinary consumer needs.

Efforts to provide consumer services (as in the Reading senior citizen project) are still fragmentary, cautious, and lacking in overall purpose. A good part of the problem is economics: data banks and networking are very expensive operations. A mixed public/commercial coaxial-cable system proposed for the District of Columbia by the Mitre Corporation some years ago put the commercial break-even point for the system at 50% of total customers, and the public service break-even point at closer to 100%.

This gap is indicative of the economic realities behind the rhetoric that has clogged so many discussions about the new information channels. So-called "free" public services have to be paid for by taxpayers, or through some fee system. Experience with such services on cable systems in the early eighties has been too limited to provide any firm projections of the exact pattern for future services. However, there are indications that they will be tested extensively in the next few years. This will result from the trend requiring that new urban cable systems make specific provision for such services. Systems like Qube in Columbus, Ohio, which provide special information services, are expanding rapidly, particularly in urban areas.

Some of these systems have as many as 100 channels. Whether such an abundance of channels will result in a comparable abundance of information and other services, commercial or public, remains to be seen.

The issue deserves considerably more attention than it is now getting. High-capacity communications circuits and data banks are being built largely under commercial auspices. They are efficient, well-managed, and aimed primarily at individuals and organizations who can pay for them. These individuals and groups are the professionals, the information seekers. However, this pattern of development ignores the very large group of people who have neither the money nor the opportunities for access to the new resources. As a result, the gap between the information-rich and the information-poor is likely to widen rather than narrow with the introduction of the new information technologies. The question cannot be begged by suggesting that most people don't need, and don't want, access to sophisticated information resources. This reasoning is demeaning, and not particularly true in an increasingly complex society in which the range of information needed for survival is widening.

Post-industrial America cannot thrive in an environment in which there is a new kind of literacy gap based on unequal access to the resources of the new communications and information technologies. Individuals are not all equal as information seekers, but they all seek information for a variety of reasons. We need to know more about these reasons, the kinds of information services people want, and how the new technologies can be adapted to these needs. The information machines, with their flashing lights and mysterious insides, can be intimidating to many people. These paraphernalia of the new information environment should be developed in ways that make them readily accessible, inexpensive to use, and programmed to provide information people need. This will call for a different kind of public sector involvement in assuring access to the new machines. One researcher has suggested that Xerox-type copying machines be subsidized in ghetto areas, where they are generally not now available, as part of an overall information access program.[24] Whether or not this proposal makes social or economic sense is secondary to the fact that it raises a problem — information access inequality — that has not yet been fully faced in considerations of the role of the new high-capacity circuits and machines.

In the absence of a national consensus on the goals of the new information age, economics and technology are now shaping the future. They are the major forces propelling us into the new age. Experience with earlier, less complex technological advances has shown, however, that at least some of the unexpected, unwanted results could have been modified, and perhaps turned around, by some intelligent prior planning. As *Fortune* editor Max Ways points out:

> The range of possible consequences presented by the new information technologies is so varied and subtle that no society would be expected to

have ready-made solutions to the main problems presented. But as the employment of these technologies continues to spread rapidly, it will be disgraceful if policy questions generated by them are not soon identified, discussed and dealt with.[25]

There are sensitive politial, economic, legal, and social issues involved in any attempt to develop a viable national approach to information and communications resources. The participants in the debate tend to polarize their positions. On the one hand there are the enthusiasts who exaggerate the influence of the new information machines as solutions, rather than mere necessary supporting resources, for complex problems. At the other extreme are the skeptics who fear, with some justification, that more active public sector intervention is this area could lead to undersirable government controls and erosion of constitutional freedom.

The answer lies, as usual, somewhere in between. The critical issue is whether everyone in this society — both chief and Indian, the powerful and the powerless — has equal rights to the basic information he or she needs to survive and thrive. No society has even come near this goal. The United States has come the closest, and our national experience has shown us that expanding the information base, plugging everyone in, is the best policy. Moving more rapidly toward this ideal is our biggest challenge in the new information environment.

NOTES

1. For a useful overview of interrelated communications and information policy issues, see Glen O. Robinson, ed., *Communications for Tomorrow* (New York: Praeger Publishers, 1978).

2. Harold Black and Edward Shaw, "Detroit's Data Banks," *Datamation*, March 1967, p. 27.

3. Karl W. Deutsch, *The Nerves of Government* (New York: The Free Press of Glencoe, 1963).

4. John DeButts, "Policy, Not Technology, Will Shape the Future of Communications in the U.S.A.," *Communications News*, June 1975, p. 47.

5. Erik Barnouw, *Tube of Plenty* (New York: Oxford University Press, 1975), p. 39.

6. The dispute surrounding the formation of the Communications Satellite Corporation is described in Wilson Dizard, *Television — A World View* (Syracuse, N.Y.: Syracuse University Press, 1966), pp. 263–267, and in Brenda Maddox, *Beyond Babel: New Directions in Communications* (Boston: Beacon Press, 1974), pp. 82–90.

7. U.S. Executive Office of the President, *Final Report of the President's Task Force on Communications Policy*, (Washington, D.C.: U.S. Government Printing Office, 1968).

8. Anne W. Branscomb, "Communications Policy in the United States," in Patricia Edgar and Sayeed Rahim, eds., *Communications Policy in Developed Countries* (Honolulu: East-West Center, 1981).

9. U.S. Executive Office of the President, *The Radio Frequency Spectrum: United States' Use and Management* Office of Telecommunications Policy (Washington, D.C.: Government Printing Office, 1975), p. D–18.

10. Testimony of Harold Brown in U.S. Congress, Senate, Communications Subcommittee of the Committee on Commerce, *Space Communications and Allocation of the Radio Spectrum*, 87th Cong., 1st sess., p. 17. A critical description of the evolution of the National Communications System can be found in Herbert Schiller, *Mass Communications and American Empire* (Boston: Beacon Press, 1971), pp. 63–78.

11. "U.S. Scuttles Plan for IRS Computer," *New York Times*, 7 January 1978, p. 1.

12. "AT&T Continues to Head Companies on Federal Advisory Boards," *Defense Space Daily* (Washington), 28 October 1977, p. 3. Also "Advisers Are Fewer but Expenses Mount," *Washington Post*, 26 March 1978, p. 52.

13. U.S. National Commission on Libraries and Information, *National Information Policy*. Report to the President submitted by the staff of the Domestic Council Committee on the Right of Privacy (Washington, D.C.: Government Printing Office, 1976), p. vi.

14. U.S., Congress, House Subcommittee on Communications, Committee on Interstate and Foreign Commerce, *Options Papers*, 95th Cong., 1st sess., committee print 95–13, May, 1971.

15. For a useful summary of the checkered history of rewrite legislation, see Manny Lucoff, "The Rise and Fall of the Third Rewrite," *Journal of Communication*, 30, no. 3, (Summer 1980): pp. 47–53.

16. Kurt Borchardt, *Structure and Performance of the U.S. Communications Industry*. Division of Research, Graduate School of Business Administration, Harvard University, 1970, pp. 152–56.

17. St. Paul, Minnesota, and Patterson, New Jersey, are cities that have adopted this option. Municipal ownership of cable systems is, of course, strenuously opposed by the commercial cable television industry.

18. Simon Ramo, "Technology and Resources for Business," *Horizon*, U.S. Information Agency publication no. 4, (Washington, D.C.: 1975), p. 32.

19. Quoted in John F. Judge, "The Complexities of Seeking a Policy," *Government Executive* (Washington), June 1976, p. 44.

20. A strong case for electronic publishing is given in Peter Jay, "The Future of Broadcasting," *Encounter* (London), April 1977, pp. 68–79.

21. Edwin Diamond, "Media Myths That Limit Free Speech," *TV Guide*, 5 November 1977, p. 44.

22. Douglass Cater, "A Communications Revolution?" *Wall Street Journal*, 6 August 1973, p. 18.

23. Edwin B. Parker and Donald Dunn, "Information Technology: Its Social Potential," *Science*, 30 June 1972, p. 1399.

24. The suggestion is made in Susan Krieger, "Prospects for Communications Policy," *Policy Sciences* (Amsterdam), no. 2 (1971): p. 312.

25. The Conference Board, *Information Technology: Some Critical Implications for Decision Makers*, report no. 537 (New York: The Conference Board, 1972), p. 6.

CHAPTER EIGHT

EXPORTING THE INFORMATION SOCIETY

FIRE FIGHTERS IN Sweden have an ingenious system for assuring efficient responses to fire alarms. A computer data bank keeps records on each building — its construction features, number of occupants, and any special characteristics (combustible chemicals, for instance) that might be important if a fire breaks out. The data bank also records the quickest route from the nearest fire station. When a building catches fire, this information is instantly retrieved on a computer terminal at the station.

The Swedish fire data bank is an imaginative application of computer power. But the project is interesting in another way: the computer containing the data was originally located in Cleveland, Ohio. The 8000 mile electronic round trip involved in the transmittal of information to and from the Cleveland computer was not a deterrent in awarding the data bank contract to an American bidder, the General Electric Company. The information could be retrieved as quickly as if its source were in Stockholm or another Swedish city. Similar computer data banks are being developed for American fire departments.

The Cleveland computer's role in Swedish fires is only one example of a new phenomenon — the internationalization of communications and information. It was also an example of the problems of electronic internationalism. Despite the fact that the Cleveland fire data base worked efficiently, there were complaints in Sweden about having information regarding Swedish buildings stored in a foreign computer. As a result, the arrangement with General Electric was ended.

When airline clerks make reservations for passengers in Warsaw or Tokyo, they are probably unaware that they are connected to a computer in Atlanta, where a large share of international flight reservations are stored. Nutrition researchers in Rome, searching for technical data in the new European regional computer network ("Euronet") may not know that they are dealing with a data base in Amsterdam. These networks are, in a very real sense, indifferent to time, place, and distance. They have, as anthropologist Edward Carpenter has remarked, made free spirits of us all, not in a Sunday school sense of having wings or being good, but in the sense of being pure spirit, divorced from flesh, capable of instant transportation anywhere.

Free spirits aside, international computer networks are part of a pattern of dramatic changes in global communications and information resources in recent years. To a considerable extent, this pattern was developed first in this country; most of the rest of the world is only beginning to catch up with us. Over and above the effect this pattern will eventually have on our own information environment, the change represents a strategic new element in the American global equation. The United States needs a strong world communications network to support its overseas interests. Economically, the export of communications goods and services is increasingly important. Politically, communications are the nervous system for the interdependent world order to which this country is committed, and particularly important to this world order are improved links between the industrialized and developing nations.

The expanded world communications network will amplify American ideas and values in a more forceful way than has ever been done before. As in the past, these ideas will evoke reactions ranging from admiration to anger — often at the same time. "What makes America unique in our time is that confrontation with the new is part of the daily American experience," Zbigniew Brzezinski noted. "For better or for worse, the rest of the world learns what is in store for it by observing what happens in the United States."[1] University of California communications researcher Herbert Schiller, a critic of American communications practices abroad, makes the point that the United States does not simply export products and services in this field. It exports a *system*, including a heavy ideological bent favoring American values and attitudes which, in Schiller's view, are not in the best interests of other cultures, particularly those in the developing nations. The evidence Schiller cites to support his observation may be debatable, but his basic thesis has merit.[2]

In assessing the American role, three major trends should be considered. The first of these is the pell-mell growth in world communications and information resources, particularly in the last 2 decades. Accurate statistics are often hard to come by, but taking one measure — volume of global communications traffic — it becomes obvious that growth is occurring at a rate of between 10 and 15% annually, roughly doubling every half-dozen years. Whatever measures are used, communications and information emerge as major growth sectors that have been uniquely immune from the economic turbulence affecting other industries in recent years.

The second trend influencing American interests are the changes taking place in the geographic pattern of global communications. 20 years ago, this was a neat, orderly business, confined largely to the North Atlantic area and a Japanese extension. By present standards, volume was low, consisting primarily of business traffic passing through government owned or controlled networks. Again, the exception to government control was the United States, whose overseas communication circuits were (and still are) owned by several firms operating under light federal regulation. Nevertheless, the American firms worked efficiently with their foreign government counterparts in what was essentially a gentlemanly division of the world market, dominated by American interests.

Today economics, politics, and technology are pulling these patterns into different shapes. The market is becoming geographically more diverse every year, thanks in large part to the 110-nation *Intelsat* satellite network, which provides high-grade communications wherever there is an earth terminal. Among other changes, the satellite network has reduced the importance of the "gateway cities" in Europe, the United States, and Japan through which communications traffic to the rest of the world was formerly channeled. Until the advent of the satellite network, for instance, all international traffic between the east and west coasts of South America was routed through gateway cities in the United States. Similar changes in Asia and Africa have given Third World countries direct communications with each other for the first time, thus lessening their dependence on the industrialized nations. Another satellite development which promises to change old patterns is the regional satellite networks that will operate outside the *Intelsat* framework. The Europeans are building several such networks now. The Arab states have built a regional system and there are proposals for similar networks in Africa, Latin America, and Asia.

The third significant trend in international communications is the threat of political restrictions on the growth of the world system. The United States has taken the lead since World War II in advocating the elimination of restrictions on communications flow internationally. In the late 1940s, it used its then dominant influence in the United Nations to get international approval for the concept of "free flow of information." Our democratic partners approved, while the poorer areas of Asia and Africa were either still colonial states or regarded the issue as irrelevant. Only the Soviet Union and its client states objected, a predictable reaction given the need for tight internal controls over domestic information channels in order to maintain the communist parties in power. Although American advocacy of open information channels reflected deeply held national convictions, it also provided the ideological underpinnings for the postwar expansion of American information influence throughout the world.[3]

Until recently, this influence was welcomed, or at least accepted as a normal consequence of American power and influence. Now it is being questioned in ways that could affect United States interests in international communications as well as overall prospects for an open world information order. The reasons for this development are complex, but they center around new perceptions abroad of information as a political, economic, and cultural force. Increasingly, information is being viewed as a strategic resource that, like oil or nickel, is a measurable element in calculations of national strength. As a result, it is a newly contested factor in international affairs. As communications consultant, Andrew Aines, has noted:

> The battle is to use modern information technology most advantage-ously. It involves out-and-out espionage, military and industrial. It involves the quest for scientific and technical data of all kinds and for all purposes. It involves the delivery of political information.... It in-volves the United Nations, COMECON (the Soviet economic bloc), the Common Market, military alliances and many other international bodies.[4]

This battle has, in turn, led to a new concept of information sovereign-ty, defined as the right of a society to protect itself against what it regards as unwarranted intrusion by outside information and communications influ-ences. The concept arose originally during the early seventies when Third World countries complained that their information and communications resources were dominated by American and European interests. The charges originally focused on the influence of Western mass media, particularly film, television, and news agency products. In particular, Third World spokes-men argued that the American free-flow concept did not take into account the massive imbalance in information flows between the West and other parts of the globe. They saw the free-flow thesis as a rationalization for what they regarded as cultural and economic imperialism. The debate went beyond rhetorical charges and countercharges. In recent years, Third World countries have taken a series of steps to gain more control over foreign influences in their domestic telecommunications and information affairs.

The information sovereignty question is also being seriously discussed by European nations, although their perspectives and motives are generally different from those of Third World countries. Confident that they can hold their own in this field. Europeans are considerably less worried about American cultural influence. Their concern is to protect themselves against what they regard as inordinate outside (that is, American) control over their information resources, particularly in computerized data banks and circuits. American companies have been particularly successful in marketing goods and services to industrial nations abroad. Some analysts estimate that between 50% and 60% of European *domestic* data records are processed by United States companies.[5]

This worries the Europeans, both in terms of the privacy rights of their citizens and the newly perceived strategic importance of information and communications as a national resource. This has led them, as we shall see later, to consider regulations on controlling international data flow. At another level, the Europeans are particularly concerned about the dominant role of American industry in computer hardware. They have taken steps to strengthen domestic computer production through government subsidies and other programs. Through the European Economic Community (EEC), they are also developing their own regional computer data network, partly in response to American competition. Taken together, these moves reflect a growing feeling that in the future, as an Organization for Economic Cooperation and Development (OECD) report on European industry has stated, "information and knowledge rather than capital and production of manufactured goods will become the central issue around which sharp competition will develop."

These world trends toward protectionism and control of information flow across borders have not yet reached a critical stage. However, they are a potentially serious problem for the United States in advancing its political, economic, and cultural interests favoring an open global information pattern. Not only are other countries taking a closer look at their own national interests in this area, but the subject is being debated here. A 1976 Defense Department study suggested that the United States was too liberal in sharing its science and technology know-how with other countries. The report declared that a significant "leak" in this area was created by the large number of foreign students — most of whom are studying technical subjects — in United States universities. While it is improbable that the United States would ever adopt general policies restricting information exports, over and above longstanding controls on technology flow to Communist countries, there is increasing concern about the rate at which certain technologies are exported, cutting into the competitive edge for American products.

Rapid growth, changing patterns, challenges to American leadership — these are the conditions that will set the agenda for United States strategy in the global information and communications field during the 1980s. American decisions in this area will be an important element in determining the future pace and scope of world communications growth. No other country has the technological and economic strength, or the political will, to assume the lead in this area. The Soviets are ideologically incapable of taking a major role, given their own inhibitions about information and communications matters. The Europeans have not been able to develop a consensus, much less take actions, in this area. The Japanese look upon the issue primarily in terms of trade.

If the United States takes on a greater leadership role, it will first have to address the fact that it does not now have an articulated national policy in this area. Its primary interest in the past two decades has been, with good reason, to provide support for the international expansion of the American communications and information industries. Government policy has essentially reacted to commercial needs. In most cases this has been done successfully and in one instance, it was done brilliantly — in the Communications Satellite Act of 1962, which provided the legislative authorization for America to develop a global satellite system. The legislation was a triumph of pragmatism over a formidable list of reasons why it couldn't be done. However, no effective attempts have been made to develop a comprehensive policy approach in other global communications matters since then. One effort to develop such a policy in the late sixties, by the presidentially appointed Rostow Commission on communications which we discussed earlier, was unsuccessful because some of its recommendations clashed with strong communications industry interests in this country.

As in the domestic policy area, international communications responsibilities are divided among a number of federal agencies. The overall responsibility in the executive branch rests with the State Department. Within the department, however, this authority is fragmented among a number of offices. In February 1978, Secretary of State Cyrus Vance took a first step toward improving the department's handling of communications matters by appointing his deputy, Warren Christopher, coordinator for the subject. Although the Federal Communications Commission's (FCC) primary responsibilities are in the domestic field, it has become increasingly involved in international matters in recent years as a result of the expanded foreign activities of the domestic companies it regulates. This wider involvement led former FCC chairman Richard Wiley to propose that the commission be authorized to negotiate agreements on communications matters directly with foreign governments — a function normally carried out by the State Department. The department did not take kindly to the proposal and the matter was dropped.[6]

A dozen other agencies have fragmentary roles to play in overseas communications matters. The Defense Department, manager of its own large global communications system, carries weight in any discussion of the subject involving its many interests. The Department of Commerce, the Federal Aviation Agency, NASA, and the Central Intelligence Agency contribute their particular interests. The United States Information Agency has a mandate to advise the President and foreign affairs agencies on foreign communications matters. The National Telecommunications and Information Administration (NTIA), created in 1978, also has international responsibilities as part of its charter to coordinate overall government communications policies. Its authority is limited in practice, however, by the resistance of other agencies, notably the Defense and State Departments, to NTIA activities in areas traditionally assigned to these agencies. NTIA also is inhibited by its bureaucratic location at the second level of the Department of Commerce.[7]

The overall fragmentation of United States Government responsibilities was summarized several years ago by Senator Ernest F. Hollings, then chairmen of the Senate Communications Subcommittee: "No single agency of the United States government has comprehensive authority over international communications, nor was the distribution of functions among several agencies the result of planned allocation. Rather, it grew like Topsy, responding to particular technical or industrial problems as they arose."[8] A significant step to correct this situation was taken by the House of Representatives' Subcommittee on Information Policy in a 1980 report suggesting the establishment of a top level office for communications policy in the State Department, and a White House level interagency coordinating mechanism.[9] After much pulling and hauling among agencies attempting to defend their bureaucratic turfs, a permanent office designed to coordinate United States government international policies was set up in 1983 in the State Department. Diana Lady Dougan, a communications executive from Salt Lake City, was appointed first head of the office, with the rank of ambassador.

Meanwhile, the controlling factor in United States overseas communications is that these communications are private sector responsibilities, with government in only a minor supportive role. This is unlike the situation in most other countries, where governments control or tightly regulate all international communications. A significant exception to private sector dominance in this country was made in 1962, in a decision to make the Communications Satellite Corporation (Comsat) a government mandated "chosen instrument" to exploit the then-American monopoly on advanced satellite technology. The Comsat exception was a compromise between competing claims within private industry on how best to manage the satellites commercially.[10]

In the absence of any grand design for public policies, the communications industry is the prime mover of American overseas interests. It is big, wide-ranging, and cockily confident of its capabilities. It has the advantage of operating from a strong domestic base, the biggest market in the world. Almost half of total global communications equipment production is absorbed by the United States market. This ratio has dropped to about 40% by the mid-eighties, still an advantage no foreign competitor will come close to matching. American industry had a running start in the early postwar decades, before competitors in other industrialized countries had geared up. Riding the technological lead provided by their research and development laboratories, United States firms dominated most segments of the overseas communications field until the seventies. Competition is more rigorous these days, and the American lead is narrowing in the three key sectors — equipment production, message distribution, and information products and services. Since United States industry plays such a dominant role in world communications, it is useful to take a look at its place in these three sectors.

Providing reliable overseas communications circuits has been a complex, risky business since the 1850s when Cyrus Fields attempted to lay the first transatlantic cable — a primitive telegraph wire wrapped in gutta-percha. The cable snapped, and Fields and his associates went bankrupt. A later project was successful, providing the first oceanic link in what has become a cat's cradle of international circuits throughout the globe. The first cables were simple wires that were later supplemented by unreliable radio circuits. This changed in the 1950s with the development of high-capacity submarine cables and, in the 1960s, with satellite microwave links. Thus the technical base for a dramatic expansion in global communications was opened.

American firms were in a strong position to exploit this advantage. In the early 1960s, when expansion began in earnest, over half of all international communications originated in this country. Yet, international telephone and telegraph traffic was, and is, only a small part of the American communications pattern. Overseas traffic accounts for only about five percent of total national service in the mid-eighties.[11] These figures do not accurately reflect the quantum jump in American overseas communications in recent years, paced largely by business requirements as American firms expanded abroad. Telephone calls are a good indicator. In 1950, the annual number of overseas calls was one million; by 1975 this had jumped to 75 million, and projections for the mid-eighties are for over a quarter billion calls. The increase in data communications, the fastest growing area of international traffic, is even more impressive, with an annual growth rate of over 10%.

The United States share of the market is split among a half-dozen established firms headed by AT&T. Until recent years, this market was divided between the AT&T monopoly over international voice communications with record (telegraph, telex, data) traffic carried by the other companies. This distinction is breaking down, as will be seen, but it still holds for most overseas traffic. AT&T currently links its circuits to 99.5% of the world's telephones, over half of which can be dialed directly. During the eighties, direct dialing will become nearly universal, with the introduction of a worldwide dialing code developed by the International Telecommunications Union.[12] A world telephone number will have up to fourteen numbers, making it possible to reach any dial phone anywhere. Taken together with rapid telephone growth overseas, the result should be a massive increase in world telephone traffic. AT&T will continue to be the dominant United States connecting link to this market.

Transmission of American telex and other text and data traffic is largely in the hands of three "international record carrier" (IRC) firms — RCA Global Communications, ITT Worldcom, and MCI International. The Communications Satellite Corporation has served primarily as a "carrier's carrier," providing satellite circuits for this traffic. Starting out with traditional telegram traffic, the IRCs branched into the telex business in the postwar years. Following the domestic trend, the telegram share of the business is headed for extinction in the coming years. The telex business is now the biggest part of the market, and it is currently being transformed from the clackety-clack printer terminal into a variety of high speed services. The IRCs are playing a high-stakes game in this field, much of it pointed toward the development of international computer-to-computer links.

A transitional step in this direction was taken by the three big firms in the late seventies when they offered roughly similar high-speed terminal-to-computer data transmission services over leased lines.[13] Computer-based links will be the primary growth area in the coming years. A European study found that data processing services will have four times the traffic volume of any other data services by 1985, with a 28% annual growth rate projected up to that date. A 1980 American survey of world data communications prospects projected a 16% annual growth in the eighties, with estimated total revenues of $14 billion in 1985.[14]

This growth will be paced by technology and by economic pressures for better international communications. It already affects the way in which international carriers do business. The development of high-capacity cables and satellite circuits have effectively broken down the distinction between voice and data services, the line which divided AT&T from the data carriers for decades. A leased line can be used for both services. The data carriers have been in the telephone business *de facto* since 1964 when the FCC gave them access to what is known as the alternate voice/data service, in which a customer can, with appropriate equipment, use the channel for both voice and nonvoice purposes. The service can provide, in effect, a private telephone line, to AT&T's loss but to the profit of the record carriers, which do about a quarter of their international business in leased lines. The technology cuts two ways however. In 1976 AT&T received FCC permission to begin international data service through its Dataphone system, which operates through the company's normal switched service. In 1980, the FCC took further steps to expand competition among the international communications carriers by giving AT&T and another domestic firm, Western Union, wider authorization to operate international services.[15]

More recently, the Commission eliminated most other regulatory controls on competition among international carriers. An interesting side effect of this deregulatory trend is the pressure it puts on public telecommunications authorities in other industrialized countries to take similar steps toward matching the freedom accorded to United States firms to provide innovative services. In common with bureaucracies everywhere, government-controlled telecommunications agencies abroad are reluctant to surrender control over their domains. However, the pressure to do so is there. Prime Minister Margaret Thatcher's pro-business Conservative government took a series of dramatic steps in 1983 and 1984 to privatize the government telecommunications agency, British Telecom, and to permit private carriers to operate in competition with it. In Japan, the Diet (parliament) in 1983 ordered an inquiry into the issues involved in providing more competition for government-operated telecommunications agencies. Other governments, notably the French and German, have been more resistant to suggestions to give up state control over telecommunications. Nevertheless, these pressures will increase in the coming years, both in response to competition from the outside and to domestic demands for better services.[16]

Another significant set of FCC decisions in recent years authorizes domestic specialized data networks such as Telenet and Tymnet to operate internationally, using packet data technology. This will expand public information networks to global proportions in the coming years. The

Telenet network, for instance, includes access to the *New York Times* Information Bank, Lockheed Information Systems, and other publicly available data resources. Customers here and abroad can dial into these services from their own private dials or leased line facilities, or they can go to what Telenet calls "public dial ports" — the computer network equivalent of a public phone booth. Telenet has expanded its public dial ports to 450 cities, with dial port access available in over 33 countries abroad.

The international telephone and data transmission system is clearly in transition from the low-volume elite services of two decades ago to a new kind of mass communications network. The changes have sharpened the competitive edge of the American firms involved, each of them pushing hard for a bigger share of what is, despite all the neat statistical projections, a market whose size and pattern is still unclear. The trends point upwards; the question is how far up? An important part of the answer will depend on the willingness of foreign governments to provide, through the telecommunications structures they control, the facilities the American companies need to extend their new services abroad. During the seventies, government controlled post, telegraph, and telephone agencies (PTT) were reluctant, and sometimes hostile, toward American proposals of new services. Traditionally conservative, many PTT's were generally in no hurry to upset their highly profitable telecommunications services (which normally subsidize postal services).[17] This element was mixed with their governments' information sovereignty fears about the rapid spread of American data processing services in Europe. The result has been to inhibit but by no means to halt the growth of international information networking.

Building a full-scale world information network will require a staggering amount of new machinery, from satellites in space to telephones in African villages. Parts of the network are already in place, but most of it still has to be constructed. One recent estimate puts the construction cost for a minimal world network, with the emphasis on telephone service, at nearly a trillion dollars in the years leading up to the year 2000.[18] In the fast-moving communications and information field, the telecommunications equipment industry will be one of the high-growth sectors. Any growth projections involve educated (and usually conservative) guesses; what is more certain is that the major growth will be abroad in other industrial countries and, increasingly, in the Third World.

Equipment markets were dominated handily by American manufacturers in the early postwar decades. This is no longer true: European and Asian firms are now stiff competitors. The ability of Japan and other Asian countries (Taiwan, Korea, and Singapore, among others) to produce cheaper, quality consumer goods has resulted in a net deficit in the United States communications equipment balance of trade in recent years. The American industry's strength is in high-technology products, but even here the advantages provided by innovative research, quality engineering, and patent protections are shrinking. "The world is regressing to the speedy technological transfer of the 15th century, when patents did not exist," the London *Economist* notes. "Electronics, where patenting is nearest to collapse, is recreating that vanished age. In electronics, the technological lead time is usually only 18 months."[19] The result is, increasingly, a global free-for-all as telecommunications firms (and the many governments that subsidize their efforts) scramble for bigger shares of an expanding market.

The market involves a bewildering variety of products, but most of them are grouped around two familiar items — telephones and computers. A century after Alexander Graham Bell's invention, the rest of the world is moving into the telephone age. The phone has been an elite instrument until now in all but a handful of countries — the United States, Canada, Sweden, and several others. Despite its advanced industrial status, West Germany did not have phone service for 40% of its families in the late seventies. Moving down the economic ladder, telephone services range from the inadequate to the near-hopeless in most Third World countries. What phone services exist are patchwork systems, often in an advanced state of decay.

The rush is on to build new systems as scores of countries, both the haves and the have-nots, realize that a good telephone system is not only a national status symbol but also an economic necessity. They want their new systems quickly, and they often opt for the latest models, which means expensive, computerized, all-electronic exchanges. (In the case of technology-poor countries, this high initial expense can make sense since electronic exchanges, with fewer moving parts, are considerably easier to maintain with a small trained crew.) Building a minimally adequate world telephone system in the next decade — amounting to roughly a billion phones compared to half that number in the mid-eighties — will be one of the biggest telecommunications projects ever undertaken and will cost perhaps $750 billion.

American industry will provide equipment and services for large parts of the new network. The three big equipment firms are Western Electric, General Telephone and Electronics (GTE), and International Telephone and Telegraph (ITT). GTE and ITT are traditional exporters; Western Electric, the manufacturing arm of the Bell System, is reentering the overseas markets it dropped out of in the 1920s. The firm is one of several Bell organizations operating abroad through a new Bell subsidiary, AT&T International. All three equipment companies begin with the advantage of serving a strong United States market. Although this country may seem to have become telephone saturated, with over 95 phones per hundred households, the market continues to absorb more. In a recent year, 6.5 million new phones were installed, more than there are in all of Africa outside of South Africa.

The overseas market is big, and competition from European and Japanese manufacturers is sharp. Working in Third World countries is difficult. Technicians who are used to neatly phased domestic construction programs find themselves enmeshed in management and technical nightmares compounded by strange political, economic, and cultural customs that, in theory, have nothing to do with building a phone system. One experienced United States executive compares the experience to wrestling with a jellyfish.[20]

Although American firms win big contracts (ITT's in oil-rich Nigeria, for instance), they often lose bigger ones. The classic confrontation took place in the late seventies over modernizing the Saudi Arabian system, a project that involved a series of contracts totaling over $4 billion. All of the major American firms were involved in the bidding as were Sweden's L. M. Ericsson, Germany's Siemans, and Japan's Nippon Electric. The struggle was epic in its proportions, involving low intrigue and high diplomacy. The final contracts went to a consortium of Ericsson, Philips of Holland, and Northern Telecom, a Canadian company.[21]

At the beginning of the eighties, there were growing doubts among some U.S. economic experts about whether American firms were being aggressive enough in the competition for the overseas equipment market. Many of them were concentrating their efforts on the domestic market, still the largest in the world though its growth rate is slower than the offshore markets where there is more pent-up demand. In a 1980 survey of American prospects in this area, *Business Week* noted that the American firms' superiority in technology was offset by weaknesses in the marketing of their products abroad.[22] Furthermore, American sales were often hampered by tariff and other measures designed to protect local manufacturers. This led to a special effort by the Reagan Administration, through the White House Office of the Special Trade Representative, to negotiate more favorable conditions for United States electronic exports. The initial target was Japanese restrictions, which had virtually closed off opportunities for many American firms seeking to sell in that lucrative market.

The economic stakes are equally high for American firms in another equipment area — computers. Here the Americans took an early lead and have kept it. Computer power is a new index of national strength. American dominance is, for the present, formidable. The reasons are not hard to find. Much of the technology was developed here followed by a strong investment program during the fifties and sixties. The major companies have large distribution and servicing organizations here and abroad. The domestic market gave them a strong starting point for what has been, almost from the beginning, a major international market. Finally, American computers have, by and large, set the world standard, making foreign competitors follow in their technical footsteps. As a result, in 1976, United States computer equipment firms accounted for 87% of the sale of the world's computers, by value. In the mid-eighties, the American share will drop to less than three fourths of the international market due to increased foreign competition.[23]

This is still a healthy lead — but it is also one that will be increasingly challenged during the eighties. No longer can the United States computer industry automatically count on its technological and merchandising superiority to win international orders. The industry also has to cope with foreign government policies designed to curb dependence on American computer equipment and to build up national capabilities. The result, as with telecommunications equipment, is a complex series of steps, — involving subsidies, mergers, cartels, quotas, and restrictionist devices — aimed at limiting American computer products and services.

"Watching the movements made by companies and governments in the computer industry worldwide is like watching 15 chess matches going on at the same time," says international computer expert Angeline Pantages. "Every match has one thing in common, though. IBM seems to control both queens on every board."[24] If most computers have a "Made in USA" label on them, they usually also have the clinically efficient IBM logo. The company has its share of the world computer market that starts at more than 50% in most major countries; it is almost totally dominant in many smaller markets. Half its sales and half its profits normally come from overseas. With over one hundred thirty thousand employees abroad, 21 plants, and 10 laboratories, it has a worldwide reach and flexibility unmatched by any other firm. For example, a new model, the 3033, was introduced in 1977 with a $3.38 million price tag for the smallest version and simultaneous production at factories in Poughkeepsie, N.Y.; Havant, England; and Yasu, Japan. The project was typical of the kind of global strategy that has given IBM such a strong lead in research, manufacturing, distribution, and servicing of its products.

IBM may be, as Pantages suggests, the queen of the international computer chessboard, but a more fitting analogy may be that of a Gulliver beset by Lilliputians. The Gulliver image applies to both domestic and overseas markets. IBM's traditional strength has been in the big mainframe computers; as noted in the previous chapter, it has now established its credentials in the growing small computer market against a proliferating number of competitors.

IBM faces other similar problems in the future. In Europe and Japan, a combination of government and private strategies have been developed to reduce the company's dominant position. The first moves were made in the sixties in France, prompted by President Charles de Gaulle, who cited both French *gloire* and economic realities as the reasons why IBM's near monopoly of the French market had to be ended. This resulted in a cycle of mergers, licensing deals, and other arrangements, all designed to create a workable domestic alternative to IBM.[25] The results were mixed: IBM's long lead had been cut back, but it still dominates the French market. In 1976, the newly elected President, Giscard d'Estaing, ordered a comprehensive look at the entire French communications and information structure. (His motivation, in part, was to redeem an election promise to improve the French telephone system, whose condition was summed up in the popular complaint, "Half of France is waiting for a telephone; the other half is waiting for a dial tone.") The resultant government study, the 1978 Nora Minc

Report, was a prescription for transforming France into a modern information society.[26] The code word was *télématique*, the integration of communications and information resources into a powerful strategic national utility. The immediate result of the report was a dramatic improvement in the French telephone system. Within five years, subscriber lines were doubled and a host of high-technology innovations were introduced.

However, computers were the main focus of the Nora Report. The future of France as a political and economic power, the report said, rested on decisions in this area. IBM was, predictably, portrayed as the villain, the most formidable factor in American domination of French computer resources and of the data banks on which French industry and research facilities were forced to rely for specialized information. France had to develop its own resources in these areas in order to maintain itself as a healthy society. Although the report concerns technological and economic matters primarily, it includes valuable sections on the cultural implications of the *télématique* society that offer many insights useful for our own American dialogue on the new information environment.

The Nora Report also encouraged a series of French Government initiatives in advanced communications, including increases in subsidies for research and development, and a renewed attempt in 1981 by the new Mitterand government to reduce the large American minority share (held by Honeywell) in the biggest domestic computer company, CII-Honeywell Bull.[27] President Mitterand nationalized the major French electronic firms as part of an effort to develop a strategic base for strengthening national resources in this area. His efforts were hindered by a stubborn recession, labor union opposition and a continuing wary attitude on the part of the *patronat* — French big business — towards government controls. Despite these difficulties, the French are positioning themselves to play a strong role in world telecommunications through aggressive marketing of advanced high-tech products.

In the meantime the European Economic Community was also taking steps to counter the influence of IBM and other American firms in the Common Market, motivated by the fact that the EEC accounts for only 15% of the West's production of computers and 26% of consumption in the early eighties. The negative European trade balance in electronic products went from $200 million in 1970 to $6.5 billion ten years later.[28] At a 1980 summit meeting in Dublin, the EEC determined that its members should aim for a third of world communications and information resources, both in production and consumption by 1990. In 1983, the EEC announced a $1.3 billion program, code-named Esprit, to encourage regional cooperation in advanced computer research.[29]

More recently, both American and European attention has been focused on a new competitive force in the high-technology international markets — the Japanese. A more than symbolic turning point in Japan's role as an information power occurred in 1980, when IBM's leading place in computer sales within the country was overtaken by Fujitsu Ltd. The shift also signaled Japan's entry into world markets, competing against the Americans and Europeans both on their home grounds and in the export trade.[30] The aggressive Japanese push in computers will be an increasingly significant factor in the next few years. The more important Japanese impact may involve the basic microelectronic module, the semiconductor chip, with Japanese firms challenging the hitherto massive United States dominance of the field, both technically and economically. As noted earlier, the Japanese firm, Nippon Electric, began construction on the most advanced semiconductor plant in the United States in late 1981.

The Japanese challenge has its roots in a 1971 Ministry of International Trade and Industry "white paper" on information and communications.[31] The report set goals for the conversion of Japan to an information-based economy, with due attention given to high-technology electronics. Large-scale government assisted research and development during the seventies paid off in a wide range of technologies. When United States manufacturers could not meet the demand for microelectronic chips in the late seventies, Japanese manufacturers jumped in and captured 40% of the United States memory-chip market by the end of 1979.[32] The Japanese also moved actively into Europe, staking a claim to the growing microelectronics market there. In the process, they forced Common Market economic experts to adapt their strategies to a new non-American challenger.

The United States electronics industry has reacted vigorously to the Japanese initiative in the early eighties. Capital spending to expand facilities rose to record levels, as did investments in research and development. Major firms began pooling their research and development efforts, usually under university sponsorship, modifying their previous practice of individual research competition in this area. This shift moves American firms closer to Japanese and European methods of pooling technological resources. The best-known of these efforts is Microelectronics and Computer Research, the joint research entity set up in 1983 by a consortium of leading computer and semiconductor companies. In addition, the University of Minnesota's new Microelectronics and Information Science Center is underwritten by Control Data, Honeywell, Sperry, and other firms; IBM, Xerox, and Burroughs are among the companies jointly underwriting basic microelectronics research at the California Institute of Technology.[33] In the meantime, the industry was considering political action, in the form of advocating protectionist trade legislation. In May 1981, the Japanese took steps to ward off such a move by agreeing to more liberal trade rules.[34]

However, the strongest weapons United States firms have in meeting Japanese and other foreign trade challenges are still aggressive competitive merchandising and a leading edge in technology. Two leading American firms — IBM and Intel — have demonstrated this dramatically by expanding their operations in the Japanese market against formidable local competition.[35]

These developments reflected the high stakes involved in the future of the United States semiconductor industry. Its health, both economically and technologically, will directly affect any American strategy for the information age, since it is essential to a productive electronics industry whose annual output may reach $400 billion by the end of the decade.[36]

Despite challenges from overseas competitors, United States electronics equipment manufacturers will continue to have the lion's share of the world market for some time to come. The pattern will change as more competitors enter the field and as the market itself changes to accommodate the new minicomputer, microcomputer, and microprocessor technologies. Not all the competition will come from Europe and Japan. Many ambitious Third World nations want a computer industry in much the same way that they had originally sought steel mills, airlines, and Hilton hotels.[37] Brazil, in particular, has developed firm national policies for building up a computer industry, including protectionist measures against foreign competitors. Other developing countries have invited Western manufacturers in to develop joint venture projects. In some instances, countries have sought to take over majority control of local foreign plants. Almost all of ITT's Latin American production facilities were nationalized or placed under local majority control during the 1970s. IBM pulled out of India in 1978 after refusing to accept 60% Indian ownership of its local subsidiary, as the country's government had ordered.[38]

Beyond hardware, there is a new and rapidly expanding export market in information services. Selling (or giving away) information is an old American habit. The United States is the largest information market in the world, a condition that has had incalculable consequences for our political structure, economy, and culture. We have not been shy about sharing this resource with others: until recently two thirds of all international communications originated in this country. Three major changes have taken place in this pattern in the past two decades. First, the United States share of this information transfer has decreased as other nations build up their information resources and make them available internationally. Secondly, a larger share of information is moving electronically across borders and increasingly between computers. Finally, the volume of this information is expanding exponentially, probably at an annual rate of 10%.

The net result has been the creation of global information networks of all sizes, patterns, and purposes. One of the largest is the World Meteorological Organization's massive world weather watch, which gathers information from thousands of stations on earth as well as from weather satellites in space, analyzes the results, and retransmits them all over the globe. Another is the United States government's Medlars network, a computerized data base of over four million research reports from 3,000 medical journals and other sources. Medlars is "searched" a million times a year by doctors and hospitals in North America and abroad, either by mail, telex message, or direct on-line access.[39] Another United States government information facility, the National Technical Information Service, makes available reports on all research funded by the government. It is heavily used by foreign governments and institutions for its access to a significant portion of United States technological and scientific research.

These and similar public data banks are made available without cost, or for a relatively small service fee. They are an important part of the new electronic information services. Even greater expansion is taking place in the commercial sector. Information is a highly salable item, and this country has traditionally held the lead in making technological data available for a fee. The United States is responsible for almost half of the global trade in the licensing or sale of technical know-how.[40] This is sold in many different forms, but increasingly it is moving as data between computers.

This has spawned a new sector in the information industry that provides access to specialized data resources stored in computers for a wide variety of customers. These include systems operated by such firms as Lockheed, Control Data, Systems Development Corporation, and General Electric. Most of them provide time sharing arrangements, where the customer pays by usage, although many variations for obtaining their information have been developed. The General Electric network can be accessed from local telephones in over 400 cities in North America, Europe, Japan, and Australia. The network information industry has moved up over the billion dollar sales mark with international sales accounting for about one fifth of the total.

Another category of networking is composed of private corporation circuits, heavily used by the big multinational firms for their internal communications around the globe. The Bank of America's telecommunications network stretches from Hong Kong to Vienna, involving circuits on three separate satellites. The system provides voice, data, telegraph, and interactive computing services in ways that give the bank's central headquarters in San Francisco instantaneous access to its operations on four continents. Citicorp, the largest United States bank, has a computerized global network that links its operations in 95 countries. About 700 of the world's major banks belong to a network known as SWIFT, an acronym for the Society for Worldwide Interbank Financial Telecommunications. SWIFT's global reach allows its subscribers to buy, sell, lend, and borrow throughout the world, getting an acknowledgement back five or six seconds after the transaction is made. The process is a big business version of what will eventually be a consumer-oriented electronic banking system in this country, handling similar transactions for bank customers in their homes. In New York, an electronic clearing house for international payments known as CHIPS processes $150 billion in transactions on a normal business day.

Similar services are available to smaller companies, who can plug their terminals into commercial networks for a fee. The best known of these are Tymnet and GTE's Telenet, both of which provide domestic and international electronic mail and other communications services. The future of this sector of the information services business will be set largely by the relationship between AT&T, IBM's Satellite Business Systems, and the Xerox Corporation, all of which are developing advanced telecommunications networks that may bring information service grids down to the consumer level in this country, eventually to connect with similar networks abroad.

The rapid expansion of information networks has led to the dispersal of international business to locations where there are low taxes, good communications and few restrictions on data transfer. Two such locations, popular with banks, are the Bahamas and the Cayman Islands in the Caribbean. The Bahamas has 263 banks, most of them foreign, with assets (in 1977) of $70 billion; the tiny Caymans have 260 banks with assets of $12 billion. Basically, these islands are offshore tax havens, where, thanks to good communications circuits, business can be transacted as easily as if banks were in a traditional financial capital.[41]

But not all international business can be transacted on lush Caribbean islands, whatever the tax advantages. The bulk of it is still done in the old locations, where stricter regulations apply. Foreign governments are becoming increasingly concerned about the vast amounts of computer-based data information moving in and out of their territories, affecting their economies and often their political interests. The result has been a move, particularly in Europe and Canada, toward regulatory guidelines on transborder data flows. The Canadians are concerned that too much information about their economy, and their citizens' private lives, is stored in computers in the United States. In Europe, 16 countries have developed legislation imposing specific restrictions on the electronic transfer of personal information about their citizens to other countries. The first country to approve such restrictions, Sweden, has a national data control board that must approve all such transfers. On a regional basis, the Organization for Economic Cooperation and Development (OECD) has drafted guidelines for assuring the compatibility of such privacy legislation, and is also studying more general questions of the economic impact of international data flows. The United States has been publicly sympathetic to concerns about privacy of information — which it also protects through its own legislation — but is also worried that the expansion of restrictions on transborder data flow may affect American economic interests.[42]

The most controversial area of United States information sales abroad involves the mass media — film, television, publications, and news agencies. Here the American information age is made visible to literally billions of people abroad in ways that are brash, colorful, and immensely popular. It will be generations before the impact of contemporary United States mass culture on the rest of the world can be measured. Will it be judged as the raucous noise of a flash-in-the-pan society, as critics claim, or will it be seen as the transmitter of ideas and values that created a new democratic world order? For the present judgments are mixed, but there is little dispute about the ubiquitous influence of American mass culture abroad.

In the last century, an English cleric, Sydney Smith, asked, "In the four quarters of the globe, who reads an American book? Or goes to an American play? Or looks at an American picture or statue?" It is a different story now, when American influences have been instrumental in establishing the first world cultural style. There are many sources of this impact, but a large share of it comes from the Hollywood film industry. In the 1920s, the industry produced and distributed most of the world's films, establishing the medium's artistic, technical, and economic standards.[43] This production dominance was cut back in later years as film industries developed abroad, but Hollywood continued to set the pace. It was an envious Stalin who once told a visitor, "If I could control the American film industry, I could control the world." However, entertainment rather than ideological enlightenment was what drew huge audiences to Hollywood films. Even now, when American production is down to 10% of the world total, Hollywood films — particularly blockbusters like *Star Wars* — dominate foreign markets.[44]

When film production fell off in the fifties, television programs took its place. As films had done in the twenties, American television shows provided a large share of world production in the sixties and seventies.[45] Although these products are still a healthy export market for United States syndicators, they face increasing competition from foreign producers. In Latin America, once an unchallenged market for United States television, Mexican, Venezuelan, and Brazilian producers now have the largest export share. American syndicators also face restrictions in the form of quotas on the amount of foreign programs shown on overseas stations. Many countries now have such restrictions, generally designed to encourage local production as well as to counter criticism that too many foreign (that is, American) programs are shown, with allegedly baleful effects on local cultural patterns.[46]

The old major segment of American media involvement abroad is the news business. The two large American press agencies — Associated Press (AP) and United Press International (UPI) — dominate international news flow, although there is strong competition from European agencies, particularly Britain's Reuters organization. Reuters has taken a strong lead in transforming itself from an old-line news agency to an electronic information network, particularly in supplying financial information to corporations and, more recently, directly to individuals via cable systems. By 1984, Reuters was providing 47 specialized news services to these subscribers in 74 countries.[47] A more uncertain challenge is the prospect that, within the coming decade, one or more large news agencies may be organized in Third World countries. Similar proposals had foundered in the past. In the late seventies, a nonaligned news pool, largely under Yugoslav sponsorship, was set up for news exchanges among Third World countries.

The initial results were professionally unimpressive, but the motivation behind the idea was strong enough to suggest that some form of permanent organization might develop. In 1983, after four years of preparation, a Pan African News Agency, sponsored by black African countries, began operations.

This motivation was a combination of political and cultural factors. Culturally, it involved a desire to break away from dependence on Western press agencies as news sources allegedly biased against Third World accomplishments and values. Proponents of this view invoked the concept of "information sovereignty," contending that Western agencies were only interested in reporting political unrest, earthquakes, and *National Geographic* type exotica from their countries. However justified these charges, there was also a strong underlying political motivation to curb Western reports on Third World political and economic troubles. The nonaligned news agency's output in its early years consisted largely of Propaganda Ministry handouts from its member countries. The experiment raised doubts as to whether an indigenous Third World news-reporting system — a laudable enough project — could be developed soon. In the meantime, the American news agencies and their European competitors will continue to be the dominant force in international news flow.

Another influential segment of United States international media influence involves print publications — from the *Reader's Digest* to scholarly books and journals. *Reader's Digest* is an international media phenomenon in its own right, with editions printed in thirteen languages and in 31 countries. The international editors of *Time* and *Newsweek* reach relatively small but significant elite audiences in every country. The American book industry, with over $7 billion in annual sales, relies heavily on its export trade, particularly in the technical field. United States publishers have been successful in developing cooperative production and marketing arrangements with local firms in Third World countries since the abrogation in the seventies of a long-standing arrangement that gave British publishers preferential access in large parts of the world.

The weakest area of American media influence abroad is radio. Before World War II, a number of attempts were made to develop commercial shortwave broadcasting from this country, with emphasis on transmissions to Latin America. The war halted these efforts. The only private United States stations now broadcasting to foreign audiences are evangelical-type religious stations, most of whose transmitters are located abroad. International radio is largely a government responsibility, with particular emphasis on reaching audiences in communist countries where outside news and information sources are restricted. Three government financed stations — Voice of America, Radio Liberty, and Radio Free Europe — provide almost continuous round the clock transmissions to these areas.

In summary, the United States is a major player in the business of international communications and information — from building satellites for the Arabs to selling *Reader's Digest* in Brazil. Although American activities cover a wide range of activities, they share three characteristics. The first is that American firms have a strong position in each sector. The second is that each sector is becoming more competitive each year; the easy postwar days are over. The third is that, in each sector, American products and services face, in varying degrees, threats to their access to foreign markets.

Harvard University information resources expert Anthony Oettinger sees information access as a major policy issue for the United States in the coming years. He uses a simple chronological progression to illustrate his point: in the fifties, American strategic interests centered around access to real estate for military bases; in the sixties the emphasis shifted to economic access for the worldwide expansion of United States industry and banking. He believes the problem is now shifting to threats to information and communications access, the connectors between an increasingly information-dependent American society and other nations.

One of Oettinger's colleagues in the Harvard information resources study, William Read, has suggested that we may come to a world "information crisis" roughly comparable to the oil crises of the early seventies.[48] This may seem to be a worse-case scenario, given the fact that the trend toward more communications circuits, and more information openness is running strong. There is, however, a dark side to this trend, based on the imbalance of world information resources. By and large, this imbalance has favored the United States. As foreign nations begin to perceive communications and information resources as national security factors, American strength in this area is seen in a different light. This shift lies behind the "information sovereignty" argument, or in simpler terms, good old-fashioned political and economic protectionism extended to a new field.

Fortunately, the problem is not yet generally regarded in such rigid, black-and-white terms. Information is not oil, a resource that can be easily bestowed or denied by turning on a tap. However, it would be risky not to recognize the potential of greater political control of information flow. The Soviet Union has demonstrated, over a period of six decades, the relative ease with which a determined authoritarian regime can control information flow for its own interests. The new information technologies, from the computer on down, have no ideology. They can be manipulated for various purposes. The threat is there, and occasionally it surfaces in direct form. In 1983, a number of Arab banks decided to boycott the SWIFT international payments transfer network because ten Israeli banks had joined the system.[49] In 1978, British telecommunications workers voted not to handle any international traffic to South Africa, in protest against racial policies there. The ban lasted only a short time. It is possible to imagine a similar ban against traffic to this country because of the way it voted on a certain issue in the United Nations, or because of some other political event.

The United States has indicated on at least one occasion that it would be prepared to take such action. Shortly after United States Embassy officials were seized as hostages in Tehran in November 1979, the White House ordered a study of the possibilities of cutting off all communications between Iran and the outside world. The study concluded that a complete cut-off, particularly of satellite communications, was not feasible for legal and other reasons, and the project was dropped.[50] The world communications and information networks are fragile instruments, easily disrupted by terrorist attacks. Whereas terrorists and other revolutionaries used to seize radio and television stations, they have now begun to turn their attention to computers and other information facilities as a way of seriously disrupting a society.

These kinds of assaults on electronic networks that link our social and economic activities will be increasingly common events in the coming years. Another less violent prospect will be the taking of political actions to restrict communications products and information flow. As noted earlier, this is already a problem for American firms in such areas as data communications, television exports, and computer machine exports. In each case, the aim has been to restrict rather than to eliminate American products and services. The initial effects have been economic, resulting in some loss for American industry. This is an important enough consideration, but it should not mask the overriding political issue involved. The United States is in no position — lingering superpower mythologies to the contrary — to impose its will in such matters. It does, however, have a leadership role to play in the evolution of a world communications system whose emphasis is on openness rather than protectionism and outmoded concepts of sovereignty. Clearly this will benefit our trade interests, but the United States should not be so preoccupied with short-range economic problems that it does not recognize the need for sharing information and communications resources, particularly in correcting the massive imbalance between industrialized and developing countries.

This will be a difficult, complex job. It will be viewed with suspicion by those with more narrow-minded economic interests as a do-gooder approach, one that limits their options. There is, in fact, no reason why a policy encompassing our long-run economic and political interests cannot be developed. At present, the United States lacks the coherent guidelines needed to undertake this task, over and above a cycle of tactical moves that represent reactions rather than initiatives designed to create a more stable overall environment for global communications development.

Part of the problem, noted earlier in this chapter, is the absence of an effective mechanism within the American Government to coordinate these issues. Policy decisions are spread across a dozen major agencies and departments. The problem is not how to group them in one agency — this would be an impractical and probably impossible venture, given the bureaucratic passions involved. A more realistic approach might be to establish a coordinating mechanism that operates under clear-cut Presidential directives and has strong liaisons with the private and public interest sectors. In any event, both public and private policymakers need to establish better consultative arrangements, within and between each sector, if they are to identify and implement the decisions required for a full American role in the global communications environment. Since 1981, a number of bills authorizing a Cabinet level committee to oversee United States policy and operations in this area have been introduced in Congress.[51]

A restructuring of the United States Government apparatus remains a prerequisite for handling the more difficult problem of how to improve international consultation on communications and information issues. Any domestic consensus on how to proceed will depend for its success on how it relates to negotiations with other nations, either individually or in groups. Our traditional preference has been for bilateral negotiations, where the problems (and their solutions) are usually more narrow and clear-cut. However, the trend is toward multilateral negotiations as communications and information problems spill over into regional and wider international concerns. This means that the United States will do more of its negotiations through the United Nations and related international organizations.

The number of international organizations claiming stakes in these subjects increases annually. For many of them, communications and information are trendy subjects they can invoke to extend their bureaucratic empires with correspondingly bigger budgets. Other agencies have more legitimate claims. These include such relatively small organizations as the Universal Postal Union, the World Meteorological Organization, and the International Atomic Energy Authority, each of which has performed useful, quiet service in global information cooperation. The two world agencies with the most direct interest in the subject, however, are the International Telecommunications Union (ITU) and the United Nations Educational, Scientific, and Cultural Organization (UNESCO). Most of the critical multilateral negotiations in communications and information during the eighties will be held in these two agencies.[52]

In Chapter 3, we examined the ITU's role in developing and administering global standards for telecommunications, including the equitable use of a major natural resource, the radio spectrum. The Union is a one-nation/ one-vote organization, and the new nations of Asia, Africa, and Latin America make up the majority of the membership. These nations are prepared to use their influence to seek redress for what they consider, almost without exception, to be an unequal distribution of international telecommunications resources. This pressure comes at a time when the older industrial powers have need to expand their own use of these resources for post-industrial requirements.

These pressures came to a head at the ITU-sponsored 1979 World Administrative Radio Conference (WARC), which reviewed and made decisions on the radio spectrum pattern for the rest of the century.[53] (The conference, which caused hardly a ripple in the world media, was the largest international conference ever held. It had 2,000 participants from 145 countries, 15,000 proposals to consider, and ran in Geneva for three months.) The 1979 WARC tested the world's ability to deal with its expanding communications requirements within the finite limits of the radio spectrum. This goal is technically reachable. The critical question is whether ITU's members, particularly the new nations-in-a-hurry, can resist confrontational political and ideological temptations in the interests of maintaining an orderly telecommunications framework.

The United States has its own set of temptations in the form of strong domestic pressures from industry and from public claimants on spectrum resources. By and large, the 1979 conference held to its technical agenda, avoiding political confrontation and reaching agreement on most issues. Some of the more sensitive problems were, however, postponed until a later series of specialized conferences to be held during the eighties. This will have the effect of making spectrum issues the subject of almost continuing negotiations throughout the decade. These negotiations will be a stringent test of the ITU's ability to preserve its role of maintaining a technical order in international telecommunications.[54]

The other major international forum for communications and information issues is UNESCO. Founded with idealistic hopes after World War II, UNESCO has a checkered record of achievements and failures. It has settled down to bureaucratic middle age in its Paris headquarters, peopled by an international staff who grind out documents written in a corkscrew international dialect that may, if everything goes wrong, someday become the world linguistic standard. In its early years, UNESCO was dominated by the conflict between the Europeans' esoteric cultural concerns and the Americans' pragmatic interests in literacy campaigns, scientific cooperation, etc. The organization is now dominated by Third World concerns, reflecting the majority of its members.

Communications and information issues are high on the current agenda. Developing countries see UNESCO as a useful forum for airing policies and programs to correct the communications imbalance. A corollary to this is the effort of underdeveloped countries to curb the "cultural imperialism" resulting from the current heavy flow of Western films, news, publications, and other media to their countries.[55] These concerns fall under the Third World rubric of a "New World Information Order." UNESCO was the spawning ground for the concept of *information sovereignty*, or the right to protect one's cultural heritage from harmful outside influences. This led to a move to overturn UNESCO's long-standing support for free flow of information, a concept sponsored by the United States in the organization's early years, in favor of a new emphasis on the right to communicate and on a more balanced information flow. The need to correct the imbalance was acknowledged by the United States and other democratic nations. The debates became sharp, however, when proposals for imposing international restrictions on news flow were put forward under the "New World Information Order" slogan. The subject was extensively documented in a UNESCO-commissioned report by an international committee headed by former Irish foreign minister, Sean McBride, issued in 1980. The report was, from the American viewpoint, a mixed bag. It supported the concept of open information flow and also put forward a number of restrictive proposals which had the effect of compromising this concept. Nevertheless, the United States supported the report during UNESCO's 1980 general conference in Belgrade. At the same time, the American approach has been to urge UNESCO members to call an armistice on the cyclical ideological debates in favor of practical programs for improving Third World information and communications resources. To this end, it sponsored a proposal for a UNESCO project on international communications development programs that was approved at the Belgrade meeting.[56]

Despite these and other attempts at pragmatic solutions to global information imbalances, Third World countries maintained their ideological pressures on the alleged information imperialism of the United States and other Western powers. Their grievances were summarized in an extensive resolution passed by the United Nations General Assembly in its 1980 session. In December 1983, the United States took the unusual step of informing UNESCO that it intended to withdraw from the organization within a year if significant changes were not made in the way in which the organization handled information issues.

Both UNESCO and the ITU are weak reeds on which to build an international policy structure for communications and information. Each agency is buffeted by pressures that prevent it from acting effectively, even in relatively simple matters. However, both are preferable to any of the occasional proposals for a supranational organization to guide overall global network development — a proposition that would neither serve United States purposes nor, in the long run, anyone else's.

There is one limited example of a successful supranational agency in this field. It is Intelsat, the operator of the 110-nation satellite grid that has reshaped global communications in the past 15 years. In 1984, its satellites provided over thirty-five thousand circuits, more than a hundred times the number of cable circuits that were the only reliable intercontinental connections in 1964 when the first Intelsat *Early Bird* was put into orbit.[58]

Intelsat also represents a significant political achievement, a dramatic step in the exploitation of a major technology through international cooperation. The Intelsat innovation combined profit motives, a pragmatic division of power, and a willingness by its owner-nations to forego short-term political and ideological advantages in the interests of a workable system. Intelsat's owners are diverse, ranging from the People's Republic of China to South Africa to the Vatican State. (The Soviet Union is the only significant nonmember.) Collectively they generate over 95% of all international traffic.

The Intelsat system was started by the United States and managed by it, through the Communications Satellite Corporation, for a dozen years. The American voting share, based on system usage, has dropped from over 60% in 1965 to below 25% in the mid-eighties. The surrender of American control was not the result of unalloyed altruism by any means. It was the price the United States paid for creating a network management system acceptable to other nations. Intelsat now faces different problems as satellite technology opens new service opportunities and as the needs of its member-owners grow. The organization's success raises questions about its role as a model for other global communications ventures. It is an intriguing idea, but the Intelsat experience is probably not readily transferable to other areas. The organization was a unique creation of its time, involving a technology that would not work without a high degree of political cooperation. The technology was, moreover, a monopoly of one country — the United States — which had the resources, the imagination, and the will to allow its monopoly to erode gradually in the interests of a long-term viable world system. Such circumstances cannot easily be replicated in the foreseeable future.[59]

Intelsat's status as a virtual global monopoly in satellite communications is being challenged by newer forces. A number of countries are constructing regional satellite systems which will become separate but compatible networks under the Intelsat umbrella. European countries and the Arab states have well-advanced plans for such systems. In addition, several United States commercial satellite firms applied to the FCC in 1983 for permission to operate their own satellites, servicing the lucrative North Atlantic area in competition with Intelsat. The applications set off a fierce policy battle within the American government between officials who saw benefits in a more competitive international satellite environment and those who feared that such competition would harm Intelsat's economic viability.

New technologies like Intelsat's satellites are deceptive in their promises. They encourage visions of instant hook-up, of plugging everyone in. It is a peculiarly American vision — the old electronic myth updated. Why shouldn't there be a princess phone in every Hottentot hut and Eskimo igloo, not to mention a television set and a table-top computer? Despite the new technologies, however, the world information network is going to be built through the slow, patient activities of a wide variety of organizations, techniques, and economic programs.

In summary, we have seen that the United States has a major stake in the development of a strong global communications system. Its own information society can be a general model for a new kind of post-industrial democratic evolution abroad. Access is the measure — access to information and communications resources in terms of their availability, the ability of people to pay for them, and their freedom to use the information for personal enrichment as well as community needs.

Assuring international open access may be the most difficult United States information policy issue of the eighties. It is not a new problem, but it will take different forms in the coming years. Many other cultures do not put as much of a premium on open access as we do, including otherwise like-minded societies in Europe. And the Third World is suspicious of our tendency to be aggressive in both giving and receiving resources.

A primary United States resource in promoting these interests is its industrial productivity. A world grid will not be built by UNESCO resolutions or other pious incantations. It will be built by good technology, sensible economics, and stable political conditions. This is an elusive combination, in short supply in most parts of the world. American industry has the ability to provide the goods and services needed for the network, as do its European and Japanese competitors and the new communications industries of the Third World. Assuring a reasonably open market for these United States products is an important part of overall American strategy. It should complement the major thrust of our strategy — our commitment to an open information order, one in which adequate information and communications resources are available to everyone.

NOTES

1. Zbigniew Brzezinski, *Between Two Worlds* (New York: Viking Press, 1970), p. 31.

2. For a summary of Schiller's views, see his *Communications and Cultural Development* (White Plains, N.Y.: International Arts and Sciences Press, 1976).

3. Anthony Smith, *The Geopolitics of Information* (New York: Oxford University Press, 1980), pp. 19–40.

4. Quoted in Jonathan Tourtellot, "A World Information War," *European Community* (Washington), January/February 1978, p. 12.

5. *Ibid.*, p. 14.

6. For a summary of the controversy, see *Telecommunications Report*, 18 July 1977, pp. 2–5.

7. A useful compendium of Congressional and private sector attitudes on government policy and organization in international communications and information issues is given in U.S. Congress, Senate Committee on Foreign Relations, *The Role and Control of International Communications and Information*, Report to the Subcommittee on International Operations, 95th Cong., 1st sess., June 1977.

8. *Telecommunications Report*, 18 July 1977, p. 5.

9. The basic proposals of the subcommittee are summarized in U.S. Congress, House Committee on Government Operations, *International Information Flow: Forging a New Framework*, House Report, no. 96–1535, 96th Cong., 2nd sess., 1980, pp. 55–59.

10. For a description of the debate, see Wilson Dizard, *Television — A World View* (Syracuse, N.Y.: Syracuse University Press, 1966), pp. 263–67.

11. U.S. Department of Commerce, *U.S. Industrial Outlook 1976, with Projections to 1985* (16th ed.) (Washington, D.C.: Government Printing Office, 1976).

12. "International Direct Distance Dialing Offered to More Nations," *Communications News*, November 1975, p. 42.

13. "International Carriers Looking Forward," *Telecommunications*, August 1976, p. 21.

14. "Dataquest Forecasts Worldwide Datacom Service," *Communications News*, September 1980, p. 13.

15. "FCC Seen Acting to Expand Competition Among World Communications Firms," *Wall Street Journal*, 12 December 1979, p. 44. The 1980 decision to permit Western Union entry was opposed by other carriers in the courts. Congressional legislation permitting the firm to compete for international business was introduced by Senator Barry Goldwater (R-Arizona) early in 1981.

16. For a French view of the pressure on European telecommunications organizations to allow more competition, see "Télécom: la déréglementation américaine ébranle aussi le monopole des PTT en Europe," *Le Monde* (Paris), 8 November 1983.

17. "Dealing with Foreign PTTs," *Telecommunications*, January 1980, p. 25.

18. "The New New Telephone Industry," *Business Week*, 13 February 1978, p. 69.

19. "Where Are Britain's Capital Venturers?," *The Economist* (London), 23 July 1977, p. 73.

20. "The Great World Telephone War," *Fortune*, August 1977, p. 144.

21. "Blanketing the World with Phones," *New York Times*, 2 February 1980, Special section on international economic developments, p. 12.

22. "Data Communications: A Market Where the U.S. Lags," *Business Week*, 11 February 1980, p. 57.

23. American Federation of Information Processing Societies, *Information Processing in the United States: A Quantitative Summary*, (Washington), 1977, p. 14.

24. Angelina Pantages, "The International Computer Industry," *Datamation*, September 1976, p. 56.

25. For a description of the complex maneuvers involved in the attempt to reduce IBM's share of the French computer market, see "Western Europe's Computer Industry," *Datamation*, September 1976, pp. 65–75.

26. Silmon Nora and Alain Minc, *The Computerization of Society*, (Cambridge, Mass.: MIT Press, 1980).

27. Guy de Jonquires, "French Telecommunications — The Wired Society Gamble," *Financial Times* (London), 1 October 1980, p. 14.

28. "The European Community prepares to close the widening technology gap," *Data Communications*, September 1983, p. 54.

29. "Why Europe Is Not an Open Market for Computers," *The Economist* (London), 5 April 1980, p. 83. See also "European Strategies to Fight IBM," *Business Week*, 17 February 1979, p. 43, and "Telematics Are Here: European Community Working on a Common European Strategy," *Europe* (Washington), May/June 1981, pp. 5–7.

30. "Computers: Here Comes Fujitsu," *New York Times*, 11 November 1980, p. G–1.

31. Ministry of International Trade and Industry, *The Plan for an Information Society* (Tokyo: Jacudi, 1972).

32. "Fighting Off the Japanese," *The Economist* (London), 7 June 1980, p. 80.

33. "Joining Hands Against Japan," *Business Week*, 10 November 1980, p. 108.

34. "American Electronics Industry: Fighting to Cash in Their Chips," *Washington Post*, 9 November 1980, p. G–2. Also "U.S. and Japan Plan Cuts in Semiconductor Tariffs," *New York Times*, 12 May 1981, p. D–1.

35. For a description of the two firms' successful strategies in Japan, see "IBM's big splash in the land of electronics," *Business Week*, 1 August 1983, p. 35, and "Why Intel is winning big in Japan," *Business Week*, 19 September 1983, p. 48.

36. The estimate is from electronics industry expert Warren Davis, quoted in "American Electronics Industry," *Washington Post*, 9 November 1980, p. G–2.

37. Louis Turner and Stephen Woolcock, "Emerging Nations Compete with the Industrialized World," in German Marshall Fund, *Transatlantic Perspective*, no. 3 (September 1980): pp. 21–24.

38. "Computing the Loss of IBM," *The Economist* (London), 1 December 1979, p. 77.

39. In 1980, at least ten countries had full or partial on-line access to Medlars. See "Information Biomedical Communications — the Role of the U.S. Library of Medicine," *Health Communications Informatist*, 1980, p. 212.

40. "The Trade in Technology," *The Economist* (London), 21 April 1979, p. 48.

41. "A Boom in No-Strings Banking," *New York Times*, 2 February 1980, Special section on international trade, p. 14.

42. For useful background on this issue, see U.S. Department of State. *Selected Papers: International Policy Implications of Computers and Advanced Telecommunications*, Bureau of Oceans and International Environmental and Scientific Affairs (Washington, D.C.: Government Printing Office, 1979). Also "Transborder Data Flow," special issue of *Stanford Journal of International Law* 16 (Summer 1980).

43. William Read, *America's Mass Media Merchants* (Baltimore: Johns Hopkins University Press, 1977), pp. 39–44.

44. For a useful survey of Hollywood's continuing influence on world film markets, see "Hollywood Flourishes, Its Colonies Languish," *The Economist* (London), 4 November 1978, pp. 85–87.

45. Read, *Media Merchants*, pp. 144–79.

46. The point is documented, with some ideological bias, in Jeremy Tunstall, *The Media Are American* (London: Constable, 1977).

47. "Reuters plans to go public after bonanza," *Washington Post*, 13 November 1983.

48. William Read, *Foreign Policy: The High and Low Politics of Telecommunications*. Program on Information Technologies and Public Policy, Harvard University. Publication P–76–3, February 1976, p. 2.

49. "Arab bank boycott of data links," *New York Times*, 17 February 1983.

50. "No Go for Satellite Sanctions Against Iran," *Science*, 16 May 1980, p. 20.

51. "Bills to Establish Review on FCC Clear Hurdles," *Wall Street Journal*, 17 May 1981, p. 6.

52. For a useful description of the international agencies involved in communications and information policy, see Edward Ploman, "The Whys and Wherefores of International Organizations," *Intermedia* (London), July 1980, pp. 6–11.

53. The political and technical aspects of the conference were extensively

examined in ten articles grouped under the overall title, "The U.S. Faces WARC" in *Journal of Communication* 29, no. 1 (Winter 1979): pp. 143–207. For a review of the conference results, see Glen O. Robinson, "Regulating International Airwaves: The 1979 WARC," *Virginia Journal of International Law, 21*, no. 1 (Fall 1980): pp. 1–54.

54. A useful survey of proposals for reforming the ITU over the years is contained in J. Henry Glazer, "Infelix ITU — The Need for Space Age Revisions to the International Telecommunications Conventions," *Federal Bar Journal*, 23, no. 1 (Winter, 1963): pp. 1–36.

55. This development is summarized in Jonathan F. Gunter, ed., *The United States and the Debate on the World Information Order* (Washington, D.C.: Academy for Educational Development, 1979), pp. 44–53. See also "Third World News and Views," *Journal of Communication*, 29, no. 2 (Spring 1979): pp. 134–98.

56. Philip H. Power and Elie Abel, "The Third World vs. the Media," *New York Times Magazine*, 21 September 1980, p. 116. For a useful summary of the Third World agenda in communications and information matters, see United Nations, General Assembly, Special Political Committee, *Questions Relating to Information*, Annex to Agenda Item 59, December, 1980. An American-initiated critique of attempts to curb information flows can be found in *Voices of Freedom*, the working papers of the World Conference of Independent News Media, Talloires, France, 15–17 May 1981, published by the Edward R. Murrow Center for Public Diplomacy, Tufts University, 1981.

57. Joseph N. Pelton, *Global Talk* (Amsterdam: Sijthoff Noordhoff Publishers, 1981).

58. Marcellus Snow, "Intelsat: An International Example," *Journal of Communication*, 30, no. 2, (Spring 1980): pp. 147–56.

59. Anthony Smith, *The Geopolitics of Information* (London: Faber and Faber, 1980), pp. 148–73. See also Glen Fisher, *American Communication in a Global Society* (Norwood, N.J.: Ablex Publishing Co., 1979), pp. 141–157.

CHAPTER NINE

THE OPEN-LOOP FUTURE

HAVING REVIEWED THE overseas impact of American communications and information activities, we now return to the problem of goals and policies for the new information environment here at home. International factors will, of course, influence our formulation of a domestic strategy. Until recently, this global dimension was slighted because of the geographic, economic, and cultural distances separating us from other societies. These gaps, however, are narrowing at such a pace that it is almost impossible for us to perceive the changes and their implications.

We are inclined to be impressed most by the physical components of this international outreach — the satellites, computers, highspeed cables, and other innovations linking us to the rest of the world. But the wider, more significant impact will be on our understanding of our role in a new world order as we touch the minds and emotions of men and women everywhere and are in turn touched by them.

American ideas, resources, and actions will continue to have an outsized influence on what happens abroad, given our progress so far in shaping an advanced information society at home. This does not mean that the United States pattern will or should be copied. Nevertheless, the United States can set a standard for other societies to consider as they identify their own goals and actions. Our ability to influence these societies will depend on how we develop and carry out our own approaches to the new age. Like the rest of the world, Americans face an open-loop future, in which it will be increasingly difficult to identify guideposts to purpose or direction. As physicist Robert Oppenheimer has noted:

> This world is a new world.... One thing that is new is the prevalence of newness...so that the world alters as we walk in it, so that the years of a man's life measure not some small growth or rearrangements or moderation of what he learned in childhood but a great upheaval.[1]

Communications and information are driving forces in this environment. Their technologies are no longer constrained by the linear pattern in which innovations were previously introduced over a period of many years.

The telegraph, telephone, wireless radio, and other machines evolved slowly, strengthening economic productivity without disrupting social order in an expanding democratic society. In the present age of converging technologies and greater social complexity, the balance between economic productivity and social harmony becomes more difficult to maintain.

The balance is threatened by a dilemma. Technology as a productive force rolls on, while its contribution to social stability grows weaker. And as the distance between technological promise and social effect widens, confidence in technology is eroded. The situation underscores the warnings of Jacques Ellul on the contrary effects of rapid change. Other observers, like Jay Forrester of MIT's System Dynamics group, suggest that we may have to impose what were formerly unacceptable restrictions on personal and collective freedoms to cope with the consequences of this imbalance. It is a conclusion they reach not because they are antidemocratic but because they see such control as the only alternative to social collapse.[2]

Whether right or wrong, these critics are generally wary of facile post-industrial or information society labels. Their point is valid — but only to a point. The United States is not stepping over some imaginary line in time, from materialistic industrialism into a golden epoch of white-collar ease. Such boundary drawing is simplistic, given the still fragmentary evidence of the changes taking place and our own distorting proximity to them. Nevertheless, once we get past the exercise of labeling ages and epochs, we face the fact that the current shift appears increasingly to be a departure from the dynamics that drove our agricultural and industrial past.

Agriculture is still a vital sector of the United States economy, but it is no longer a major force for innovation or for shaping social values and goals. Similarly, a loss of inner dynamism is becoming evident in the industrial sector, although this is masked by a continued high output of goods. Less than a quarter of the United States work force is now involved in primary industrial production, a ratio that reflects a steady decline in the amount of human energy being put into the production of goods in recent decades. Technological change has profoundly altered the nature and centrality of industrial activity in our society. Growth in agriculture and industry is no longer the major impetus of social development, but is being replaced by a still undefined force. This is an information-based thrust that draws on human resource capital to transfer knowledge into many forms of physical and social activities, to generate wealth in new ways, and, in the process, to profoundly alter goals and values.

Is this a permanent shift, or simply a fluctuation in our national energy that will someday subside into a familiar pattern? Improvements in information production and distribution, after all, have been part of all general economic and social advances throughout the agricultural and industrial ages. Then, however, the information factor was subordinate, in terms of applied resources, to physical activities. The shift taking place now, the one we need to know more about, is moving us toward an environment in which information production and distribution will overshadow material production.

This may be a unique moment in human history, one we cannot observe clearly because we are too close to it. Astronomer Carl Sagan has given the concept a cosmic twist with his suggestion that within the past generation we have turned a corner, developing a replication of the information coding and storage capacities of primitive life via the computer. It is, he argues, a quantum leap in the creation and storage of intelligence *exosomatically*, that is, outside the body. For the first time we have machines whose information-handling capacity is roughly comparable to the genetic memory of a living organism — the single-celled paramecium.[3]

This point is sharpened by a comparison of the progressive power of various information storage methods during the past 40 centuries. The measure is the number of binary digits, or bits, representing information that can be stored in one gram of each device, beginning with the first permanent information records developed in the ancient Middle East:

Sumerian cuneiform table	10^{-2} bits or .01 bit.
Paper with typewritten words	10^3 bits or 1,000 bits.
Electronic magnetic tape	10^6 bits or a million bits.
Ultrafine silver haloid film on which information is placed with microbeams through a demagnifying electronic microscope	10^{12} bits or one hundred billion bits.[4]

Such a leap in high-technology information and communications capacities leaves us disoriented. The familiar road markings are smudged or missing. In Marshall McLuhan's analogy, we move into the future looking through a rearview mirror.

Comforting old assumptions can no longer be taken for granted. Heirs to the electronic myth, we like to assume that information and communications factors will continue to raise our level of economic productivity and social progress. There are disturbing indications, however, that such information-based productivity gains may have reached a plateau. The introduction of more resources may not advance the gains of recent years at the same fast pace.

There is growing evidence to suggest that communications and information resources will have to be reassessed if they are to realize their full potential in the current reindustrialization effort. Edwin Parker of Stanford University sees a flattening of growth curves, indicating a point of diminishing returns with respect to investment in information goods and services.[5]

Although the information sector is now larger than the agricultural and industrial sectors combined, the costs of its labor intensive activities may outweigh the productivity gains made possible by more sophisticated technology. In particular, Parker and others have identified the braking effects of a nonproductive public and private bureaucracy, the fastest growing subsector of the information economy despite perennial attempts to control its spread. In the eighties, office work has accounted for over $800 *billion* in annual expenditures in the United States economy, 70% of which involves salaries and other personnel costs.[6] To reduce the burden of labor intensity in information growth, problems of management conservatism and other obstacles must first be overcome. Better application of existing technologies may be more productive than an accelerated pace of technical sophistication.

Beyond the question of production levels is the matter of social balance in the new information environment. Heavy infusions of information historically have had a disruptive effect on societies. The current flood of new data, increasing at a rate of about 10% annually, is unprecedented in any age. It is unclear how much of this is useful information, contributing to social productivity and maintenance, and how much simply adds a potentially unmanageable physical and psychic burden to what Alvin Toffler (*Future Shock*) and other pop analysts characterize as "information overload." In a society that gives the broadest legal protection to the most questionable fact and the most wrongheaded opinion, there is no acceptable way to evaluate information as useful, useless, or superfluous. Justice Holmes's open marketplace of competing ideas remains our ideal, whatever it lacks in standards for selection.

How much information do we need? We began this study with an analogy between the broad information requirements of our evolving society and the specific needs of the Wright brothers in the development of their first successful airplane. Theirs was an unstable machine, designed with barely sufficient information input to allow it to move successfully through a turbulent three-dimensional environment. The analogy remains apt for the perilous passage we have to navigate toward a more complex level of democratic order.

Optimism is difficult to sustain in the face of current trends. One might better take the stance of a pessimist, defined by an anonymous Polish wit some years ago as an optimist with better information. Realistically, the likelihood is that in the near future United States society will be marked by higher levels of uncertainty, a blurring of values and priorities, rising mistrust among large sections of the population, and a resulting inability to adapt private and public institutions quickly enough to cope with current problems, let alone adequately anticipate future ones. Expanded information and communications resources will tend, in the short run at least, to magnify these factors rather than reduce them to manageable proportions.

A striking analysis of this prospect is to be found in a 1978 French Government study of the effects of computerization on French culture.[7] Known as the Nora/Minc report after the two civil servants who were its principal authors, the survey was given fairly wide publicity in this country because of its strong attack on the alleged American computer dominance of the French economy. The report's sober analysis of the long-term effects of *informatisation* on French society was largely ignored here. This was unfortunate since a significant point made by Messrs. Nora and Minc was the need to face up to the negative effects of the new computer-based environment, particularly the threat of greater social alienation and erosion of traditional values. The report was a best-seller in France, and the focus of continuing debate there.

We may not be able to replicate the neat Cartesian, and somewhat authoritarian, way in which the French approach problems of orderliness, but we need a better understanding in our own context of the issues raised in the Nora/Minc study. The United States faces essentially the same situation — a massive technocratic drive, threatening to go out of control unless its potentially dehumanizing antidemocratic effects are understood and reined in. If this is not done, there is a strong possibility that broad masses of people will be cut off from adequate participation in the technological mainstream, swept along as a kind of information-poor *lumpenproletariat*.

To expect these groups to accept such a position docilely would be dangerously shortsighted. One of the paradoxes of information and communications technology is that, although it seems to benefit primarily those in power, it also provides the means for organizing previously scattered and powerless challengers into strong constituencies.

One example, yet to be adequately documented, is the role played during the Vietnam protest movement by a simple technology — the telephone — in organizing groups who reversed a major national policy. Platoons of researchers have concentrated their efforts on the role of television for having "brought the war into the American living room." Though television played a role, it was essentially a passive one.[8] As a readily available two-way technology, it was the telephone that gave politically motivated groups the means for organizing against an establishment that had infinitely more communications resources available for its own purposes. Whether or not the protest groups served overriding national interests is still debatable. Their success, however, is an effective example of the chances a democratic society will have to take in the new information environment in which established power groups may be tempted to limit access to communications channels and information resources to protect their interests.[9]

The risks of open access are substantial. Yet everything in our tradition tells us that the risks are worthwhile, that we must embrace error. A strong reaffirmation of democratic values and actions will be needed to assure social balance and, ultimately, national survival in the new information age. A pluralistic democracy such as America's needs to provide sufficient shared information, beliefs, and assumptions for its members to function as self-governing groups at many levels. "The way to prevent error is to give the people full information of their affairs" — the words are those of an eighteenth-century optimist, Thomas Jefferson. They are a reminder that a fully responsive national communications and information system is not a luxury but an imperative if we are to survive and thrive as a vital democracy.

How can our complex society come to decisions and act to make high-technology communications and information responsive to its goals? We are handicapped by the lack of an overt information or communications crisis or of a coercive fact of the kind that a pluralistic society usually requires to mobilize itself for action. Moreover, we are restricted by a special sensitivity to policy enforcement in this area. A good healthy dose of First Amendment protection buffers us from self-appointed guardians of what is right. British communications scholar Anthony Smith has identified the paradox present in any discussion of the management of communications and information resources in a free society:

> We have acquired a double conundrum: what happens to freedom of communications when the necessary instruments are concentrated inside a small elite of professionals? What obligations has a society towards policing its mass culture when that culture can exercise an influence over the attitudes, the morals, the emotional security of the mass audience? We have already lived with this debate long enough to know that these are not simple organizational questions capable of simple organizational answers. The problems are buried very deep inside our culture and like such problems in past generations they cannot be solved, only replaced with new problems and new formulations of old ones. . . . The only undisputed effect is the dilemma which it poses for all modern societies.[10]

The reality of this dilemma should be a check on any facile approach to a national strategy for communications and information. This caution applies particularly to recurrent proposals for using technocratic methodology to solve sensitive social problems. Such proposals abounded in the wake of the "optimal control" techniques used in the Apollo manned-space-program during the sixties. If computers could be used to identify a path through space that optimized manpower, fuel, and other resources, why not use them to develop policies and programs that optimize the performance of whole societies? The analogy was grossly inexact when applied to a complex civilization whose strengths lie, paradoxically, in an unwillingness to optimize its future by formula. As Nigel Calder notes, it is a wise society that believes the future is too interesting and dangerous to be entrusted to any predictable, reliable agency:

> We need all the fallibility we can get. Most of all we need to preserve the absolute unpredictability and total improbability of our connected minds. That way we can keep open all the options, as we have in the past.[11]

This does not argue against prudent planning. It does suggest hedging our bets against unknown or unforseen factors. If we choose a rigid course and are proved wrong, we all go down. Americans are steadied by a pattern of checks and balances, politically and socially, that in spite of some dangerous tilts, has kept us on keel for the past two centuries. Our stability will be severely tested in the coming years as we adjust our institutions and attitudes to information age realities.[12]

The outcome will depend largely upon decisions dealing with the distribution and use of power. In *The Nerves of Government*, published in the mid-sixties, political scientist Karl Deutsch argued that the new power was in information and communications. The groups that control the nervous system of modern society, the information networks, control the society. Deutsch's thesis was both persuasive and prescient. The proof came in the most dramatic political event of the past 15 years — the Watergate affair.

The sequence of events in Watergate began with a botched robbery aimed at collecting information about rival politicians. This led to revelations about elaborate White House operations (the "plumbers group") for stopping information leaks and, for good measure, the automated paper shredders and tape erasers designed to destroy information. The critical turning point was the public release of transcripts of tapes from a semiautonomous system of recording devices monitoring offices in the White House. And the highly dramatic culmination came in a televised congressional investigation that made the information available to a vast public.[13]

Watergate exposed the role communications and information played in consolidating political power and also, fortunately, in curbing its abuse. Future attempts at such a major power play will be more subtle, avoiding the stumble-footed flagrance of Nixon's White House. A wide range of sophisticated electronic devices can invade our lives softly and invisibly without, so to speak, leaving fingerprints or incriminating tapes. These devices can be used for benevolent purposes, or for malevolent purposes reminiscent of those employed by Orwell's Big Brother. In between lies a wide gray area, a seemingly innocuous monitoring of routine activities that are carried out in the name of efficiency but are capable of curbing personal rights. Electronic intrusions will be hard to measure and harder to resist, since they will generally involve quiet, discrete functions whose potential threat is not evident.[14]

Such Orwellian scenarios are not all hypothetical. Communications and information technology, unchecked by democratic restraints, can be concentrated in the hands of a distant, anonymous elite bent on containing innovation and protecting its own resources, nominally for some higher purpose. The efforts of any such elite will eventually fail because the new technologies are not that controllable. We have begun to see how modern anarchists, the new breed of political terrorists at home and abroad, can manipulate television, radio, and the telephone system, as well as the traditional print media, for their purposes. Such latter-day guerrilla tactics are, as defense authority Ian Smart has remarked, a lateral evasion of traditional social restraints. This capability is a new form of power, and it can be very effective. The physical fragility of most communications networks — wires, towers, and the like — make them particularly susceptible to terrorist actions which can paralyze a city or an entire region. Terrorist actions will be increasingly directed against computer installations the newest, and highly vulnerable, form of information resources.[15]

Threats from small activist groups cannot be ignored, but they are peripheral to the problems that have to be dealt with by the majority who accept the premises, and the promise, of the new information age. The central issue is power and its disposition. At this critical time in America, an awesome amount of power is concentrated in complex information technologies and the economic efforts behind them.

Can we handle this expanded power through adjustments in present policies or linear extensions of current practices? Or is a new strategy needed for a different dimension of political power? Are information trends more than a progression of technological and economic adjustments? Do they constitute a fundamental shift in the patterns and purposes of United States society? If communications and information resources are in fact pushing us towards a radically different environment, a new political consensus on their use may be needed.

A strong case can be made against a radical change in strategy, for both pragmatic and ideological reasons. The pragmatic arguments stress that the communications and information structure is naturally evolving as an open system through the dynamic interplay of economic forces. In the new competitive environment, the United States is moving toward a universal information utility that is accessible to more people more quickly than even the sunniest optimist would have predicted a decade ago.

There is a large measure of truth in that argument, but it is false to assume that technological and economic forces, however dynamic, can by themselves assure a fully accessible system. There will be gaps in isolated geographic areas and among disadvantaged groups who are bypassed for economic or other reasons. Those who are left out will not, in this day and age, be willing to accept second class status until market forces trickle benefits down to them. In a complex, interdependent post-industrial society, the risks of excluding them from mainline benefits may be too high.

The history of communications and information development in this country shows that there has been public intervention at critical points to insure a broadening of benefits. The list is long and distinguished: Congressional funding of the original Morse telegraph experiments, the Morrill Act providing assistance for land grant colleges, federal intervention to assure wireless radio development after World War I. The example most closely paralleling the current situation was public intervention to assure the development of the world's first mass interactive communications systems — the American telephone network — in the 1930s. This decision was incorporated into the Communications Act of 1934, which gave AT&T unique legal protections in exchange for providing universal telephone service, a commitment largely fulfilled. The legal decision 50 years later to break up the AT&T empire will have reverberating effects for some time to come. Meanwhile, there remains a continuing need for public study and consensus on future communications and information patterns in this country.

The ideological argument against political intervention rests on the First Amendment and its protection of individual expression. Rights of free expression, and their support in law and custom, cannot be abridged without compromising the democratic character of the new information age. In simpler times, the definitions of those rights were relatively clear-cut. These distinctions have become fuzzy, however, in the new information environment, with its complex levels of economic and political power wielded by governments and private interests, often in collusion. The line between public and personal rights blurs to the point where civil liberties arguments become a smokescreen for policies and actions that work against individual freedom.

The debate on political principles for the information age is just beginning, as a new sensitivity to the distinctions (and similarities) between public and private interests is growing. "After all," notes communications lawyer Glen Robinson, "interest conflicts do not disappear simply by chanting the words 'public interest' three times, and, indeed the public interest is not something grandly aloof from the amalgam of different private interests that lie beneath it. . . . Yet there must be something more in governance than simply the arbitration and settlement of private conflict."[16] This 'something more' is the elusive and necessary component of a coherent national communications and information policy. Essential personal freedoms must be protected against arbitrary political and economic power without sacrificing the social dynamics that have given this society the most open communications system in the world.

The outlines of a democratic strategy for the new age begin to emerge. These do not constitute a centralized master plan, but a new social compact that will provide the basis for needed policies and actions in the expanding area of information and communications. How can a consensus for identifying and realizing these needs be formed? Agreement will be difficult to bring about in a society in which much of political action is determined by organized interest groups seeking to protect and enlarge group entitlements. New approaches to democratic political strategy are needed, approaches that are not limited to problems of communications and information but recognize their central role in the process. Interest group politics has been given new force by the sophisticated use of communications in ways that often seem to favor direct self-serving actions over the more difficult, slower processes of consensus. Constructive decisions on the future of communications and information may, in fact, be compromised by an anachronistic approach to policy making. It is time for us to reevaluate the ways in which we approach our long-range planning.

The lead has to come from the top. In the United States political structure, this means the federal executive branch, and specifically the White House. Communications and information strategies should be put on the priority agenda of critical issues requiring deliberate policy attention. At present, the subject is relatively low on the political list, if only because there isn't any compelling pressure from major public or private interests. This may be an advantage for the time being. It reduces the prospect that the issue will be "discovered" for some temporary crowd-pleasing purpose. The usual result, in such cases, is to prevent any serious attention to the issue, once the clarion calls for action, the prestigious advisory commissions, and the other paraphernalia for crisis politicking are set in motion.

Long-term strategies for communications and information will be better served by a less frenetic, more deliberate approach, involving the participation of major interest groups. One way of doing this could be a presidentially appointed Communications and Information Policy Council for the purpose of defining problems, goals, and strategies. The council should not have a large bureaucracy attached to it, but it should have sufficient funds to carry out necessary research in preparing its recommendations. A credibly refreshing precedent would be set if the council's funding were shared by federal government, industry, labor, and consumer organizations represented on the council. Participation and funds should also be provided by state and local governments, a generally overlooked sector which has an important stake in communications and information strategy.

The council's primary purpose would be to serve as a sort of communal radar, tracking the implications of communications and information developments out on the horizon and making the results of its deliberations, including those concerning minority views, available to the President, to Congress, and to the public at large. It should strive for consensus, not in the spirit of surface unity, but rather in an ongoing attempt to set the agenda of issues. It should seek cooperatively to identify and address information age realities. No one public organization can encompass all these realities. However, the council could provide a highly visible public forum for identifying and developing long-range national goals and policies in this area.[17]

Meanwhile, certain policies and actions require immediate attention. Priority should be given to the ways in which communications and information matters are now organized within the federal structure. Each administration since the mid-fifties has attempted, with only partial success, to develop procedures for handling communications and information issues within the executive branch. The Carter administration's decision to consolidate many federal programs in a single National Information and Telecommunications Administration brought some order to the subject but did not succeed in providing a strong coordinating point for policy action decisions. At least 18 federal agencies, plus the independent Federal Communications Commission, remain involved in major communications policy and operational activities. In 1981, the Reagan administration moved cautiously in the face of conflicting recommendations from interest groups to restructure NTIA and other agencies. Nevertheless, there is a strong case to be made for providing a better coordinated approach to both policy making and operational needs in this area.

There are three related areas where policy initiatives are urgently required, whatever new organization structure is developed. The first of these involves both Congress and the executive branch in the problem of modernizing national communications law to reflect information age changes. Significant decisions to move the country in this direction, taken by the FCC and the White House in recent years, have been slowed down by the inability of Congress to pass comprehensive supporting legislation. Until Congress can act on many of these developments, the arbiter will be the courts, which by their own admission are unable to provide clear decisions in the absence of specific legislation. Efforts to bring the Communications Act of 1934 up to date have resulted in legislation only partially responsive to the need. This partial mandate is inadequate; only a comprehensive set of legislative actions can accomplish for the new technologies what the 1934 legislation did for telephone, telegraph, and broadcasting systems.

The second area in need of policy initiatives is the economic sphere. The impact of communications and information as vital industrial sectors in themselves and also as key elements in the current reindustrialization effort must be recognized. The 1977 Department of Commerce study on the information economy discussed in chapter 5 described the dimensions of that impact. Economic policies in this area will be critical in determining the overall growth of the economy through the end of the century.

The third priority policy area involves America's international role, with particular attention to economic factors. Information and communications make up the third largest element in the United States export pattern, after agricultural products and aviation. America's high-technology lead in this area gives us a strong competitive edge, an advantage which is being challenged by our industrial allies in Europe and Japan. This is a welcome challenge, in fact, since it is in our overall strategic interest that these countries develop comparable strengths in these sectors. At the same time, we should be pressing an aggressive trade program to capitalize on our present advantage in microelectronic-related products. Specifically, we need to see that increasing indications that we have been slipping, due in part to complacent business-as-usual attitudes, are reversed.[18]

Our international concerns should also extend to the development of more stable policies in the political area. Communications and information have become more sensitive issues as nations identify them as strategic subjects, affecting political, economic, military, and cultural affairs. We have been inclined to ignore, and on occasion denigrate, overseas concerns about the dominant United States role in these sectors. Such attitudes, and the policies that sustain them, have to be revised if we are to take a constructive lead in the development of an open global information system. In particular, we need to work more closely with our European and Japanese allies in developing long-range strategies and operations for strengthening communications and information resources in the Third World.[19]

Our responsibilities abroad are a natural extension of the democratic forces that have impelled us to develop an open information society at home. Decisions to continue to support and expand this approach, in a new era of technological abundance, are basically political. We will make them by conscious positive efforts or by default. Either way, they will be made.

The information age is only a convenient phrase to describe the climate of change in which we live. We cannot understand its full significance, however, simply by analyzing the economics, politics, and technology involved, or even by understanding the interaction of these elements. The evolving information environment is part of a larger shift, a shift in the powerful intangibles of values and purposes.

We have gone through two centuries of extraordinary change, beginning in the North Atlantic region and spreading more and more rapidly around the globe under the rubric of modernization. Modernization has many aspects, but its dynamics spring from the scientific revolution. A vision of an inflexible, precise natural order first drove this revolution and then was absorbed into social ideas. The transition was subtle, facilitated by the assumption that, having learned the rules of nature, we had only to apply them to society. Thus the valid precepts of such men as Newton and Darwin were extended beyond their original contexts.

This misapplication of scientific theory pushed us toward the brink of anarchy. We will not survive another two centuries if we continue to pursue the same social chimeras, inspired by myths of scientific and technological certitude. Fortunately, we now sense that something is wrong, and the new perceptions of science confirm our doubts. In physics, Einstein and quantum mechanics shattered the supposed order early in this century. More recently, microbiology has challenged the extremes of Darwinian social views and now offers some hopeful analogs about our human destiny.

Biologist Lewis Thomas has noted, with grace and clarity, the ways in which new studies have questioned older concepts of evolution as primarily a record of open warfare among competing species, with survival limited to the strongest aggressors. He points out:

"Now it begins to look different. The tiniest and most fragile organisms dominate the life of the earth.... [The] urge to form partnerships, to link-up and form collaborative arrangements, is perhaps the oldest, strongest and most fundamental force in nature. There are no solitary free-living creatures; every form of life is dependent on other forms."[20]

These observations from the new biology parallel the realities we face in coming to terms with the information age. The vision of thousands of Einsteins whose talents are liberated by computers, as suggested in chapter 1, will not be fulfilled if computers are used simply as sophisticated storage and calculating machines. Their greatest potential is in creative simulation — not as "artificial intelligence" but as a powerful augmentation of our own imaginations. And this means combining the computer's power with our own power of serendipity — the seemingly formless way in which the human animal arrives at its most enduring ideas, not by proceeding directly and infallibly in doing the essential business of our kind, as other species do, but by leaving well-trodden paths and exercising our gifts for ambiguity.

It is by appreciating this marvelous inherited gift that we can begin to fit the new communications and information resources into a more mature reordering of our personal and collective purposes, not as deterministic evolution but rather as a more harmonious melding of the many-colored strands of our common humanity. British scholar George Steiner has noted the importance of molding communications systems in ways that do not sacrifice diversity to the uncertain benefits of a bland global culture. He cites the role of the world's ten thousand languages in this process:

> Each and every tongue is a distinct window into the world. Looking through it, the the native speaker enters an emotional and spiritual space, a framework of memory, a promontory on tomorrow, which no other window in the great house of Babel quite matches. Thus every language mirrors and generates a possible world, an alternate reality.[21]

We may some day shape a world order in which unity not only in language but also in other ways prevails. This prospect, however, is a long way off. For the present, our best interests lie in preserving freedom through competing diversities. This is the objective Americans must keep in mind in shaping our society in a new age. Other cultures will judge us, and identify their own interests, as they see fit. It is, in the last analysis, the one sure path to expanding human freedom, permitting each of us, as Emerson urged, to produce that peculiar fruit we were born to bear.

NOTES

1. Quoted in Max Ways, "The Era of Radical Change," *Fortune*, 11 February 1980, p. 201.

2. "Probing Our Future," *Washington Post*, 8 July 1975, p. D–1. For a more optimistic view, see Isaac Asimov, "Communications and the Individualism to Come," *New York Times*, 7 January 1973, special section on direct mail advertising, p. 3.

3. Carl Sagan, *The Dragons of Eden* (New York: Ballantine Books, 1978), p. 25.

4. James G. Miller, *Living Systems* (New York: McGraw Hill, 1977), p. 12.

5. Edwin B. Parker, "An Information-Based Hypothesis," *Journal of Communication*, 28, no. 1 (Winter 1978): pp. 81–83.

6. "Death Sentence for Paper Shufflers," *The Economist* (London), 27 December 1980, p. 56.

7. Simon Nora and Alain Minc, *The Computerization of Society* (Cambridge, Mass.: M.I.T. Press, 1980).

8. Michael J. Arlen, *Living Room War* (New York: Viking Press, 1969).

9. Dallas W. Smythe, "On the Effects of Communications Satellites," *Communications Explosion* (Paper no. 9, Program of Policy Studies in Science and Technology, George Washington University, June 1965), p. 2.

10. Anthony Smith, "The Management of Television in a Democratic Society" (Paper presented at the Symposium on the Role and Management of Telecommunications in a Democratic Society, Munich, June 24–26, 1974).

11. Nigel Calder, *The Life Game: Evolution of the New Biology* (New York: Viking Press, 1975), p. 132.

12. Jon Stewart, "Computer Shock," *Saturday Review*, 23 June 1979, p. 14. Also "Who's Afraid of Video Screens?", *The Economist* (London), 16 February 1980, p. 98.

13. Watergate involved relatively primitive information technology. Computer scientist Martin Hellman of Stanford University has suggested that events would have turned out differently if Nixon and his advisers had relied on more sophisticated technology, such as computer encryption of the White House tapes rather than simple voice recording. "Scientists Urge New Laws to Curb Misuse of Computer Technology," *New York Times*, 23 November 1977, p. D–3.

14. Daniel S. Greenberg, "Molding Behavior Through Electronic Trickery," *Washington Post*, 25 April 1978, p. 22.

15. "Terror by Technology," *The Economist* (London), 19 April 1980, p. 45.

16. Glen O. Robinson, "The New Communications: Planning for Abundance," *Virginia Quarterly Review*, 53, no. 3 (Summer 1977): p. 397.

17. A useful initiative was taken in this area by the White House Conference on Libraries and Information held in October, 1979, in Washington. Its reports recommended a broad series of initiatives for making information available through the new technologies. An interesting proposal for a Temporary National Economic Committee on Computers in America's Future has been advanced by lawyers Harlan M. Blake and Milton R. Wessel in "Time for a National Computer Study?" *Infosystems*, December 1980, p. 12.

18. "The U.S. Lead in Service Exports Is Under Siege," *Business Week*, 16 September 1980, p. 70.

19. Recommendations for carrying out such an initiative are contained in U.S. Department of State, *Toward an American Agenda for a New World Order of Communications*, report issued by the U.S. National Commission for UNESCO (Washington, D.C.: Government Printing Office, 1980).

20. Lewis Thomas, "On the Uncertainty of Science," *Harvard Magazine*, September/October 1980, p. 19.

21. George Steiner, "The Coming Universal Language," *Atlas World Press Review*, October 1977, p. 26.

SELECTED
BIBLIOGRAPHY

Bell, Daniel. *The Coming of Post-Industrial Society*. New York: Basic Books, 1973.

Brock, Gerald. *The Telecommunications Industry*. Cambridge, Mass.: Harvard University Press, 1981.

Deutsch, Karl W. *The Nerves of Government*. New York: Free Press of Glencoe, 1963.

Devtouzis, Michael and Moses, Joel (eds.). *The Computer Age: a twenty-year view*. Cambridge, Mass.: M.I.T. Press, 1980.

Edelstein, Alex; Bowes, John E.; and Harsel, Sheldon. *Information Societies: Comparing the Japanese and American Experiences*. Seattle: School of Communications, University of Washington, 1978.

Eisenstein, Elizabeth L. *The Printing Press as an Agent of Change*. New York: Cambridge University Press, 1979.

Ellul, Jacques. *The Technological Society*. New York: Alfred A. Knopf, 1964.

Estabrook, Leigh, *Libraries in Post-Industrial Society*. Phoenix: Oryx Press, 1977.

Evans, Christopher. *The Micro Millenium*. New York: Viking Press, 1979.

Ferkiss, Victor C. *Technological Man: The Myth and the Reality*. New York: George Braziller Inc., 1969.

Fisher, Glen. *American Communication in a Global Society*. Norwood, N.J.: Ablex Publishing Co., 1979.

Forester, Tom, ed. *The Microelecronics Revolution*. Cambridge, Mass.: M.I.T. Press, 1981.

Hamelink, Coes. *Cultural Autonomy in Global Communications*. New York, Longman Publishers, 1983.

Hammer, Donald P., ed. *The Information Age: Its Development and Impact*. Metuchen, N.J.: Scarecrow Press, 1976.

Innis, Harold A. *Empire and Communications*. Toronto: University of Toronto Press, 1972.

Kuhns, William. *The Post-Industrial Prophets*. New York: Harper & Row, 1971.

Machlup, Fritz. *The Production and Distribution of Knowledge in the United States*. Princeton, N.J.: Princeton University Press, 1962.

Martin, James. *The Wired Society*. Englewood, N.J.: Prentice-Hall Inc., 1978.

McLuhan, Marshall. *The Gutenberg Galaxy*. Toronto: University of Toronto Press, 1962.

Mumford, Lewis. *The Pentagon of Power*. New York: Harcourt Brace Jovanovich, 1970.

Oettinger, Anthony; Berman, Paul; and Read, William. *High and Low Politics: Information Resources for the 80's*. Cambridge, Mass.: Ballinger Publishing Co., 1977.

Pelton, Joseph. *Global Talk*. Rockville, Md.: Sijthoff and Noordholf, 1981.

Phelan, John M. *Mediaworld*. New York: Seabury Press, 1977.

Pool, Ithiel de Sola, ed. *The Social Impact of the Telephone*. Cambridge, Mass.: MIT Press, 1977.

Pool, Ithiel de Sola. *Technologies of Freedom*. Cambridge, Mass.: Harvard University Press, 1983.

Read, William H. *America's Mass Media Merchants*. Baltimore: Johns Hopkins University Press, 1976.

Schiller, Dan. *Telematics and Government*. Norwood, N. J.: Ables Publishing Corp., 1982.

Schiller, Herbert I. *Communication and Cultural Domination*. White Plains, N.Y.: International Arts and Sciences Press, 1976.

Scientific American, Communication. A special issue, September 1972.

Smith, Anthony. *The Geopolitics of Information*. London: Faber and Faber, 1980.

Smith, Anthony. *Goodbye Gutenberg*. New York: Oxford University Press, 1980.

U.S. Congress, House, *Options Papers*. Prepared by the staff for the Subcommittee on Communications of the Committee on Interstate and Foreign Commerce, 95th Cong., 1st sess. Committee Print 95–13, May 1977.

U.S. Department of Commerce, *The Information Economy*, 9 vols. Office of Telecommunications Special Publication 77–12, 1977.

Wangermée, Robert, and Lhoest, Holde. *L'Aprés-Télévision*. Paris: Hachette Littérature, 1973.

INDEX

WILSON DIZARD is both a practitioner and a student of communication and information affairs. From 1951 to 1980, he served as a Foreign Service officer in the Department of State and U.S. Information Agency. His overseas assignments included Turkey, Greece, Iran, Pakistan, Viet Nam, and Poland. Since 1965, Mr. Dizard has specialized in communications policy issues involving satellites, computers, radiocommunications and international developments. He was vice-chairman of the U.S. delegation to the 1979 World Administrative Radio Conference in Geneva.

Dizard is currently vice-president of Kalba Bowen Associates, a research and consulting firm in Cambridge, Massachusetts. He is also adjunct professor of international affairs at the School of Foreign Service, Georgetown University, and a member of the university's Center for Strategic and International Studies.

His other writings include, *The Strategy of Truth and Television: A World View*, as well as numerous articles in scholarly journals and other publications.